From Hurt To Joy

How to Transform Self-Defeating Patterns With Energy Dynamics

From Hurt To Joy

How to Transform Self-Defeating Patterns With Energy Dynamics

Sarah Gillen, LMFT, PCC

Distinction Press
Waitsfield Vermont

From Hurt to Joy: How to transform self-defeating patterns with Energy Dynamics
Sarah Gillen, LMFT, PCC

Published by   Distinction Press
                  354 Hastings Rd
                  Waitsfield Vermont 05673
                  www.distinctionpress.com
                  kitty@distinctionpress.com

Cover design by Serena Fox, Serena Fox Design Co, www.serenafoxdesign.com
Cover photo © 2011 Marcus Lindström, iStockphoto

Designed and typeset by RSBPress LLC

Interior Photos and their copyrights: pgs 18, 156, 212, 302 © 2011 Terrence Keeney, pgs 28, 66, 107, 190, 296, 315, 324 © 2012 Sarah Gillen, pg 46 © Kreefax bigstockphoto, pg 84 © BrendanHunter iStockphoto, pg 144 © coyote bigstockphoto, pg 172 © 2011 emsee photos, pg 256 © 2009 kgtoh bigstockphoto, pg 257 © 2007 Eraxion bigstockphoto, pg 278 © 2011 Isidro Dias dreamstime, pg 290 © 2006 Atlantic View bigstockphoto, pg 330 © 2008 JLV Image Works bigstockphoto, pg 332 © 2011 hospitalera bigstockphoto, pg 332 © 2006 Florin CC bigstockphoto

ISBN 978-1-937667-08-5

Dedication

This book is dedicated to my husband and daughter
who show me every day that life can change and be wonderful,
and for their support, patience, and help.

Acknowledgements

I owe a huge debt to my clients, past, present and future. I value your courage, fortitude, and grace, and all that you teach me.

I'd like to thank my dear friend, Beth Bradfish, for her editing, endless enthusiasm and encouragement. She made sure this book saw the light of day.

And my publisher, Kitty Werner at Distinction Press, for her skill, friendship, and generosity.

To Serena Fox, for the most beautiful cover ever.

To my many readers and constructive critics, especially Diane Sue and Kathy Brue, and to everyone who helped during the many go-rounds about the title.

To Christiane Northrup, MD, for reminiscences about our childhood and encouragement about the book; to Jack Kornfield, PhD, whose support and advice were generous and invaluable.

And to my Guides,

Thank you.

Contents

Introduction

MILLIONS OF PEOPLE wrestle with emotional and physical pain that are leftover from past events. Their outlook on life is often severely affected by the intrusion of emotions and memories from the terrible things they have experienced. To them, others appear to live with an optimism that seems impossible to attain.

> Do you have painful, maybe even traumatic memories that hold you back from living the way you want?

> Do you find yourself repeating unhelpful patterns in your work or relationships?

> Do self-defeating beliefs hold you back from realizing your full potential?

It *is* possible to feel joy, even if you are carrying the weight of old, painful occurrences. It *is* possible to release the hold that serious hurt has had on you, to stop feeling tossed by stormy seas or frozen for fear of being annihilated by pain. It is also possible to transform patterns and experience life as wonderful and full of promise. Even if your past was free of trauma, but you feel stymied by the obstacles that your patterns of behavior throw in your way (as everyone's do, sometime or other), the information in this book will help you develop your gifts and enrich your experience of life.

From Hurt to Joy will show you how, in this moment, to have choices and the power to move freely in your life. You will learn to use your own Energy Dynamics, made up of breath, physical and emotional energy, mental awareness, meridians, chakras, your immune and nervous systems, as well as spiritual energy. You will explore specific skills that will help you develop a new base of strength, safety, clarity, and optimism. You will also learn effective ways to resolve the obstacles that typically crop up for you when you are trying to accomplish something, so your efforts are not short-circuited.

Trauma can be caused by horrific events such as rape, war, or child-abuse. Such common occurrences as car accidents, hospital stays, divorce, chronic illness, natural disasters, terrorism, and abusive marriages can also cause trauma as well. People often find their sense of safety, and their expectations of the world to be radically skewed going through these events. It is not the event itself that determines whether you are traumatized. It is how you personally have been impacted by it. If you formed negative beliefs about yourself or the world as a result of those events, they can stunt your self-expression, your expectations, you health, and your sense that you deserve to succeed and receive good things.

In my struggle with my own trauma, I fell into many quagmires and explored many healing methods, some of which helped, and lots which did not. I spent thousands of dollars trying to work through my pain, so that I would finally feel free to live a life that felt fully mine, as opposed to one run by old beliefs and other peoples' demands. The only psychiatrist I ever worked with was completely puzzled. "Why is it that it seems as if it all happened yesterday for you? Why can't you take the 'catbird seat?' Since catbirds perch on the highest branches, he meant that I should have been able to peer at past events as if from a great distance. But that is the issue with trauma. You cannot just reason yourself out of it. And memories of trauma are stored in the brain differently from regular memories, so the effects do continue to grab you as if they were happening right now.

This book is the result of my own search, and of over thirty years working with thousands of clients from all over the world who had very different stories. My goal was to help them not only relieve hurt but to change the way they felt about themselves and about life. Sharing in their work helped me grow tremendously. I also trained in many modalities and followed other professionals' clinical research. Friends and mentors added some crucial insights that led me to see that it is truly possible to overcome trauma and embrace one's gifts with a positive outlook.

As well as having an advanced degree and clinical licenses, I am a medical and psychological intuitive. I perceive subtle layers of energy and how they are affected by the far-reaching effects of the past. I look for interrelationships and overlaps as well as the root causes of symptoms. I have been trained in many healing traditions across the spectrum. Because I look from different theoretical angles at the same time, and my perspective melds disparate areas of theoretical knowledge, I often perceive causal issues and interrelations that others have missed.

Over the years, I developed an Energy Medicine approach for working with trauma and other stubborn baggage. My method is a synthesis of Eastern and Western theory and techniques, as well as energy-based practices. It has two aspects: the healing work that I do in concert with the person, which is the Energy Medicine, and the skills that I teach people so that they can change their habits and help themselves, which I call Energy Dynamics. When clients and students use these tools, they describe feeling empowered, safe, free, and relieved. And *whole*. Their self-awareness and optimism have blossomed.

These Energy Dynamics skills are what you will find in *From Hurt to Joy*. I have taught them to thousands of people, including children, couples, executives, and political leaders. My goal is not just to describe theory. You will learn about your own energy systems and how they work for you and sometimes against you. You will see how to resolve old patterns. You will develop some new dynamics—new ways to use your energy and build new neural connections. In each chapter, you will find suggestions and exercises to practice. The skills build on each other, so skipping around is not a good idea. Take your time and move through the chapters in order. The more you practice, the more the skills will grow, and the more you will be able to rely on them in stressful moments. The CDs that will be available make it easy to practice the exercises, so that you'll be able to have your eyes closed or move around. Other CDs will be available to assist you in deepening your exploration in specific areas.

From Hurt to Joy will be useful in conjunction with work you may be doing to address specific concerns, such as divorce, having alcoholic parents, or spousal abuse, to name just a few.

This book is not intended to replace psychotherapy. Its purpose is to educate, not treat. Uncovering the joy that hides within you involves processes of discovery and growth, of opening and allowing, as much as of focusing energy and intent. Have fun exploring and finding out that you have access to more skills than you may have been aware of, knowing that you are responsible for your own journey. I hope that, in the process, you gain more sense of empowerment with which to approach and move through your own painful material. Remember, though, that many times, the most loving and caring thing you can do for yourself is to enlist the aid of experienced helpers. Even in a therapist's office, healing is not something that can be done *to* you. A healer supports the innate healing capacities of your own system, even if she or he uses surgery or verbal techniques to clear the way, so that your system can do its job. If you have uncontrollable flashbacks or triggers, then you probably have post-traumatic stress which necessitates working with a good trauma therapist. One who understands the relation between energy and traumatic memories would be best. The ideas in this book will at least give you a sense of what is possible. They can show you many ideas about supporting yourself through and beyond the therapeutic process.

Healing from hurt and trauma takes work. Many survivors feel as if they have been slogging through the muck for such a long time that they should be done by now, and so they are very discouraged when they still hurt. Unfortunately, many of the instinctive ways that people wrestle with pain do not help the past release its hold. What really helps is often not what you would expect.

In *From Hurt to Joy,* you will learn to:

- move into your body, rather than cutting it off to get away from sensations,

- live in the present, while resolving and releasing the past,

- identify and undo the automatic protective energy patterns that are your reaction to stress,

- discover what really protects you and what does not,

- transform your opinion of, and learn to value, yourself,

- develop a deeper relationship with who you really are, and

- turn toward the positive in you, in others, and in circumstances.

You will also learn to alleviate physical pain, lower anxiety, become less hyper-vigilant, replace self-defeating beliefs with ones that support you, identify your strengths and use them to improve your life, and respond in the moment in ways that build you up, rather than tearing at your self-esteem.

Some notes about the book's organization

The chapters have specific directions to help develop each skill in the "How To" sections.

Toward the end of many chapters there are exercises with which to deepen the learning, with which you can continue to build skills over time. These are labelled "Practices."

When I refer to information gathered from other sources, rather than giving the full reference, (which interrupts the flow of what we're talking about) I'll give the name of the author. You'll find a bibliography and suggested readings at the end of the book.

Many chapters have Endnotes of ideas that relate to the topic by would be too tangential in the chapter itself.

I hope that *From Hurt to Joy* will help you move past obstacles, treat yourself compassionately, claim your innate goodness, support and value yourself, feel more comfortable in the world, and embrace your life with optimism and a renewed sense of wonder and support.

Part I

Setting the Stage for Change:
What You're Starting With

Photo © 2011 Terrence Keeney

Terrible or not, difficult or not, the only thing that is beautiful, noble,
religious and mystical is to be happy.

—Arnaud Desjardins

Joy *IS* Possible 1

TANI WAS A talented, attractive woman in her early thirties who
cared fervently about the natural world and about helping people.
But, over and over again, she held herself back from using her talents
by becoming anxious and self-critical. She second-guessed herself
constantly, in the guise of trying to improve herself so that she'd be
acceptable. Her childhood had led her to anticipate hostility, so she
tended to react defensively. Tani avoided working in group settings
for fear that she'd be as ridiculed and rejected as she'd been in her
family. In groups she was always on the alert for the need to prove
herself.

Tani started an appointment by saying, "I can imagine why you've
asked me how I want the rest of my life to be and what my dreams are.
But you know, it's really hard to come up with any. It was never okay in
my family to have my own desires. I protected myself by rationalizing
that their nasty behavior was reasonable and trying to placate them.
Now that I'm an adult, when something would be worthwhile to do,
I talk myself out of it by thinking that I couldn't possibly manage
dealing with the pressure, the people, and the politics. I think I've cut
off the part of myself that should feel that I can have a life based on
what I want."

There are many reasons why people often believe that emotional peace
is out of their reach. To them, the notion of being joyful is a cruel

joke. Really bad things have already happened that seem impossible to overcome. Some people have learned from painful experience that they must shut down on themselves in order to be acceptable. And many disconnect from their feelings as a way of avoiding pain. They then develop distorted views of themselves. As Mark Epstein says in *Going to Pieces Without Falling Apart*, "In coping with the world, we come to identify only with our compensatory selves and our reactive minds." For them, getting through each day is a huge task. Happiness doesn't come into it. Escape looks like the only possible relief.

What would it mean to think that joy is possible? And what is it anyway? We're aiming at something more profound than pleasurable reactions to things that we do, or buy, or achieve, not that I have anything against those! Such activities and accomplishments are fun, fulfilling, can be thrilling and even inspiring. But there is a deeper, more long-lasting joy, even for those of us who have endured terrible things.

At the center of each person is a still place, a well of deep and abiding bliss. This feeling-state emerges when we are at peace and deeply connected with our true selves. Even when we feel miserable and over-burdened with pain, or with old patterns that don't seem to go away no matter how hard we try, the still place is there. It is where our true selves, our being, can be found. It is also the place in which we can access greater physical, emotional and spiritual energy, in which we connect, through a deep contact with our true nature, with all-that-is.

So, joy *is* possible. Joy simply is. Waiting for us to find it. Joy can also increase. It grows when it is fertilized with our conscious attention. The discovery that joy is not dependent on our attainments, or things, or other people, gives us more power to uncover and experience it. We can get there. All we have to do is dig through the pile of pain and unresolved issues under which it is buried.

Well, *that* was easy to say. It's not as if we've all been sitting around doing nothing. So why has emotional freedom seemed pretty impossible in the past, and what makes it easier to attain?

Our systems do have emotional and neurological resources for working through and resolving hurt when it happens. However, if we we can't face all of it in the moment, then the effects are locked away inside us, ostensibly so that we can work through them later when we have the resources or a calm stretch of time.

Mostly, though, people do not get home, pull those memories out of the old stomach storage locker, sit themselves down, and let the feelings flow. People tense against their memories, trying to annihilate them by cutting off awareness of their bodies. It's as if distancing from the body that feels the pain will make the pain cease to exist. When the body persists in doing its job, signaling more and more loudly if necessary, that there is something that needs attention, people often come to blame their bodies as the cause of the pain. Having stored the hurtful memories or emotions away, folks tend to blame themselves if they leak or blurt hurt feelings without knowing where they came from. And around it goes again, as they try to disconnect more strenuously in order to put the lid on those old sores.

The many books on happiness available today tend to gloss over the struggle, with no model for getting from here to there. The exercises they contain are often valuable, but they are of no use until we can begin to see our way out. The path from hurt to joy requires some extra steps, and if we have been traumatized, these steps are even more essential.

Energy Dynamics are helpful for anyone wanting to change their experience of life and to feel better in themselves. They are not only for those who have survived seriously damaging experiences. For those who are wrestling with the aftermath of trauma, however, it is worthwhile at this point to clarify our working definition. Trauma is any stressor or event that overwhelms the system's ability to deal with it, thereby causing lasting and substantial psychological disruption.[1] In situations in which we feel some sense of control, at least of ourselves, we do not become traumatized, no matter how awful the circumstance. It is when we feel helpless and overwhelmed, when the event blows past our emotional and mental capacities to tolerate it, that our systems shove it away into a specific portion of our brain, causing it to be stuck not only undigested, but unresolvable simply by talking or with psychotropic medication. So, conventional therapies that rely on talking and medication alone to relieve symptoms are not the most reliable in releasing trauma.

Bessel van der Kolk is a foremost researcher on trauma and traumatic memory. His long-term research on Viet Nam veterans has shown that neither approach has a significant impact when it comes to releasing traumatic memories or the ways that our bodies react to them.

Unfortunately also, the sense of helplessness stymies our efforts to struggle past the pain and self-loathing that are the most pernicious waste products of trauma, so we often feel hopeless as well. (And that helplessness also fuels a tremendous amount of pleasure-seeking. In reaching too much outside ourselves to feel better, we inadvertently strengthen the idea that we are lacking, that we are intrinsically inadequate. Then we find ourselves going after more things to make up for the emptiness we feel.)

To free ourselves from the effects of stubborn old baggage, including trauma, we need to introduce movement into the frozen portion of the brain where overwhelming hurts are shut away. Energy is what breaks up the ice and makes things move. Our energy systems can be trained and augmented, so that we move beyond old, self-defeating beliefs and turn our attention to what is positive and supportive. We then lessen the power that the memories have over our emotional well-being and can include them in the story of our lives in a way that adds meaning and depth to how we define ourselves, rather than diminishing us.

A free and full life is not without crisis and difficulty. Some trouble comes to us all. But, do we have to be contorted and arrested by those sorrows? It takes determination to remove the distorted lenses that have affected our view of life, making it look as if our old pains repeat over and over. All of us who have gone through horrific times have been handed the assignment of coming to terms with them rather than being diminished.

How do we deal with crisis and loss in such a way that we can be self-supportive and confident, having made peace with what happened? How we deal with pain and loss is directly related to how much joy and richness we are able to allow ourselves to experience. It is possible to reassert our sovereign place in our own story. Optimally, we'll resolve suffering and integrate what we learned, and know our own value, moving forward more connected with ourselves and with life, with a larger sense of who we are, and with more sensitivity and empathy.

Joy comes as a result of our effort, effectively applied. The paradox is that joy is always present in us. Under all the layers of pain, unresolved feelings, and beliefs that life is hard and we don't deserve to have it be easy, there it is. Waiting. As soon as we do the work, sometimes, just a piece of it, we can be flooded with contentment, gratitude, and yes, joy. It doesn't matter what we've been up against before, or even what our life circumstances are now. There it is.

You may have seen an example by watching an acquaintance fighting against grief. When people react to the loss of a loved one by hiding from it, they become stuck in the painful memories. They can't remember the good times. Their outrage and dismal outlook grow. Alternatively, when they allow grief to run its course, they start recalling happy times and the blessing of having had that person in their life. The loving feelings surface, seemingly of their own accord, because they have been there all along, hiding in the bedrock. The grief and rage simply covered them over. The psyche seems to have a mandate to make sure that we face things, so it continues to present us with the unfinished business before we can get to the fun stuff.

Joy is a deep, abiding feeling of happiness grounded in peace and bliss. It is our felt perception of the creative and sustaining energy that the Universe is made of. When we are centered deeply within ourselves, we feel true joy. It does not depend on any external circumstance. When we are settled in the still place and in that feeling, we feel nourished and held, even when circumstances around us are less than optimal. Enlightenment is being able to experience this on an on-going basis.

We, as regular humans, can experience this kind of joy. A worthy goal for life and for the development of our spirits is to do the work that increases the time that we spend within this joy and express it through the way we live our lives. And yes, here, at the beginning of this journey, you may not know yet how to access it. You may have had so many painful things happen to you that you are far from seeing that it has anything to do with you. You may even have piled bad behavior on top of your pain. You may be so lost in shame, despair, and self-doubt, that you think you don't deserve it.

But, the fact is, joy and connectedness lie at the heart of everyone. In the course of this book you'll see how to uncover the joy that is already in you. Doing the work to resolve the feelings heaped on top starts to build a renewed sense of your ability to act on your own behalf. In doing so, you engage the healing process. As you go on, you can change your outlook on life, learn to value your true nature, trust in your strengths, and see your opportunities. Shift your viewpoint just a little, and you'll see that the struggle itself is evidence that you still have hope that, with enough work and the right tools, it is possible to be happy.

But first, we need to look at how the brain works, and how it keeps us stuck. If we understand that, we can see how to use our own neurology to help us release baggage, rather than carrying it everywhere.

A word about reading this book

Reading it may very well be an emotional experience. In order to illustrate the points, it is necessary to describe what does not work. This will involve examples of people who don't have the skills. And there are examples of people who have experienced trauma, with its effects on their lives and functioning. Some people's stories may remind you of your own, and some stories may stir your feelings, simply because you are a person who is sensitized to the effects of painful situations. The up-side is that you will be able relate to the examples. It may be that your painful memories are triggered, so there may be discomfort in reading it. When I describe sensations, yours may be roused.

So *From Hurt to Joy* will not only give you some information. By reading it, monitoring your responses, and working through the exercises, you will be improving your own experience and hopefully beginning to reduce symptoms.

One of the key points of Energy Dynamics is learning to manage your level of sensation, including those generated by this book. Keeping the levels of arousal of your symptoms and memories manageable, and processing only as much as you can at a given moment while staying connected with yourself, is what makes it possible to release old, stored feelings. Not being washed away or overwhelmed will be addressed in chapter seven, entitled BWITSY. One goal in reading (and writing!) the book is to learn the important skill of monitoring how stirred up your body is while still functioning well in various life situations.

Here are some guidelines while you read the chapters. Even if you don't expect to have any difficult reactions, these steps will give you a head start in learning the skills and also in being compassionate and caring toward yourself.

1) Keep some attention on your body. Notice your heart rate, where tension may be building, if you suddenly feel tired or drained, if you start feeling fullness or pressure. It'd be a good idea to get a baseline, so note now how your body feels. Then practice staying in touch with yourself while doing something else, in this case reading. Start at the top of your head and notice how you feel in your skull, your ears, your face, and down into your neck. Notice if areas are warm, cold, full, airy, tight, achy, whatever sensation you have in each area. Don't try to change them at this point. Just notice. Keep checking into your shoulders, upper back, upper chest, into your rib cage, solar plexus area, abdomen. Check in with your shoulder blades, spine, mid-back, lower back, sacrum and all through your pelvic region. Notice your legs and feet.

2) Make sure that you keep breathing. Notice if you stop, when you read some passage. Take some deep breaths into the places that tightened. If your breath feels constricted, keep attention on it and exhale long and slowly through your nose until your breath deepens again.

3) If you start feeling reminded of your old stuff, or upset for any reason, press your feet into the floor. Keep your connection to the here-and-now by feeling the connection between your feet and the floor.

4) Purposefully notice the room around you. List items you see, as a way of pulling yourself into your present reality. Remind yourself that you are a fully grown person, reading in a nice, safe place. Really see the lamp, the pillow, the table, the picture. It helps you not get lost in the past if you consciously ground yourself in the present.

5) If necessary, take a break and walk around, and tell yourself that's what you are doing. Make it a conscious choice, rather than finding yourself rummaging in the freezer for the ice cream. Moderate the amount of stress your system needs to deal with at any given time by dividing it into chunks and absorbing it on your terms. Move enough to get your blood going. Swing your arms. Movement and exercise are sure-fire ways to come back to the moment and to shake off tentacles from there-and-then.

6) Also tell yourself specifically when you will return to the book. It won't help in the long run for whatever triggered your old material to loom larger and larger in your subconscious and become a barrier that keeps you away from the helpful information in the book.

7) Then come back to read some more. You will feel stronger, knowing you can control the process of reading and absorbing the information. As an added bonus, you'll be giving yourself a clear message that you are taking care of yourself.

With these notes in mind, let's get started on the adventure of moving from hurt to joy.

Endnotes

1 Interestingly, this definition implies an explanation as to why an event may traumatize one individual and not another. If we have the outlook and tools necessary to work through a particular type of crisis, we do not become example,

a group of Tibetan nuns came to the United States for a Buddhist retreat organized by Jack Kornfield and other Western spiritual leaders. They were asked to give talks on their experiences in Chinese prisons. Some of them had been arrested as young as seventeen years of age. All had been in prison for years, beaten, tortured, and raped for the crime of practicing their faith. What was interesting was that they came out of their ordeal with physical but not with emotional scars. Hurt, yes. Lasting psychological trauma, no. When I discussed this phenomenon with Jack, he mused that their world view included strong beliefs that there must have been a karmic reason for their going through those ordeals. Buddhists are taught that the best way to deal with karma is to acquiesce to the experience as graciously as possible, remaining aware of one's innate goodness (one's Buddha nature) as fully as possible, and centering in Spirit. The nuns were full-grown at the time, and the aggressors were strangers. As well, they had each other, as well as the structure of their religious practice to count on. The conclusion I drew from this was that they were not, it turns out, traumatized in the fundamental way that we are discussing, because the events, horrific as they were, did not overwhelm their ability to cope.

@ 2012 Sarah Gillen

Alice knew it was the Rabbit coming to look for her, and she trembled till she shook the house, quite forgetting that she was now about a thousand times as large as the Rabbit and had no reason to be afraid of it.

—Lewis Carroll, Alice's Adventures in Wonderland

The Real Purpose of Self-criticism, Shame, and Other Forms of Heavy Artillery   2

CONNIE WAS A college student at a large California university. One night, walking home after partying with friends at the local hangout, she was violently raped. Her roommates insisted she call the crisis hotline and then accompanied her to the hospital. At least, in this day and age, she was much less likely to be accused in court for provoking the attack and having the district attorney question her sexual history and choice of clothes as if she caused the attack. And there was a hotline, run by people who understood the severity of the ordeal.

Yet, months afterward, Connie still blamed herself. She wondered how she could have been such an idiot as to walk home (although she always had before), why alone, why she'd stayed out so late, why she didn't carry mace, why she'd worn that dress, and on and on...

What was she doing with all these questions? Were they useful and productive? Was she making progress in finding the real reason she was attacked? All victims of violent crimes go through this self-catechizing. It is an automatic reaction to feeling emotionally assaulted. People grieving over the sudden loss of a loved one do the same thing, as do people who have experienced more chronic, long-lasting trauma.

Why do people criticize and blame themselves when they've been hurt?

Connie's preoccupation with self-blame illustrates one of a handful of mechanisms that people automatically use in an effort to come to terms with distressing events. They seem to work in the moment. However, just because they occur automatically does not make them effective or healthy.

In order to come to terms with stubborn pain, it is necessary to look at the tools you have been using to manage it, whether they support how you want to live, the purpose they attempt to serve, and their actual results. In the next chapters we will look at more effective approaches.

While Connie's defense mechanism is automatic at this point, unconsciously she is trying to achieve four goals through blaming herself:

First, she is distracting herself from seemingly intolerable emotions. Facing the feelings that keep surfacing after an event that already has you burdened with horrible visuals seems much too terrible. Our impulse is to do anything rather than feel helpless and violated. Under the circumstances, blaming the victim seems like a acceptable price to pay. And the problem is, it works great! In fact, nothing is as effective for turning our attention away from unacceptable feelings as blaming ourselves. Nothing grabs our focus more completely. However, doing so does not lay the incident to rest or help us move on. Like alcohol, drugs or other addictions, it simply covers the hurt with a maladaptive habit.[1]

Unfortunately, when we beat on ourselves, we close the doors of awareness. We don't see the emotions lined up needing to be dealt with. We see no options, no real opportunities to improve the situation or to get the heck out of there. We also do not accurately perceive what is going on in the present.

Second, she is trying to gain some control over the situation, after the fact. There is nothing like being violently attacked to make you feel completely out of control. Helplessness is one of the least acceptable and most intolerable emotions. In order to counter it, people develop self-blame as a management technique very early in life. Children blame themselves for everything, both because they feel helpless and therefore endangered when bad things happen (and they hate it as much as we do), and because they naturally are self-centered: they have not yet developed the ability to see things from others' points of view, so they assume that everything that happens relates to them. When children blame themselves for events, they are trying to assure themselves that they have some power, rather than being at the mercy of grown-ups and circumstances. If the child is at fault, then she believe that she can change events by affecting the only thing under her jurisdiction—herself. The psychological assumption is that if she can figure out what she did to make it happen in the past, she can stop a bad thing from happening in the future by changing her behavior, thus placing her in charge of the outcome. Survivors of violent or chronic abuse blame themselves for the same reason.

🐾 **Third, it displaces danger, making it seem less threatening.** Victims focus on trying to keep bad things from happening in the future in order to block out the fact that the bad thing has already happened. Hypervigilance, which is about seeing the future before it gets you, seems less threatening than realizing that they have already taken a hit. The problem is that displacing the danger onto the future makes what is coming much scarier, affecting their adrenals and their outlook, inadvertently loading their sense of life with more danger and helplessness. And they are not taking care of the business already on their plates.

🐾 **Fourth, it perpetuates the fantasy that they are loved and safe.** Children also blame themselves for circumstances because they cannot tolerate feeling unloved. They cannot wrap their minds around the notion that an adult might not care about their well-being. It is impossible for a small child to face living in a world in which care-givers or other adults could be harmful. After all, children's survival depends entirely on the concern of adults. They know this. If they can believe that something is their fault, then they can continue to see their parents as loving people who would behave lovingly if only they had a decent child to deal with.

Adults blame themselves for the same reason. Psychologically, it seemed much better for Connie to blame herself. Doing so allowed her to maintain the unconscious belief that, if only she were not an idiot and could figure out what she had done wrong, she could maintain a vision of the world as a safe place in which people do not violently attack innocent strangers. Blaming yourself is a (futile) effort to gain some sense that the world is an okay place to live, and that you have some say in everything that happens.

Connie had become hyper-vigilant. At the first glimpse of any man walking by who remotely reminded her of the attacker, Connie would dart into the street rather than stay on the sidewalk. She was almost hit by cars several times. She changed the way she dressed, now covering herself as much as possible in baggy sweaters and pants. She stopped meeting friends at the local hangouts, staying in her room whenever she did not have a class or work.

These behaviors were similar to her unending self-analysis in that she was unconsciously attempting to prevent future occurrences as if it was her fault she was attacked. Unfortunately, she was not addressing the real situation. The longer she continued to do this, the more harder it was to face the fact that she had already been attacked. She had feelings and hurts that needed to be addressed, before she, and her body, could realize that the attack was over.

What is accurate?

The parts of your nervous system charged with keeping you safe perceive danger based on what gets your adrenalin and anxiety going, whatever that may be. When you can take a deep breath and step back enough to see that your self-criticism and self-blame are not the voices of incontrovertible fact about you or about a situation, it is possible to notice that the criticism is trying to protect you from the perceived danger of your own painful emotions and memories. The voices of your own armament of self-blame don't care about external proof at all. They will say anything in order to get you to step away from internal unrest. When you see that the actual effect of that type of protection is that it holds you in an endless feedback loop, in which the trauma is always present and looks as if it will repeat in the future, then you may be more able to mobilize your strength to risk questioning the veracity of your self-blame and eventually give it up. There is huge freedom in doing so. It is such a relief to experience the reality that you are not to blame for everything, and that in fact, not that much is yours to control. It is a major milestone to realize that feeling helpless, while painful and scary, is preferable to beating ourselves up. It is more effective too, because it allows the release of the stranglehold of painful memories and allows us to move on. We feel more powerful when we learn effective ways to work with emotions, with the past, and with future situations.

Anxiety, the Red Flag

More people are medicated to get away from anxiety than almost any other emotional state. People view anxiety as bad; that it means that something is wrong. Many people experience what's called "free-floating anxiety," meaning there is no obvious cause. The problem is that people don't see the cause because they have disconnected from their bodies and feelings, so they aren't aware of their reactions to events when they happen. They are not getting any information, so their reactions seem to come out of the blue. Not knowing why they are agitated makes people feel out-of-control. That leads quickly to seeing any anxiety as a sure sign that their lives are out of control. They try madly to figure out what's going on and avoid any situations that they think may cause the anxiety. Then they have more and more anxiety.

Anxiety actually has a crucial purpose. It is supposed to be uncomfortable. It is a function of activity in the amygdalae, part of what has been called the limbic system in the central part of the brain and whose purpose is to deal with emotional reactions. The amygdalae are activated when we are startled or when we anticipate an event. These could be surprises such as a car back-firing, or the phone ringing at 3:00 a.m., or an event that we've chosen, such as taking part in a local production of "Rosencrantz and Guildenstern are Dead"; going out the door into Manhattan at night; or taking the SATs. The amygdalae's job is to focus our attention on possible dangers. We have a choice, once they have been activated. We may go on automatic and react with fight-or-flight, or we may engage the assessment functions of our more advanced brain centers. Those will help us weigh the reality of the danger, check that our costume is on straight; be on guard around strangers on the street; or have our pencils sharpened. Our job is to moderate the instant alert system using assessment—consider the stimulus; memory recall—compare it to other events we've gone through; and strategizing—think about the best response given all the information. Otherwise chances are we will find ourselves running madly away from slamming doors or taking a swing at a bratty brother when he comes up behind us unexpectedly. Or we may freeze, unable to remember our lines. One thing is for sure: we'll constantly over-estimate the amount of danger in any given situation.

Mislabeling the Cause

It is not the street, or the test, or the stage that actually causes the anxiety. The triggering of the amygdalae is supposed to give us the chance to check it out. But so many people back away from the situation as if that will reduce their anxiety. And it does, for a moment. But it doesn't handle the real situation. It only makes people believe that pulling back from things will make them feel safer. We automatically believe that what causes a feeling is whatever is happening at the same time. If you do ascribe cause to the present circumstance, it then will appear as if the only way that you can calm down is to back away from the curtain/the test/the outing and hightail it for the exit. You will think that you are saving yourself from anxiety or fear, and then you will back away each time you feel anxious. The anxiety will become greater and kick in sooner. Over time, you'll lose your perspective and will feel smaller and smaller. Your sense of yourself as competent and up to the task will weaken. Thus is crippling performance anxiety born, the type that can ruin a performer's career, as well as agoraphobia, not to mention not living up to your potential.

That is too bad, because every time someone backs down from a challenge, their sense of agency diminishes, and their fear increases. They lose touch with themselves more and more, mesmerized by the scary image in their mind's eye. And unless they examine this reaction in the light of day, they won't see that they are really stuck in past fears and past events; that they are not really reacting to the one in front of them. The performance doesn't cause them to feel anxious. Their anticipation and their history do. As they stand there sweating, their third grade production of "The Princess and the Pea" suddenly flashes across their mind, not to mention their embarrassment when their costume caught on the stage flat and pulled the whole thing over on top of the class bully, who then hassled them for a month. If all this is triggered as they wait in the wings, no wonder they find themselves tremendously anxious. *Danger! Humiliation! Threat!* telegraphs from deep in their stomach where it's been buried for fifteen years, along with shame and a belief that they can't do anything right. If they give in, rip off their costume, and run for the stage door, they will not have conquered the anxiety. They will have missed the message.

The purpose of anxiety is to be a red flag sticking up on top of the time capsule or garbage can in which we have buried unexamined reactions and emotions. When a memory is triggered by a present event, and it starts rising toward the surface, the red flag breaches first. It grabs our attention quickly, telling us to be alert, that there is something we need to look at, maybe not right now as we're about to go on stage, but soon. The ideal response would be to turn toward it, say, "Thanks for the heads-up," and make sure we find some time to deal with those memories directly.

Problems occur when we react instantly by backing off or panicking, rather than taking the waving flag as a sign that the capsule is coming and needs to be opened and cleaned out. The more we give in to anxiety, the more our reaction to it becomes automatic. If that happens, as soon as we feel even the tiniest bit, we rush for Quick Fixes (more about these in a moment). We react as if the anxiety is the real issue, to be avoided at all costs. If we go on automatic every time it appears, then we undermine the reliable emotional clearing systems that we have available to us as human beings. We become terrified of the messenger and try to kill it. And if we avoid our real emotions as dangerous, they never have the chance to speak. We never learn from them, and they never ease off.

Heavy Artillery

Tani was the queen of heavy artillery. Her parents acted outraged and contemptuous of her normal child needs and behavior. She had internalized the message from childhood that not only was she never good enough, she was toxic and despicable. Her friends joked that, while others who criticized themselves harshly used words like knives or bludgeons, while Tani used machine guns, grenades and nuclear bombs. She'd second-guess herself for any effort, and if she thought she'd messed up somehow, her inner critic was vicious and unrelenting. "When I was a kid, I got so much hell when I was good that I never dared do anything bad. Now I treat myself the way they treated me."

It is important to recognize if you use heavy artillery, if your self-criticism is of the mercilessly attacking variety. As you go through exercises in following chapters, it will be necessary to treat yourself with extra kindness, in order to release the stored hurts and patterns. With practice, you will learn to be compassionate with yourself and see what a valuable and worthwhile person you are.

Exposing shame for what it really is

Another universal reaction to chronic or overwhelming hurt is shame. Marisol knew shame intimately. When just out of college, she fell in love with a man who was involved in a religious movement. Marisol became a member of the cult at 22, gave all her earnings to the leader who inflicted psychological cruelty and brainwashing on his followers. He kept her and the others cut off from their families and told them they were too unstable to ever marry or have children. In this way, he acted as abusers usually do—by undermining their victims' self-esteem and making them believe that no one else will want them, and that their misery as a result of the abuse is because of their own faults. It took Marisol years to fight her way free of the cult, and still she was afraid of this man and the prestige with which he was viewed by the world at large, which knew nothing of his cult practices. She carried within her a well of shame.

Let's clarify the difference between shame, guilt, and remorse. Guilt is feeling that you have done something wrong, based on standards of behavior learned from others. It is imperative to society that people be able to feel guilt. It indicates that people have consciences. Properly used, it leads to remorse, which is feeling badly about having done something wrong and wishing that you could undo the damage caused by your actions. (Improperly used, guilt occurs when we go against the expectations of our parents which may have been for their benefit and not necessarily in our best interest. Guilt that you feel when you break those internalized messages and act to further your own life will be dealt with in a later chapter.) At the other end of the spectrum, psychopaths do not feel guilt, so they have no compunction about hurting or using others. They do not see people as real with rights of their own. So there is an important place for moderate guilt and remorse in the development of civilization.[2]

Shame is not guilt or remorse. Shame is self-blame. Shame develops often when children are overwhelmed by events and believe, or are made to believe, that the pain is their fault. Shame grows when they go from feeling badly to believing that they are bad. Shame builds when they not only see it as their fault that some event occurred, but when they see events as proving that they are wicked. As grown-ups, they often have had so little real training in working through their feelings and supporting a positive self-image that their systems run instantly to that childhood mechanism of self-blame. Over time, any uncomfortable emotion becomes a trigger to blame themselves again. It comes quickly to be interpreted as, if they feel badly about something, or in reaction to something, it means that they are bad. So many people I've worked with have a hidden belief that, if they feel badly in response to things—hurt when someone says something hurtful; angry when their rights are infringed upon; sad when they lose someone—that feeling is a sign that there is something wrong with them. "You ought to be ashamed of yourself!" has such a powerful effect on people as an epithet, because it is a demand that you define yourself as bad. Their only recourse is then to attack themselves as the source of pain and evil in an effort to change into what their critic sees as acceptable. And, we're now back to the topic of trying to find control when the issue is really powerlessness.[3]

Self-doubt

Tani's father, Malcolm, was handsome, charismatic, and boyish in more ways than just his looks. He acted as if the world was there for his enjoyment and people were there to entertain him. He reacted to his children's needs as outrageous obstructions to his freedom. Tani's mother, Alexandra, believed that her children's job in life was to make her feel loved so that she'd never feel lonely. Alexandra masked a deeply hidden depression with hyper-enthusiasm and hostility.

She attacked Tani especially (the only girl child) for any needs she had. So Tani grew up reacting to any urge to further her own life with anxiety and suspicion, because it had gotten her into trouble to pay attention to herself rather than focusing on the needs of her parents. She worked hard to overcome the effects of her childhood, but she did not realize how deep and pervasive the *fiat* to deny her autonomy was. When she made a decision, no matter how small, she doubted herself. If she started washing the car, she thought she should be cleaning the basement. If she tried to relax, she berated herself for not doing something to further her career. It wasn't that she couldn't make decisions. It was that she gave herself such a hard time for them. She'd revisit each one over and over, telling herself that she'd made the wrong one and that her thinking process was faulty. When she started moving in a direction, she attacked herself harshly. Every move was complicated by the thicket of self-doubt ingrained in her.

She was missing out on supporting herself and moving through life with a positive foundation, so that she could focus on her own goals and use her talents and energy to further them. What Tani knew but couldn't get a grip on was that doing something to further her own life, moving in her own direction, broke all the rules of her childhood. By denying herself, she attempted to be a good daughter and get her parents' approval.

Narcissistic parents demand that their children live as extensions of them, meeting their own needs for gratification. The children's developing their own direction or sense of themselves is perceived by the parent as a betrayal. The children grow up fighting against their innate urge to grow and develop, because they have internalized the demand that they live to meet their parents' needs rather than their own. *(Galomb)* What they don't see is that this battle with themselves keeps them distracted from the reality of the pain of having parents who did not see them as people with their own lives and who did not support their individuation or development.

Tani is just one example of someone with painful experiences whose past pushes her to turn against herself in an effort to manage deep trauma. Self-doubt makes it very difficult to make decisions and to succeed at our own goals. Shoving down our feelings because they are painful makes it much harder to live our lives based on what is true for us, for it cuts us off from pleasant emotions as well as painful ones. We will see, in the chapter on how the brain works, why it is essential to be in touch with our emotions in order to make any decision whatsoever.

The most important thing to know about self-doubt is that it is a way of trying to protect ourselves by distracting us from our painful feelings. When we doubt ourselves, we get so caught up in the back-and-forth of our thoughts that we assume that we are engaging in a valuable assessment process. Not so. We need to take a deep breath and step back and see that self-doubt really has nothing to do with whether we are making the right decision. Either choice would lead to the same agitation. Self-doubt is designed to keep us from putting ourselves in danger, as our most primitive protection mechanisms define it. Going against our parents is dangerous. Being visible is dangerous. Standing up for ourselves is dangerous. Saying no is dangerous.

But undermining ourselves robs us of our lives. Not standing up for ourselves saps our energy and sense of self. Doubting ourselves is a sign that there is something else going on that we need to look at, if we want to be free and to uncover joy.

The hidden gratification of self-hatred

If self-hatred hurts so much, why do people sometimes seem as if they are wallowing in it? Observers, and the suffering folks themselves, don't recognize that there is a very deeply hidden reward in it. When we see ourselves as so dastardly, so toxic, having so much negative effect on events, subconsciously we are ascribing an amazing amount of power to ourselves. This comes with the territory when we are children, for kids think in universal terms—always, never, everything—and they do perceive everything as being about them. When we mire ourselves in self-hatred as adults, we unconsciously lock in that same out-sized childhood assumption in the amount of influence we have over others and over events. It seems to allay some of the helplessness and shame we feel if even unconsciously we see ourselves as having such grand effect. Yet, we lose sight of any awareness that others are responsible for their own behavior and that they react to their own preoccupations. Relying on self-flagellation to try to get us on the right track, we do not allow ourselves to experience ourselves as valid and valuable.

Quick Fixes: what happens when we don't do the real work

Over time, unless we have done the work to process painful feelings, we more and more quickly react to discomfort of any kind by using Quick Fixes. A Quick Fix is whatever is fastest, easiest and most pain-suppressing at the moment. It could be ice cream, instead of having an overdue conversation. It could be drugs, rather than tolerating the embarrassment of being rejected. Quick Fixes seem to work so well because they reduce the first flare of feeling by distracting us with instant gratification. They remove just enough anxiety that the real issue sinks out of sight. They lull us into a false sense of having gotten the problem to go away. Then we feel betrayed when it rears up again.

Rationalizing: another form of Quick Fix

Rationalizations are excuses we tell ourselves to justify our behavior. Some that are used often are:

- There's no point in feeling anger/loss/sadness. Crying doesn't help either. It won't change what happened.

- There's no point in dwelling on the past. I have to cut my losses and move on.

- I've have been slogging through the pain for ages, so I should done, already. I shouldn't have to feel more of it.

🪶 If I were over it, I'd be totally fine all the time. The fact that I still feel sad sometimes proves that nothing really works.

🪶 I'm the victim. It's not fair that I have to work to get over this!

While these statements illustrate normal reactions, they also are often used to justify taking the easy way out. It seems quicker to drink, sleep around, cut oneself, or hide in the house reading murder mysteries and eating potato chips, than it does to do the work of facing the deep hurt.

The problem with any form of Quick Fix is that it adds to our troubles in the long run. As well as becoming dependent on this habit of avoidance, it leads to feeling fatalistic, depressed, and despairing. QFs make it harder to recognize underlying issues, because we employ them so fast. As the unreleased feelings push up over and over, we start believing that there is no successful method of resolution, and that we must be too weak and ineffectual to face or tolerate the real issue. We don't see that the emotions are coming back precisely because we have not really addressed them. So QFs turn out not to be such quick fixes after all.

What causes people to do bad things

I'm convinced that a primary reason that people do really bad things to others is in order to avoid deeply buried emotions. It may be that they never learned to deal with feelings, or were overwhelmed by trauma themselves, or don't see others as human. But with all of these, there is the function of avoiding deeply buried self-hatred, shame, or a sense of howling emptiness. To hide from these feelings, they blame others; try to prove themselves at others' expense; or convince themselves that others cause their discomfort. Or they try to bolster their sagging self-esteem by joining a bigger force that makes them feel powerful, such as a street gang, proselytizing group, or invading army.

The problem is, in doing so, they try to deny that we feel such pain by acting out on others. People who are violent often are actually avoiding simply feeling angry or hurt. Those who target others, on whatever level, often feel justified because they have denied their own emotional reactions so much that they have conned themselves into believing that others cause them to feel that way. Blaming others keeps them distracted from the real issues as completely as does self-blame.

When you avoid discomfort, you can't resolve issues or support yourself

Cameron had spent his childhood being labeled by his high-powered father as the weak link in the family. His father did not realize that he maintained his own self-image by belittling others. When Cameron went off to college, his natural drive to develop and succeed threatened his father-generated self-image as a failure. After all, when he was the ineffectual problem-child, he had a place and the role of making his father feel good about himself. Cameron subconsciously became threatened by growing up and tried to revert to his old way of being. So he developed physical symptoms. In graduate school, he began to have terrible back pain. In his thirties, he developed complex health issues. As the years went on, even though treatments successfully dealt with his illnesses, he maintained a pessimistic attitude, feeling done-to by circumstance. He felt knocked down by fatigue and every ache and pain. He reached the point at which he could not work, and even household tasks seemed too much. He viewed his frailty as caused by illness rather than the fact that he had not exerted himself to act on his own goals in years. He thought he had come to terms with his father's intolerance, but Cameron could not see the way he held himself in the role of useless child. He avoided the fear that was generated by starting his own life by sabotaging himself.

This was not someone who was exhausted and wasting away due to a complex medical problem such as Chronic Fatigue Immune Dysfunction Syndrome or Lyme Disease. Rather, Cameron was so stressed by an unconscious desire to hold himself down that his immune system was compromised. Eventually it complied by creating symptoms that made him into the helpless, weak person his dad saw when he looked at him.

When we blame ourselves, we often get into a pattern of becoming very attentive to our physical discomforts or health issues. Unable to support ourselves as worthy, it's the only way we allow ourselves to pay attention to our well-being.

This pattern comes back to shame. When we believe deep-down that we are damaged, we may scrutinize ourselves for any sign that we are not all right yet, that we are still affected by the trauma, that we don't know how to handle ourselves, or to live. We are not okay. That's the bottom line. We may become hyper-vigilant about discomfort and not believe that we can tolerate it in order to reach a goal. We are caught in a belief that life will continue to feel terrible, so we want to delay engaging with it again as long as possible.

We all have painful things to deal with. When we're up against something, the only real choice is this: in what way do you want to feel uncomfortable? Do you want to saddle yourself the kind of discomfort that comes from hiding from the real issues? Is the pain of having an alcohol problem, or of being lonely because people don't stick around after being blamed for your stuff easier to deal with than the alternative? Do you want to believe that you are too small and weak to deal with terror, grief, abandonment?

Or are you brave enough to bear the discomfort inherent in looking directly at your stored memories, and allow yourself to process the pain and learn from it, resolve it, and move on?

We all, when we are not paying attention, make do with what looks easiest and most comfortable, which is really choosing what's least uncomfortable. We get more and more sensitive to the smallest irritants, and then to the slightest reminders. When our chief motivation is to avoid discomfort, everything has power over us. All it takes to make us jerk like a marionette is for something to look as if it is going to be a bit uncomfortable. Our lives shrink as we tolerate less and less, and fear more and more.

Practice: The next time you notice you are berating yourself for something, ask what you are claiming power over. Do you really know that that guy cut you off simply as a comment on your lousy driving? Do you know that Susie hates you because your off-hand comment offended her? Do you know that your boss is going to take your project away because you laughed too loudly in morning meeting? Do you know that someone would not have been hurt, or have died, if only you had done such-and-such?

- Pull back and identify what superpower you are ascribing to yourself. Did you make it rain? Are you responsible for others' moods? Do you determine others' choices?
- Think of other reasons why they might behave that way that only have to do with them.
- See if it is a relief not to be the sole reason why people do what they do or events occur as they do. See if you relax. You may not.

When you stop taking responsibility for things that you have no real control over, you may start becoming aware of what you are avoiding by taking the blame for everything.

Practice: What have you backed off from recently, thinking it was too scary, or that the feelings it aroused in you were too uncomfortable? Identify some activity or goal that you would like to engage in that you have been putting off because you feared it would be too uncomfortable.

Practice: Make some sign or arrangement that will remind you that the very things that you do to hold yourself away from pain are the very things that hold you in the pain, and hold the pain in you.

Practice: Plan for self-criticism. Notice when you tend to do it. For a while, be conscious before the completion of every activity that might lead to that reaction and counter it before it happens. Ride right over it, every time. Focusing on doing it every time can break the habit. It's okay if maybe you counter a judgement about something that you aren't proud of. In the course of your life, you can afford to support yourself about everything for a while.

Now, let's look at what it is about the way our brains function that keep us feeling traumatized and stuck in old patterns; and what we can do to harness that set-up to free ourselves.

Endnotes

1 I won't go into the prevalent uses of alcohol, drugs, sex, self-mutilation, or targeting others as defenses against one's own pain. There are plenty of books on these topics and plenty of therapists who are skilled at working with these issues. I will mention that they do fall under the category of 'heavy artillery.' I see them as an extra layer of distraction from the ones discussed here, because in using them people further externalize their problem, taking their attention several degrees further away from the real issue. So on top of the issues and the distraction, they must wrestle with the destructive behavior.

If you use any of these, apply what is in this chapter, knowing that you will have the added job of recognizing the protective purpose of your obsession, and you will have to do the work to stop using it as a fogging device before you can make significant gains with these Energy Medicine techniques.

2 Guilt can be induced by manipulation, in which the one feeling guilty believes that they are responsible for the emotional well-being of another, and so must limit their actions or growth in order to palliate the other. Folks in this position would do well to notice that the times when they feel guiltiest are when they are trying to act on their own behalf, instead of doing what was expected of them to benefit or appease the guilt-tripper. It still is not the same as shame.

3 Dan Hughes, PhD, is a psychologist who trains therapists, agencies, and parents to help kids who have been through the ringer and ended up in foster care. He states that shame inevitably occurs in children who have been abused. He stresses the importance of helping the children learn to tolerate shame enough that they can work their way through it, now accompanied by a loving adult, to the reality that they feel terrible but it was not their fault. Dr. Hughes shows how blaming themselves leads to the oppositional-defiant behavior that gets many kids in trouble. They act out in order to put distance between themselves and the belief that they are horrible. They attempt to control all situations in order to counter their lack of control over their immensely painful feelings. Shame is the outcome of their anxious or severed attachments—of the kids not being able to trust that care-givers will be there for them or actually want to take care of them. They act out their lack of trust and their fear of feeling close and vulnerable and dependent. Shame does not lead to healthy development. It obstructs it.

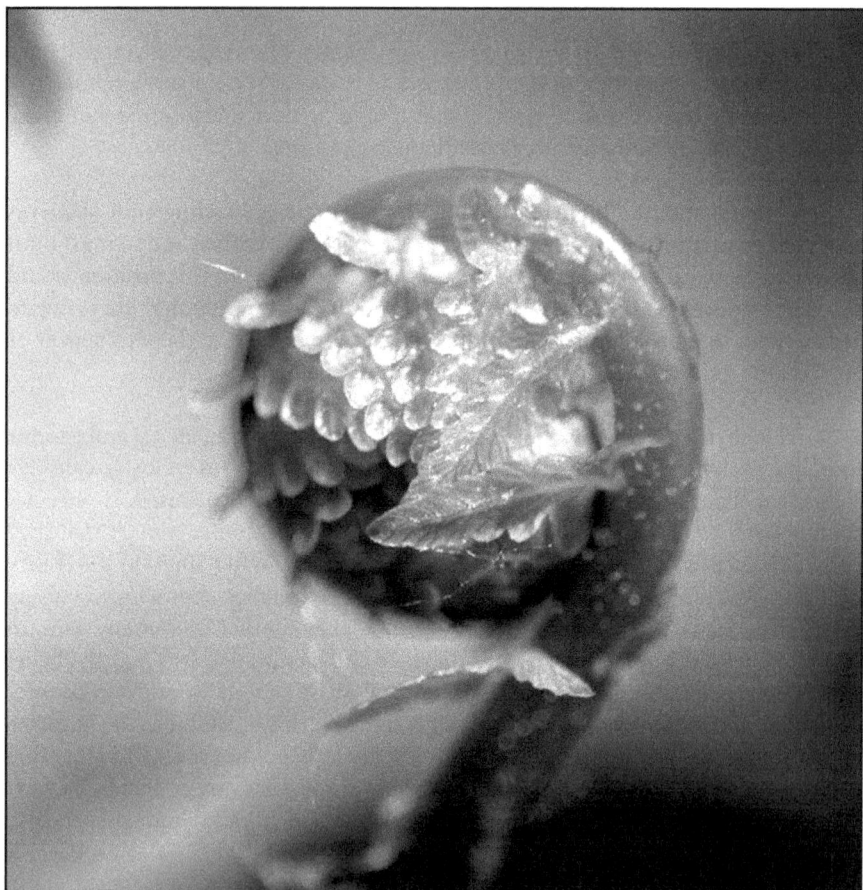

Your brain never stops developing and changing. It's been doing it from the time you were an embryo, and will keep on doing it all your life. And this ability, perhaps, represents its greatest strength.

—James Trefil, physicist and author

The Brain's Role in Change: 3
why it holds onto pain, and
how to use it to feel better

As YOU MOVE through later chapters devoted to releasing pain and anxiety, acquiring new skills, and experiencing joy, each topic will involve the nervous system and brain functions. The nervous system is an energy system. Along with the electrical and chemical wiring involved in sending and receiving messages, triggering actions, organizing and retrieval of information, assessment and interpretation of experiences, the brain orchestrates the complex movement of energy in our bodies, minds, and emotions. Your nervous system affects how you store different types of memories, how you build new skills, what habits you change easily and what you seem stuck with. You *can* change your experience of life. It can begin to transform when you realize that happiness is truly attainable and increase-able. The more you understand specific ways in which the brain behaves, the more effectively you can counter particular functions that hold you back and make better use of the ones that help you move forward. There are several mechanisms in the neurological setup that keep you feeling traumatized. Understanding those functions allows you to unwire them more easily and thereby create some space for new patterns to take hold.

Your brain, emotions, and decision-making

Physicians and scientists have performed research on brain-damaged people since the 1800's in order to learn how the way the brain works. When people survived severe accidents, such as a Phineas Gage's railroad tamping iron through the skull, doctors had a chance to map the functions of different areas of the brain by noting in what ways their functioning was affected. Other patients studied were those whose brain damage had been purposefully inflicted. These were mental patients considered incorrigibly dangerous who underwent prefrontal lobotomies.[1] The prefrontal cortex has been called the "seat of civilization," because the mature reflective functions occur here. It is the seat of decision-making. It is the location of gathering and synthesizing information from many sensory and cognitive areas and then giving you the chance to consider options before acting. In a lobotomy, the connection between the prefrontal cortex and the emotional centers, such as the limbic system, were severed, so that the primitive emotional reactions would no longer overpower the not-fully-developed reasoning processes in these individuals.

Such surgeries were considered successes (even though there many were serious side-effects) because patients exhibiting delusional behavior or violence went from being raging and out-of-control to laid-back (or vegetative). One very interesting and devastating side effect occurred that the doctors had not anticipated: many of these patients were unable to make even the smallest decision. They could weigh pros and cons and discuss various possible outcomes, but they could not decide whether to have eggs or French toast for breakfast. Why? In order for people to make a decision, it is imperative to be in touch with their emotions. If they are not, for whatever reason, there is no way of determining what was right for them.

The felt sense of what is best for you is vital in making a choice. After all the gathering of facts and weighing of options, the real decision-maker is your sense of what feels right to you. Your emotions give you information about the world and about your experiences. They let you know the impact and importance of things. They also show you the bottom line on what is best for you, at the time.

Traumatic memory

It is not your imagination or some lack of effort on your part that makes traumatic memories stick around (and jump out and derail you) no matter what you've tried. Bessel van der Kolk's team discovered that traumatic memories are stored in a different area in the brain than are regular memories. While we are remembering something untraumatic, our brains are active, firing, maybe hundreds of synapses as we watch the movie in our minds.

In his research, van der Kolk found that, when people are in the midst of a traumatic memory, all firing stops except for a few functions maintaining the body. As the brain stops practically all activity, trauma survivors are frozen in a state of hyper-arousal, but with a lowered ability to move, experiencing the memory as if it's happening right now, unable to move, think or shake it.

So their normal processing and resolution systems cannot be accessed. That trauma storage location of the brain is not accessible by Broca's area, the portion involved in speech, so verbal therapy alone does not get those memories to loosen up. The experiences remain stuck as graphic visual images and sensations—glimpses of something, sounds, smells, bodily sensations—visceral memories easily triggered by sensory events in the present, and always replayed as if occurring now. As Dr. van der Kolk said, "These 'memories' typically remain unintegrated and unaltered by the course of time…Traumatized people are prone to have intrusive memories of elements of the trauma, to have a poor tolerance for arousal, to respond to stress in an all-or-nothing way, and to feel emotionally numb." (*van der Kolk & Jose*)

Often their minds are flooded with the event as well. Examples include Viet Nam veterans who suddenly throw themselves flat on the beach when they see a horseshoe crab, certain that they are about to be blown up by a land mine. "Hyperarousal causes memories to be split off from consciousness and stored as visual images or bodily sensations. Fragments of these "visceral" memories return later as physiological reactions, emotional states, nightmares, flashbacks, or behavioral reenactments." (*van der Kolk & van der Hart*)[2]

Connie would find herself suddenly in the middle of cars in the street. Her body figured it was safer in traffic than on the sidewalk near some guy who looked like her attacker. Or she'd find herself hyperventilating in an elevator, afraid of being confined.

People with stubborn hurts unconsciously rehearse beliefs that come from those experiences, such as "I will never be safe," or "No one is there when I need them," or "I will always be alone." In saying it over and over subconsciously, they build more dendrites on the nerve line on which the belief is stored. Dr. van der Kolk stated that the most pervasive, destructive and tenacious emotional effects of trauma, and the most difficult to alter, are self-doubt and despair. But it doesn't have to stay that way. You are not stuck with the effects of whatever hurts you have experienced.

Your brain continues to develop—neuroplasticity

Early scientific studies led to the belief that the adult human brain is unchangeable except through damage or decay. The prevailing opinion was that it is not possible to grow new areas, and that each area is for one purpose and can only addresses that purpose. For example, the visual cortex can only be used for sight. Some textbooks still used today state that brain development gallops along in early childhood, slows toward adulthood, and then stops. (*Cohen*)

These scientists based their hypotheses on brain size. They believed that, since 95% of volume is reached by age five, there must be little change thereafter, so that by the time we reach adulthood we are pretty much stuck with what we have. Based on this volume assumption, medical researchers and psychologists concluded that such things as children's intelligence and abilities, as well as their sense of themselves socially and psychologically, were fixed by age five. They also believed that the nervous system does not grow new cells, that older adults can't learn as well as young people, that neural connections are pretty much fixed throughout life, and that intelligence is determined at birth by the number of neurons you have and how fast they fire. (*Cohen*), (*Dweck*)

We now know that these assumptions are untrue. Recent research has found that size is not the determinant of function. What matters is structure, the formation of neurological components capable of advanced activities. Two primary examples are the *corpus callosum*,

—the bundle of nerves that connects the two halves of the brain so that we can combine information and perceptions of both; and the prefrontal cortex, seat of emotional control, impulse restraint, and rational decision-making. These two structures begin construction in adolescence and are not completed until around twenty-two years of age or even later. (*Bradley*)

Countering other erroneous assumptions about brain function, it is now known that:

- Experience and practice of activities over time change the brain, which continually redesigns in response to thought patterns and motions that we engage in.

- Neural cells do form throughout life.

- The brain continues to organize itself as we age and continues to develop more ability to work with input from its many parts as we grow older. The two hemispheres are used more equally as we get older than when we were young, and we are more balanced, more mature, and more able to access more varied types of information, and utilize functions more fully. (*Cohen*)

The fact that the brain and nervous system are able to change is called neuroplasticity. The change in neural structure and function occurs in response to experience or environmental stimuli. (*Rapoport & Gotgay*) The first discoveries of neuroplasticity occurred when researchers studied how different messages received through the senses alter the brain's structure and function. In the mid-1960's Marion Diamond, a professor of anatomy at the University of California, Berkeley, found that when rats were placed in a more stimulating environment, their neurons sprouted new dendrites and produced higher levels of acetylcholine, a neurotransmitter. Since then researchers have noticed that older people who have dedicated years to certain activities have dramatically different brains from younger, less experienced people. Examples are taxi drivers, pianists, scientists, writers, cooks, electricians. The older we get, the more our specialized activities cause our brains to specialize as well. The parts of a mature person's brain in which there are the neurons (brain cells) that rule that specific action look like a dense forest with many branches on each tree. The area that the forest takes up also is vaster than in other people and often spreads into neighboring areas of the brain. So, the brain actively changes and grows in response to use, learning, and stimulation, and does not necessarily limit itself to a rigid map for different functions. (*Maguire, et al*), (*Ungerleider, et al*)

At the Harvard Medical School, neuroscientist Alvaro Pascual-Leone discovered that thoughts can alter the physical structure and function of brain cells. He had one group of volunteers practice a five-finger piano exercise for two hours for several weeks. Another group learned the exercise and then imagined playing it without moving their hands. Both groups' brains were then mapped. It was found that both groups had expanded the region of motor cortex that controls the movement of the fingers. "Mental practice resulted in a similar reorganization" of the brain as did actual playing, Pascual-Leone wrote. This, of course, supports what we see on television every time the Olympics come around. We can see all those athletes mentally running through their event before they actually perform. For years, sports psychologists have touted the benefits of mental practice on performance.

Other research speaks even more directly to our goals of being able to alter our moods and our experience of life. A growing body of evidence indicates that there is a 'happiness set point' to which a person returns after either a deeply painful loss or a wildly happy experience. People eventually tend to return to this level no matter whether they have won the lottery or lost their spouse. Richard Davidson, of the University of Wisconsin, Madison, did a good part of this research. He found that having more activity in the left prefrontal cortex than in the right correlates with a higher baseline level of contentment, so this relation of left over right cortical activity came to be seen as a marker for the happiness set point. At first it was believed that this set point was immutable as were other brain functions. (*Davidson*), (*Peterson*)

He then studied the research done by Dr. Schwartz on patients with obsessive-compulsive disorder, in which it was found that after ten weeks of cognitive therapy (which works with patients' thought processes and trains them to counter negative messages with more reality-based positive ones), twelve out of eighteen patients improved significantly. Before-and-after brain scans showed that activity in the orbital frontal cortex—the core of the OCD circuit—had fallen dramatically and in exactly the way that drugs effective with OCD affect the brain. Schwartz called it "self-directed neuroplasticity," concluding that "the mind can change the brain."

Upon studying the effects of cognitive training on the outcome of OCD and depression, Davidson wondered if meditation or other forms of mental training could produce changes in the base level of people's experience of happiness. With the permission and encouragement of the Dalai Lama, Davidson studied Tibetan Buddhist monks who had spent years training their minds and emotions through meditation. The comparison group was made up of undergraduate students with no prior experience of meditation who were then taught basic techniques.

Davidson gave the subjects functional MRI's while he measured their brain activity during various meditation practices. One monk engaged in specific lovingkindness techniques while scientists mapped his brain activity. After three hours of testing he was pulled out of the machine. "That felt like going on retreat! I feel fresh and rested," he said. (If you have not had an MRI, the machine makes a large pounding sound, several times per second.) Finding it relaxing meant that the monk was able to use the external pounding as a constant reminder to stay focused on his meditation rather than be pulled into fighting or avoiding the hammering. The time length alone that the monk was able to tolerate in the machine is enough to indicate something amazing about the monk's brain structure.

The researchers found that the monks had significantly greater activation in a brain network linked to empathy and caring-based (as opposed to erotic) love. The more years the subject had engaged in meditation practice, the larger and more developed were the connections between the prefrontal cortex and the brain's emotional regions. There were also more synapses devoted to moderating emotional reactions with the thinking and assessment functions of the cortex.

As well, there was a striking difference in the monks' left prefrontal cortex—a site of activity associated with happiness and contentment. While they practiced a compassion technique, activity in the left prefrontal area overrode activity in the right prefrontal (associated with negative moods) to a degree never before seen in subjects. The comparison group of students showed no such differences between the left and right prefrontal cortices. So, while the monks had a full range of emotions, like anyone else, they were happier and less inclined to fall into despair or other painful states, because their meditation practices had altered their brains to support and return to happiness.

Davidson concluded that both these research studies indicated that happiness is a skill that can be learned. For the monks, as well as the patients with depression or OCD, the conscious act of training themselves to think in a particular way rearranged the brain.

What we practice with conscious awareness, as well as what we repeat not so consciously in the back of our minds, affects the structure and connections in our nervous system and how much real estate is invested in different brain centers. Our repeated thoughts, whether conscious or not, affect how we feel and how we see the world. People who work carefully with their thoughts are calmer, happier, and less reactive. They have more chance of responding in the ways they want, rather than being triggered by situations into old habits or off-balance retorts. Clearly, the implications of the brain research, for those of us who have felt traumatized by our pasts, are huge.

The brain looks for disaster first

When babies are born, the parts of their brain that are fully functional are those involved with survival. Their heart and other organs work, and they quickly pick up breathing and digestion. The first emotional systems formed are those that will help them stay alive. Getting the attention of caretakes is essential. When something goes wrong—they are uncomfortable or scared—the tone of their crying sounds as if they are thinking, "Help! Danger! Hurry up! I'm dying!" This is very effective, as it gets adults to come running.

What babies do not have is the ability to understand that a dirty diaper is not life-threatening. They actually develop the ability to calm down about events when they watch their care-givers respond calmly and lovingly, and when they grow old enough to develop more sophisticated brain parts. But that's another matter. What is pertinent now is that the first emotional mechanism is one lodged in the brain stem, or the "reptilian brain"—the one that reacts to everything as a life-and-death crisis.

So the disaster voice is always loudest, first, and fastest, because it is fully operational at birth, has had the most practice, and is the simplest of any reaction system. Any other coping mechanism that we developed that tells us we are okay came later and is a more complex neurological event. These more reasonable (and more accurate, most of the time) voices will always be softer and a bit slower. It is only with time and growth that people develop the synaptic capacity to see that things are not so bad, that they can tolerate waiting, or remember that good things do happen. As a matter of fact, the higher functions that control decision-making, the accurate reading of emotions, and being able to balance emotions with considerations specifically about those emotions, will not be completely developed until about age 20 or even later!

We can see this in sports, as well. There are three stress windows that the body goes through during aerobic sports. The first one is the anaerobic threshold, and it comes when your system depletes its store of oxygen stored in your blood and must switch to the aerobic system—your breathing. This occurs around two minutes into a hard workout. At the two-minute mark, you will hear a voice in your head crying, "Danger! I can't breathe! I'm gonna die!" If you work out regularly, you know that this happens, so you stay calm and you keep going for the five to fifteen seconds it takes your body to switch over. Then you are fine, until you reach the next threshold at roughly twenty minutes to a half-hour in, which is when your muscles run out of glycogen and your system needs to turn to using fat stores for fuel. Same thing happens—a voice starts shrieking. You rely on your experience to calm yourself, the system switches over, and you continue your workout.

We need to learn to do this same thing when the brain stem shrieks about events. If we know that the disaster voice always gets there first, we can learn to stay calm enough to monitor a situation and give ourselves a reality check as to the real danger level. Then we can keep moving toward our goal. It also means that, even though they aren't as loud or as pushy, these more positive messages we develop for ourselves are legitimate. Remembering this will help you give them a chance to be heard. They are valuable and worth listening to. It just takes practice to listen, and to strengthen them.

The amygdalae, fear, and anxiety

The *amygdalae* are known to be involved in reactions to fear, anxiety, and depression. They are two almond shaped bunches of neural nuclei in the limbic system, located in the forward section of the temporal lobes on the hippocampi. They are triggered by the thalamus, which receives information directly from sense organs when something happens. They in turn trigger the hypothalamus, which prepares the body for action by activating the sympathetic nervous system. The amygdalae are able to receive information from the cortex after the cortex has assessed the arousing event and compared it to memories and thoughts. If developed (meaning if we have practiced stopping ourselves and assessing a situation), and if our history of trauma does not overwhelm it, this second pathway gives the brain a moment to analyze the stimulus to determine whether or not the threat is real and how big it really is.

This double system is great, but there are also some problems. The path from the amygdala to the cortex is the survival one already active at birth, so it is more developed than the one from the assessment centers (some of which only finish developing with the onset of adulthood). So it is harder to stand down than it is to fire up. The amygdalae also have a function in causing you to freeze, which may be fine if you are a deer or find that moving gets you hit worse, but it's not so fine if you want to mobilize newer thought processes so that you remember that you are okay now, in the present. As Doug Holt says, "Freezing is a robust index of learned fear," which means that, if your history has taught you to refrain from defending yourself when you are threatened, you may find yourself going numb a lot. Freezing externally does not mean that inside all is quiet. "Concurrent with immobilization caused by sympathetic system arousal are hyperarousal of the nervous system, high emotional reactivity, and racing thoughts. It may be followed, when the parasympathetic system takes over, by lethargy and numbness."

The amygdala reacts just as enthusiastically to memory as to present events (and also television images), so it can misread the present level of danger. Since it also stores remembrances of fear, it can misinterpret signals from the body. This can lead to panic, which can be defined as fear-thoughts which feed on themselves and get you more riled up, since being caught in them makes it hard to settle enough to look and see what triggered them. (We'll look more at anxiety and panic in chapter nine.) Traumatic memories are not stored in the same part of the brain as normal memories, and they are not "remembered" in the same way. They are stored more as the bodily reactions, including the emotional ones. Normal memories take time to be organized and consolidated. Since traumatic memories are by definition overwhelmingly upsetting, they do not get processed or organized into story lines with resolutions and wrap-ups about what they mean to us. They are not integrated into the narrative of our lives. So, they do not present themselves as memories of things long past. They seem to be happening in the present, because they usually are roused by some current event that triggers the body physically and emotionally in a way that seems similar to the first event. As Bessel van der Kolk says, "These 'memories' typically remain unintegrated and unaltered by the course of time." When we are in the grip of these "memory" events, we often find ourselves reacting before we know what we are reacting to, or out of proportion to what is going on in front of us.

What it comes down to is that the amygdalae are involved when we're startled, anticipating danger, ruminating and panicking about danger, or reacting to fear. From an experiential standpoint, as long as you are anticipating a scary event you may continue to build yourself up into a frenzy of fear, even if it is one that you want to do, such as, say, performing violin at Lincoln Center. Being anxious before a performance is a good thing, in that it gathers your energy and attention, and raises your adrenalin to ensure that you do a great job. But, if you stew in it too long, or don't counter it with pep-talks, you are likely to go beyond a tolerable level of arousal and run out of the stage door in a panic.

The way to end anxiety-extending perseveration in the amygdalae is to take action to change your focus. Walking onto the stage, bowing, and starting to play moves your neural firings out of the anticipation-of-danger center and into the involvement-with-what-you-are-doing brain systems. Movement stimulates the brain so that the impulses stop being sent to the amygdala and move to monitoring your actions. This is why you feel more involved in what you are doing and less concerned about the opinions of others or of your own resistant thoughts after the first few minutes of an activity. As Doug Holt says in his article on the amygdalae, "Through testing with laboratory animals, it has been determined that when attention is shifted away from the anxiety-provoking stimulus, less fear is observed. When a novel stimulus is presented slightly before or at the same time as a well-trained condition stimulus, the condition response will be disrupted." Translating that to our needs, it means that it is possible to change patterns and attenuate upset reactions. You can interrupt the anxiety and panic of anticipating danger by grounding and centering. Grounding and centering not only change your mental focus, they return you to yourself and connect you with your energy. They stop the endless feedback loop of fear-reinforcing thoughts. In following chapters, we will discuss the skills that will help you

1) access the prefrontal cortex, so that you can accurately assess present situations,

2) gather yourself so that you can walk on your chosen stage in the first place, and

3) feel collected and focus on the task at hand, rather than your fear.

But first, let's look at brain functions that help us build these skills.

Bunching

Why is it, when we have just run into a difficult situation, we find ourselves obsessing about all the things we suddenly need to take care of *RIGHT NOW*? All at once, that will we've never written, our lack of savings, the weight we haven't lost, our kids' lack of manners, the mess in the basement, the career tracks we haven't explored, *and* the problems in our marriages must be fixed. Why is it that, right when you least need to be swamped with painful memories, they all come flying in? Is it that our past experience is trying to show us that it's hopeless? People often complain that one thing that keeps them from changing their experience of life is this phenomenon of inundating with negative memories and demands. I'm sure we all have had the experience of having our car not start or having a fight with a friend, and then finding ourselves flooded with an entire list of problems, or with our negative beliefs. It is almost as if our minds are bound and determined to bury us under piles of insurmountable sludge.

It helps to understand that the nervous system organizes memories of painful events by bunching. Just as you put all your socks together in one drawer and keep all your bills together in a different one (presumably), your nervous system organizes events, memories, and learned lessons by type. If you have a memory of being ridiculed, and you have other memories that remind you of being ridiculed, they all are bunched together on the same nerve strand. When one of those memories is triggered by a person who looks like someone you felt ridiculed by, then the whole strand is triggered. Many of those memories are not even of being ridiculed. They may be of being treated badly, or ones in which you interpreted what was said as ridicule due to the lens through which you perceive the world,. But, when the whole strand is triggered, you then feel flooded with all the memories bunched on the strand. The survival mechanism may be to help us pay attention to learned dangers, but in modern life you may conclude that you are right in believing that everyone ridicules you and you are not treated fairly by anyone. Next stop, fatalism.

People feel overwhelmed and unable to cope because they think that they must attend to every thought on the string. If you can remember that memories and thought patterns—those you repeat a lot—are bunched, then you can train yourself to witness how your system throws all the bunched thoughts at you. You can learn to stop the string. You can remind yourself that, in the present, only one event is occurring. You can stop your mind from catastrophizing. You only need to attend to the one issue in front of you right now. By centering and grounding, you can stay in the moment and remind yourself of healthy beliefs that support your developing foundation of joy.

Practice: The next time you feel bummed by something, notice if your mind starts loading on all sorts of unrelated tasks with which to berate yourself. Remind yourself that your brain bunches thoughts as an organizational tool, not because it is a good idea to try to juggle all of them right now. Stop and take a deep breath, and then gently insist that you stick to the one task you need to do right now. Tell yourself that you can handle that one thing. See what happens to your stress level.

Grooves

When driving on a dirt road, your tires slide into the ruts made by all the other cars that have traveled that way. Grooves are what I call the neural pathways that are formed through repetition of conditioned reactions to old memories, thoughts, and triggers. They are the neurological basis for habits. Grooves are lines that, once developed, we run along automatically. They are like the tracks in a vinyl record. When we are engaged in one, we feel as if we are sliding into a familiar, well-worn chute to a predictable endpoint, which sometimes is the mire of our old, painful, hopeless beliefs.

The good news is that by practicing new behaviors, we groove in new pathways that are based on safety, joy, and optimism. As we develop these new grooves, we can choose to glide along them more and more easily, until *they* are the familiar tracks. I call this "grooving in a new neural pathway." When we use the old grooves less, they atrophy. Like old roads in the forest they gradually succumb to weeds and saplings, filled in with dirt from spring rains until they become less automatic and a less likely route to travel.

You'll actually start grooving in new paths for yourself as you practice the skills in this book.

Developing the Witness

One of the key elements to recovering joy, or developing it for the first time, is to increase your awareness of your thoughts, emotions, and behavior. You can't change what you can't see. If you are not able to witness yourself, you will assume that the unexamined reactions, beliefs, and thoughts that fly into your head are accurate. You won't have any chance to assess and counter them with new learning. Bringing conscious attention buys you time in which to choose how you want to respond. It also gives you a chance to treat yourself with more compassion and gentleness, moving from fighting with yourself to choosing to be on your own team.

Connie worked to develop her internal witness—her calm, non-judgmental way of being aware of herself. First she practiced it during yoga or when walking, then when she did mundane tasks, such as washing the dishes. It was a struggle at first to be a witness and not a self-castigator. Gradually she found that she was becoming aware of the times when she went on automatic, as well as what happened when she did—she'd chow down on chips or overreact to somebody. She worked at being more kind to herself about those occurrences, which added to her learning to be compassionate toward herself. Still, she had a long way to go to feel resolved about the attack.

Mindfulness enhances the effect of any activities. You increase the benefit of your effort when you pay attention. Conscious awareness augments the action of energy, so that biological processes, as well as mental or emotional ones, are enhanced when you pay attention while you do something. Have you noticed that you get more out of a workout when you keep your mind on the workings of your muscles, your breathing, and your alignment? Scientists have known for years that their attention changes outcomes of experiments. Doctors, physical therapists, and massage therapists, as well as alternative health practitioners, notice that patients who keep their awareness on procedures enhance their healing work.

Practice: Pick one activity to which you want to bring more mindfulness. While engaging in it, stop for a second. Breathe. Notice what is in front of you, behind, at the sides. Notice what it feels like to be doing what you're doing. Do it a bit more slowly, just for now. Notice the sensations in your body. Keep your mind focused on the activity, rather than wandering to what you'll have for lunch after. Feel the air on your skin, notice any smells. Then, notice how it is for you to be keeping yourself more company.

We will address self-attention, grooving in new habits, and freeing the stuck memories much more thoroughly in following chapters.

Endnotes

1 Plastic is defined as *capable of being shaped or formed* (American Heritage Dictionary). The substances we call plastic are called that due to their malleable, as opposed to crystalline or fibrous, structure. Clay when wet is plastic.

2 Prefrontal lobotomies cut the connection between the prefrontal cortex and the limbic system and the brain stem where emotions such as anxiety, anger, etc., are triggered and processed.

3 Also, as Bessel van der Kolk realized, it is possible to release traumatic memory if you can succeed in introducing movement into that stalled part of the brain. Energy Work is one of the few modalities that can get the energy in the brain to move. We will look at this in chapter seven.

4 "The signal that punishment is imminent activates two related mechanisms, one of which inhibits ongoing behavior, while the other increases the level of arousal. The behavioral facilitating system (BFS) (which is mediated by NE fibers emanating from the LC) activates the CNS structures necessary for emergency responses. The BFS is activated when specific goal-oriented aggressive attack patterns require motivated motor support (Dupre & Spoont, 1989). The opposing system, that of behavioral inhibition (BIS), is mediated by the septo-hippocampal system, primed by ascending serotonergic and cholingergic mechanisms. The crucial role of the septo-hippocampal system is to activate a descending inhibitory pathway which prevents initiation of emergency responses until it is clear that they are needed… Current clinical trials of (serotonin reuptake inhibitors) in people with PTSD suggest that they are by far the most effective biological treatments of PTSD currently available. This makes us believe that in traumatized individuals decreased serotonin decreases the influence of the Behavioral Inhibition System, thereby disposing the septo-hippocampal system to interpret ordinary stressors as recurrents of traumatic experiences. Thus we postulate that lowered serotonin activity in PTSD is responsible for the continuation of emergency responses to minor stresses long after the actual trauma has ceased." (*van der Kolk*)

Part II

The Crucial Skills for Resolving
Pain and Changing Your Life

@ Sarah Gillen

If you know the techniques of mindful breathing, mindful walking, mindful smiling, you can bring your mind back to your body and you become truly alive.
                                            —Thich Nhat Hanh

The Art and Energy of Breathing 4

GWYNETH BLEW INTO my office like a blonde whirlwind. Here was a pretty woman in her thirties with a neat figure dressed in the latest style. She was director of online applications at a trendy design company. Even though there were difficulties at work since the new CEO had come on board, what brought her into my office was the recent breakup with her boyfriend, Max. They'd been together for two years. He insisted that all their plans revolve around his ten-year-old son's schedule, dictated by Max's ex-wife. Gwyneth had been the one to travel every weekend. Max had also insisted that she be in the extra bedroom in the basement in the morning, because he worried that Billy would be confused if he found them in bed together. After two years, she finally questioned the necessity of the sleeping arrangements. She had no practice speaking up for herself (and had an unconscious belief that she didn't have the right to do so), so by the time she did say something, she was pretty worked up. Max accused her of being too emotional and broke off their relationship.

Max's rejection was the last straw. Now she had trouble sleeping, felt rudderless, anxious, and blamed herself for the breakup (as well as for pretty much everything else in her life).

Lawrence was laid off when the economy tanked. He was bound and determined not to be brought down by all the negativity in the news. At first he pounded the pavement and networked every day, working longer hours than he had at his job. When a friend said he should take a little vacation, Lawrence retorted that he had to keep moving. He held a lot of tension in his body, stiffening his torso and clenching his breath as well as his jaw. It was as if he would beat the job market into submission through force of will. But as time went on he went out less and less. By the time he came in to see me, he felt drained, listless, and depressed. His body was in knots, constricted energy and oxygen flow having depleted his system.

Jane had just become the proud grandmother of twin boys. Her daughter's pregnancy had been precarious, so Jane helped as much as possible to take care of the new babies. When babies scream, new mothers often become agitated. Babies sense their mom's tension through her body and energy and become more upset, which makes it even harder for the young mother to cope or comfort her baby. But Jane was experienced. "I've been practicing with them. When they need to relax, I know that I need to, too. I've been focusing on my breathing and using a louder breath out. They're really responding to it and calming down, and I feel better too."

Marisol, a composer, saw a dance performance in which breath was part of the choreography. Then she happened to have a conversation with a woman who had had a lung transplant. "I realized how important breath really is. It inspired me to write a composition in which musicians breathe as part of music. The piano plays nervous lines, while other musicians play different types of lines, as well as breathing, which is written into the score. It has been amazing to explore consciousness and breath."

Why focus on breathing?

We are alive, so we must be breathing, right? Why do we need to study breathing at all? Breathing is a good example of a function in which there is an unconscious, taken-for-granted level of activity that is has less benefit than the same action when we bring conscious attention to it. Until we do, we can't see how we impair our breath in unconscious reaction to emotions, tensions, and to being caught up in thinking.

People don't even realize that they hold their breath most of the time. Virtually everyone I work with tamps down their breath without realizing it. There are all sorts of affects to our breath that occur automatically in reaction to experiences. As only one example, when we impinge on it and limit air flow, tension builds up in many parts of the torso, with a corresponding lack of tone or energy occurring someplace else.

When we learn more about the breath, we can release tension and heal long-standing pain or weakness. Breathing becomes an art, a science, the basis of a more advanced relationship with our physical and emotional selves. Several traditions have noticed that you can affect your energy, health, awareness, and spiritual development through the practice of breathing techniques. Yogic tradition has delineated the most examples of types of breath and their uses in building and balancing pranayama, or life force. The benefits of conscious breathing can be as simple as noticing when we tend to hold our breath, or it can progress to being a tool to adjust our moods, to calm or energe ourselves, to change our chemistry, enhance athleticism, and deepen meditative states. The more you get into it, the more benefit you can gain and the more complex can be the effects.

You can only get there from here!

Crusty New Englanders might tell you on a muddy, rocky road through the woods that *"you cahn't git theyah from heyah."* But if your work depends on the accuracy of your perceptions, or you are on a journey of self-growth, you can get to the most amazing places, but only if you start from here—where you are, right now. It doesn't matter if your goal is to enhance the joy in your life, increase productivity, communicate more effectively, be a healer, improve athletic perfomrance, develop your intuition, or feel better in your body. True perception requires knowing where you are in space and in your physical body. You must have your awareness open, clear, and firmly planted in the present. Only then can you be accurate about what you perceive, where it originated, and what it means. Is it yours or are you picking up someone else's emotional state? Is it an intuition, or a reaction triggered by your past? Is it a response to a preoccupation or passing thought, or is it an insight into the situation that you are exploring?

Gwyneth had to look at what her people-pleasing pattern cost her and discover what its purpose was. Like many people who focus solely on the opinions of others, she had many acquaintances and did very well at work but did not have really close friends that she could count on. She talked about her parents and her philandering ex-husband as if she was silly to have any bad feelings about such good, well-meaning people. She criticized herself for being too demanding and emotional, just as Max had. She had no idea how to support herself in the face of Max's overreaction, no idea that her upsets were legitimate.

We all unknowingly try to soothe ourselves by distancing from our feelings and bad memories. We also get thrown off when we are not aware that we are being swayed by others. As Ramorrah said in a class in which I taught coaches to use Energy Dynamics, "Our bodies are crucial to help us know when we're authentic, aren't they?" By connecting with our present bodily experience, we land ourselves in the real present, not philosophically, but concretely.

Our bodies are the locus of all the information we receive. By being willing to be present in our bodies, we connect more fully with the present moment. We also are more able to release blocks and to counter distortions in perception, including those caused by the past.

It is the most direct way to become more adept. And the best way to come home to our bodies, to relieve any discomfort we find there, to increase our awareness, is through our breath. Breathing is a ongoing practice for every level of practitioner, no matter how long they have worked on mindfulness. As with piano, practicing not only improves your results, the very act of practicing carries the inherent benefit of the activity.

To build a strong foundation of experience and understanding, let's now investigate breathing, as well as quite a few exercises that you can explore. Each is aimed at achieving a different purpose, depending on your circumstance. Let's look at some examples of applications of different techniques.

Many Breaths, Many Results

Besides calming children and yourself (as valuable as those are), there are many other results that can be accomplished by using breathing techniques. Some of them include:

- Firing up *prana*, or *qi*. These exercises stoke the "fire in the belly." They often are used in yoga classes or by athletes when they are about to try something tougher that requires concentration and power. They can also be used to overcome depletion. They tend to be powerful techniques that require training, as the effects on the body can be quite pronounced. It is helpful to work with a skilled yoga or meditation teacher, so as to enhance the system and not overwhelm or drain it, if it is not yet strong enough for the exertion.

- Clearing out stagnation. In Chinese Medicine, stagnation causes pain. A breathing technique that gets things moving will then help in releasing pain.

- Aligning both sides of brain. Breath techniques that alternate nostrils stimulate first one side of the brain then the other. The corpus callosum—the bundle of nerves that cross the divide between the sides of the brain, is thought to be stimulated, so that information can travel more easily across, and you will then have the benefit of aspects of information and perception from more areas of the brain, and they can work together to provide more options and better solutions.

- Relaxing. When you want to enjoy some quiet time, sleep, meditate, or pray, Energizing, or preparing to exercise, or when you want to ease out stiffness

- Reducing stress, calming yourself when you want to settle down after something riled you up.

- Clearing mind fog. If it is mental stagnation that has occurred, and you have zoned out a bit. When you want to settle down to focus on something. Enhancing whatever activities you'll do later.

❧ Facilitating exercise by maintaining focus within our bodies and relaxing un-needed muscles while working hard.

❧ Reducing injury by releasing unnecessary tension at the same time as you expand energy, as well as by reducing the chance of injury due to a lapse in focus.

❧ Optimizing attention. Mihaly Csikszentmihalyi, in his inspired book *Flow: The Psychology of Optimal Experience,* talks about the type of attention that helps people to do their best and enjoy themselves the most in their activities. He originated the term "flow," defining it as a type of attention that is very focused, the result of years of training, but that is not tight or straining or clenched. He describes optimal attention as, "Not too tight, not too loose. You must develop a relaxed concentration on the task at hand. Attention cannot be wandering all over the place. But it also cannot be held too tightly." If it is held too tightly, the attention then shifts to the gripping, rather than staying on the activity. This tension limits the amount you can hold, as we see when we scoop sand with a loosely cupped hand versus a clenched one, or when we try to control love, or the outcome of an event. Athletes and performers get much better results when they focus on enjoying themselves and playing their own game than they do when they focus on winning. In yoga, this concept is one aspect of *aparigraha,* or non-grasping. Practicing yoga and meditation can teach this type of relaxed presence. Learning to breathe with more attentiveness and less constriction can also develop it.

The parts of the breath

There are several aspects of a breath through which we can affect the breathing to obtain different results. These include:

❧ Inhale and exhale,

❧ Mouth versus nose breathing,

૪ The muscles surrounding the lungs, from the neck and shoulders, back, sides, upper chest, to the diaphragm, belly and lower back,

૪ Rhythm and timing,

૪ Where in the body you focus your attention and breathe into. The part to which you bring attention and breath has the chance to move more, which frees your energy. You also become more aware of that part of your body from the inside. One step in increasing your breathing dexterity will be imagining that your breath occurs in various areas in your body. When you do this, you actually will use the muscles in that area more and change the way that you breathe. For example, if you focus your attention in the tops of your shoulders, you will breathe very high in your chest, moving the muscles in your shoulder, while not using your lower muscles much. Your breath may tend to be shallower. Often certain types of chiropractors, massage therapists, and energy workers ask clients to breathe into the part of the body on which they are working, because they know that having the client bring their attention to that part of the body and "breathe into it" helps move the tightness or constriction in that area.

We will be working with these different aspects of breathing in order to meet our goals, and also talk about how these aspects bring about different results.

What messes up the breath?

The biggest barrier to efficient breathing, the one everybody uses in reaction to any stressor, whether it is being startled, under the gun, or having to hold on for the long haul, is unconsciously freezing our diaphragms. The diaphragm is a sheet of muscle suspended horizontally across the bottom of the ribcage that acts as a flat balloon. Its purpose is to make us exhale without having to think about it. When we breathe freely, the diaphragm is pushed by the expanding lungs and bells downward. The vacuum thus created helps us pull more air into our lungs. As with any muscle, after it has expanded, it must contract back to its original position. As it does so, it pushes the air in the lungs (which has quickly made the oxygen/carbon dioxide swap) back up and out of the lungs. When we are at rest, exhalation is designed to be a passive event.

But this mechanism changes when we are startled, shocked, or scared. Our instinctive reaction when we go on red alert is to gasp—a reflexive, sharp intake of breath triggered by an adrenalin surge in which the diaphragm moves up rather than down. As a survival mechanism, the value of gasping is that it draws air quickly into the lungs in case we need to run or fight. As air quickly surges into the upper part of our bodies, energy is pushed upward as well. Vision sharpens and blood rushes to the head and heart for apprehending danger and preparing to act.

In our non-hunter-gatherer society, fighting or fleeing are often not options. The adrenalin is still pumping, though, so what are the alternatives? Whether we react or freeze, very often the diaphragm remains stiffened in the drawn-up, gasp position and is not released. That often becomes chronic in our startling and crowded world. Over time, most people have compensated to their diaphragm's not being released by breathing in their upper chests and shoulders, continuing to hold their diaphragms frozen. So many people go through life with severely limited air circulation. This is one reason why aerobic exercise feels so good—it gets the diaphragm moving and frees the breathing.

There is a problem energetically in freezing the diaphragm. As breath, blood, and stress hormones surge upward, so does our energy. It also remains stuck as we over-think in reaction to the conflict between adrenalin surges and modern options. What started as a safety reflex becomes a barrier that greatly limits the flow of energy and awareness between the upper body and everything below. Blood flow is lessened to the lower body. People lose bodily awareness of practically everything below the chest, going through life with very little sense of any part of their bodies that does not hurt. The survival tactic that was meant to focus our attention and energy on meeting a potential threat from outside comes to be used as a defense mechanism to keep us away from any awareness of emotional discomfort. We keep our diaphragms frozen to cut ourselves off from what we feel.

Our systems stay in crisis mode, which then becomes chronic over-arousal. Problems occur when our bodies never have the chance to find out that the threat has passed. If we limit our awareness of our feelings, we limit our awareness of every aspect of ourselves. We don't get to choose what we shut out and what we do'nt. If we shut down, we shut down. People come into my office having no connection to, or awareness of, their hips, legs, or feet. Or they say, "You know, I really only live between here (the top of their head) and here (the neck)." Yet they have all sorts of pain. As they shut down on their connection with their physical selves, the energy is constricted in that area. When the amount of energy flowing through an area is reduced, stagnation occurs. As Chinese medicine says all too well, stagnation, whether from constriction, excess fluid, or any other cause, causes pain. It often takes people quite a while to learn to inhabit their lower bodies rather than living in their heads, looking down from at the rest of them "down there."

So, ironically, it is the very mechanism that people most use to keep themselves away from pain that causes pain. Not only does lowering energy and blood flow set you up for physical aches, staying out of your body and unaware of emotional pain keeps them stuck and keeps the effects in your body. People are afraid it will never go away and then stop it from leaving. You cannot change or process what you cannot see. As we say in the therapy world, what you resist persists.

As she perched on the edge of the couch like a bird ready to take off, Gwyneth's bright and keyed-up persona hid a large well of pain, panic, and despair. She had to learn some skills before she could learn to calm herself. Gwyneth was surprised to find how unaware of her body she was. As she had clamped down on her feelings and her needs, she had also limited the amount of space she inhabited and the air she allowed in and out. We started with the breathing exercises, and the first thing that happened was that her exhaustion came to the surface. As she made more room for her breath, and her muscles started relaxing, she found what that brittle, energetic persona cost her. Freeing her diaphragm and allowing her chest muscles to move, she connected more with her physical body, and gradually with her psychological and emotional self as well. Over time there emerged an entirely different view of her past history—a story of pervasive, unbridled neglect. She'd been fed, clothed, and housed, but all her life her mother had said, "She's my mistake." Her father was a hard, loud, unpredictable man who had lost his mother when he was five. Gwyn's mother's family-of-origin was abusive and uneducated. She was resentful and unforgiving and blamed others for everything that happened. One small transgression and she'd refuse to talk a child or grandchild (when she was lucky enough to have some) for months at a time. Both parents saw no problem with saying "I love you" and then calling their children horrible names.

Letting the memories sit on the sidelines for a bit, Gwyn gradually learned to use breathing exercises to relax her muscles. When she felt wound-up at work, she gradually found that that she could make herself feel more settled and present. Rather than using tenseness to keep from being in touch with herself, she learned that her tension level went down when she became more aware of her body. Soon, she found it easier to sleep. Yet her energy level and her hyper-vigilance were not going to improve until she understood why she tied her energy up and gave it away, which would come later in her work.

Other ways that we limit the effectiveness of our breathing come from patterns such as concentrating so hard on a task that we lose track of ourselves. Getting too locked into any activity can make us unaware of our surroundings, our bodies, our other needs. I know that I'm too locked in if, when our sweet boy cat leaps into my lap while I am working, I see him as a nuisance. Rather than getting in the way, he is doing me a huge favor by reminding me of the world around me in a loving way and giving me a chance to lower my heart rate, unglue my eyes from the computer screen, soften arm and shoulder muscles, and remember to breathe more deeply. If I had an investment in staying out of touch with myself and held onto my work tension, I might have pushed him off my lap, hurting his feelings, making him less likely to approach me (and then I'd think he was aloof). How many times do people do this to a child, spouse, or coworker? It is an example of the detriments of holding concentration too tightly.

At one time I saw a physical therapist for back pain. One exercise she gave me involved my pulling on bands while bending forward and exhaling three times. "Stop and inhale in-between," she admonished. I'd been dutifully exhaling but not really taking any air in. "If you're going to take the time to do this exercise, you might as well relax and do it." People who have experienced stunning pain often inhibit their breathing by tensing the muscles of the entire rib cage region, or by clenching the jaw, or by constricting the throat. It's hard to relax and let ourselves receive things, even air, because it means we need to soften our unconsciously frozen position. It means we need to allow ourselves some ease.

We can use the breath gently to move our attention from hypervigilance, in which our energy is focused outside our bodies, to living inside our own skins. It is the only way that we can release old pain and move on, even though it means meeting the things we have been hiding from. The cost has been too great. Staying away from ourselves does not save us. It keeps us imprisoned. We fear our memories more and more, and we are increasingly limited by our withdrawal from our own experience. We want help in clearing out tension, fatigue, and pain, and in increasing well-being, feeling more present, more alive, and more relaxed. We also want techniques to use when we are in the midst of something difficult, whether it's a traumatic memory or a mind-numbing business meeting. We want ways to settle ourselves, to stay centered and grounded, and to help see things in clearer perspective.

In practicing techniques, we enhance our self-awareness. When we are clearer in ourselves, we actually see the outside world more clearly. We are less caught in anticipating danger, which distorts our vision and makes the world appear more chaotic and extreme than it usually is.

This is what trapped Lawrence, so that his job search was undermined. He had become so tense, so outwardly focused, that he acted as if he could force the world to produce a job for him. But he was cutting off all his own energy as well as trapping himself in a view of the job market as hostile and closed from him.

As he first practiced breathing, he noticed that he had no awareness of his body at all. Focusing on his breath started his new relationship with his physical self. The more he was able to breathe into and feel different parts of his body, the more he noticed how tightly wound he'd been. Several layers of tension melted away. He also noticed that his tightness had colored the way he viewed the world—the lack of job options, the meanness of interviewers, the crabbiness of people on the street, and his view of the future. As he practiced relaxing into his breath, things began to look a bit more hopeful. At first he thought it was a coincidence that he was called for three interviews the very next week.

How to Improve the Energy Dynamics of your Breathing

The first task in developing our breathing is in unlocking the diaphragm and reconnecting with the lower two-thirds of the body, and improving the movement of qi, blood, and muscle. In order to re-open the gate to a fuller experience of our own space and energy, it is vital to settle ourselves literally down. Most everyone, when tense, pulls up. We all go into our heads or numb out. The next thing we know, our thoughts are racing around like hamsters on a wheel.

To undo the effects of tension, the first step is to bring our awareness more into ourselves when we have been working or busy. By focusing on our breath, we calm our brain chatter and almost immediately start to release tension.

Below are specific exercises for clearing out tension, releasing a stifled breathing pattern, and connecting more with our bodies. You'll find in-depth directions, as well as practices for varying purposes, from quieting the body for meditation or sleep, to gathering energy to do yoga or dance, to focusing yourself to run a race. The CD on breathing will make it easier to practice, as you won't have to read at the same time.

To release tension

Here are some preliminary exercises that are helpful in letting go of the tightness that builds up when we have been too busy focusing on other things and have gotten out of touch with ourselves. They are helpful to do as a quick pick-me-up, or before going on to specific breathing exercises designed to move us into a certain state.

Practice: **Big Sighs.** Stretch your arms wide out to the sides as you inhale strongly through your nose or mouth. Then, as you exhale through your mouth, flop your arms down in front of you and round your back. Sigh vocally as you exhale, to release any holding in your torso. Try to exhale as much air as possible each time. Fill your chest as you would a big balloon, into your back and all sides of your rib cage. Do not rush or breathe too quickly.

After you have taken four or five big sigh breaths, let your breathing return to normal and notice the effects.

Practice: **HUH!** During the course of the day people breathe quite shallowly, trapping a significant amount of air at the bottom, where it may start harboring germs. Expelling it helps protect you from colds, as well as shortening the length of time that a cold may drag on. This cleansing breath clears out stale air, starts your energy building, and gathers your attention. It is useful in revitalizing your energy anytime. The speed at which this technique is done, and the fact that you are exhaling through your mouth, make your lungs transfer oxygen more rapidly than usual, so it cleans out some toxins in the blood as well as the stale air. (As a pick-me-up, find a private place at work and try this for a few seconds.)

To start, breathe in quickly and deeply through your nose, then exhale sharply and forcefully through your mouth making a loud HUH! sound with each gusty exhalation. Shouting is good. Repeat at least five times, and then let your breathing return to normal.

The Essential Step

Diaphragmatic Breathing

Next is to make sure that your diaphragm is released. Sit with both feet on the floor. Put your fingertips together, index to index, middle to middle, etcetera, though not your thumbs. Place the tips of your tented fingers gently under your ribs and fan them, with your index fingertips just under where your ribs join, and your little fingertips by your waist. Take a deep breath and focus on breathing down into your belly. See if you can feel your diaphragm muscle push down past your index fingers to your middle and then maybe to your ring fingertips. The muscle is expanding.

Then release your breath. Your diaphragm will return up to its starting position. A relaxed exhalation involves no effort on your part. Your diaphragm simply contracts to its original resting position. You can feel it move up to your index fingers again. Keep practicing until you can feel this movement. When it bells down, your diaphragm is helping you breathe deeply.

If you don't have much awareness of your body, it is easiest to feel when your diaphragm is moving freely by lying on your back with your knees bent and your feet on the floor (so your knees are pointing to the ceiling). If this position is okay for you, your diaphragm will automatically relax, and you will breathe with your belly. As you breathe in, imagine that the air you take in is clear and pure and nourishes you at your core. Then, as you breathe out, imagine that nourishment spreading out through your arms, legs, and head. Think of drawing nourishment in and then spreading it throughout your system.

Note: If lying on your back is not okay for any reason, do not do it. It is not necessary. The point right now is NOT to stress yourself.

For those who clench their jaws

As a child, I ground my teeth so badly that I would wake myself up with the noise. By the time I was fifteen, I had ground my jaw bones down flat, rather than those nice rounded hillocks for holding your teeth in your head that you are supposed to have. *Bruxism* is commonly seen in children who learn early that it is not acceptable for them to speak out, who are chronically tense due to overwhelming dilemmas that they have no way of working out.

When I met my husband in graduate school, the first thing he said that he noticed about me was how tightly I held my jaw (flattering, no?). I wore a night guard for years until I learned to relax my jaw muscles.

If you have used this adaptive mechanism, there are massage techniques that are very helpful in relaxing the muscles of the tempomandibular joint—the big muscles running vertically from your upper to lower jaw. There is, not surprisingly, a direct connection between grinding your teeth and having tension in back of your neck. The energy between your head and the rest of your spine becomes quite constricted. You may have experienced neck pain or shoulder tightness. This area may have been a focal point for numerous trips to the chiropractor.

One more point, before we get into further specifics: The sinuses are immediately next to the limbic portions of the brain. So, when you breathe through your nose, the expansion stimulates the limbic system, whose job it is to process emotions. When we are frozen in a painful memory, the only effective solution is to get movement into the parts of the brain that have shut down. Because the sinuses are within that area, breath is vital to releasing emotion.

Also, the breathing system has miraculously developed so that there are more chemical interactions that are triggered when you breathe through your nose than through your mouth. This occurs both on the inhalation and the exhalation. When you exhale through your nose, endorphins are released, so your body is more likely to relax when exhaling through your nose. When you want to energize or move energy through your body to clean out tension, breathe through the mouth. It activates the adrenals a bit and gets movement going in the body.

Some meditation teachers direct their students to breathe in through the nose and out through the mouth all the time. Because of what happens chemically, I disagree with this policy. When cleansing the system, energizing, or removing stagnation before doing more involved breathing exercises, exhaling through the mouth is valuable.

However, to lower symptoms of anxiety, stress, or panic; for meditation or relaxation; to calm yourself; and when engaged in daily activities, I suggest that you breathe in and out through your nose. And do make sure you do not hold your breath between the in and the out. You will see why in the next section.

Practice Three-part breath: This exercise helps you relax and breathe fully all through your entire torso. Focus first on filling your belly, pulling air down into your sitz bones. Expand the next breath to include your mid-section as well. On the next, expand your breath into your upper chest and shoulder area, and even into your head. Breathe slowly in through your nose, filling from bottom to top, and then exhale through your nose, emptying from top to bottom. This breath is often used at the beginning of a yoga class to establish full, deep, relaxed breathing.

Specific breathing rhythms for varied goals

In virtually any situation your experience can be enhanced by breathing consciously. The following exercises involve different rhythms of inhalation, holding or pausing, and exhalation.

Some basic rules are:

1) Start where you are. If stressed, keep your breath as it is. Focus on becoming aware of it as you do your usual rhythm, so you're breathing consciously. Once you have met yourself where you are, you can start moving in the direction of relaxing, slowing down, easing up, or energizing. Even if you are held tightly in the top of your shoulders, noticing what is going on will at the very least give you information as to your patterns. You may find that the tension starts to ease up simply by bringing your attention to your breath.

2) Remember that when stressed, practically everyone tightens up. Breathe into your belly first, in order to free your diaphragm. Once you are breathing well into your

belly, notice your attention shifting more and more to your internal sensations. Allow this awareness to extend to muscles moving as part of your breath. Imagine that you breathe into your seat, your legs, into your torso, your neck. See how far you can feel your breath in your body in each direction.

3) If you have been motionless, because you've been concentrating on something, and you want to move but your breathing feels tight, breathe in through your nose and out through your mouth, until the tension eases a bit, and your attention moves back to your body from wherever you've been.

4) Pauses, or holding your breath, are used to gather your attention, to settle you into focused awareness, or to rev you up in the same way a resistor does in an engine—by providing friction that increases and concentrates the amount of energy available. Holding your breath can be a great vehicle for learning to relax, if done correctly. In these exercises, these held pauses are not done with the tension used by kids when daring each other, or when your child thinks that turning purple will somehow change your mind about ice cream for breakfast. This holding is done in a relaxed fashion, in which you become still. Practicing this stillness increases your control over your reactions, as well as focusing your will. It can give you the sense that you are fine in yourself—that you are not so much at the mercy of the storms within you or outside of you.

Here are the exercises

The count for each will be shown as a ratio. What it shows is the number of counts for four aspects. They are

inhale : pause while holding breath : exhale : pause with lungs emptied

To relax, breathe in and out through your nose, with your exhalation twice as long as your inhalation. Breathing to relax ratio: 2:1:4:1 The longer the exhalation is, the more you relax.

If you are agitated and want to calm yourself quickly, do not hold your breath at the pauses, especially after the inhalation. When you are tense or stressed, there is much more tendency to freeze the diaphragm. Nathan, a hypnotherapist, had a client who struggled with excess weight. When he taught her this breathing technique, she finally was able to change her unhealthy habits and learn new ways to deal with her feelings. Being able to experience something normal about her body, such as this breathing, and move into her body in a connected and loving way, was the necessary step that encouraged her.

To energize and prepare for a physical task, inhale and exhale for equal counts with minimal pauses between, such as 3:1:3:1.

To oxygenate your blood quickly before a sprint or to clear your head: This is the gusty breath you see swimmers do before they take off from the starting block. Focus only on exhaling through your mouth, rapidly and with force. The inhalation will take care of itself. No pauses. Continue for only five seconds, and then burst into motion. (If you sat around doing this for longer, you'd probably hyperventilate.)

During Pilates, strength training, or isometrics, modify the same pattern—in through nose and out through mouth, but purse your lips to constrict the air flow during the exhalation, and make sure that you breathe out as much air as possible. As you exhale through pursed lips, making the sound air escaping from a pinpoint hole in a tire—"ffffff." You'll get more work out of your abdominal muscles. Timing: 2:0:__:0 — the blank equals your exhale, which lasts as long as the weight, arm, or leg is moving away from your torso.

For stressful situations in which you want to be relaxed but alert and possibly on guard: A courtroom would be a good example. You don't want to be too relaxed or introspective. You want to feel attentive while protecting yourself from negative or contentious events. In these types of settings, breathe nasally rather than orally: 2.1.4.1. If you become stressed by something that is said, exhale through your mouth slowly to let go of the tension caused by an adrenaline surge. Samir was involved in a legal case in which neighbors banded together to fight the pollution of their local water supply. While in court, he focused on his breathing as much as he could. "It works every time. After practicing for quite a while, I am at the point where I can be relaxed and alert, even in business meetings or when I'm on the spot."

To focus your energy for an exam or a project, keep the inhalation and exhalation equal, and hold only after the inhalation. A good ratio is 6:4:6:1.

To prepare for meditation, try 4:2:8:4. You see that the exhalation is twice the length of the inhalation, plus you are pausing after the exhalation twice as long as after the inhalation. This is a very settling rhythm. You can experiment with extending the exhalation to 10 or 12, for example.

Breathing is powerful. Increasing your awareness of your body by practicing breath techniques will not only help you feel more calm and confident in life situations, it will also build the basis for the next tool in releasing pain and accessing your joy, which is Grounding.

Keep your eyes on the stars and your feet on the ground.
—Theodore Roosevelt

Grounding: 5
what it really is, and how
to do it, for real

BOBBY WAS A high school basketball star with dreams of playing in the NBA. He was scouted by several colleges and earned a scholarship to a major university. He found college more stressful than he expected. He had breezed through high school, and now he was juggling classes, practices, all the social opportunities and temptations, no parental supervision, and being away from the small town that he'd thought of as boring, but now remembered as comfortable and familiar. No wonder he felt thrown off. During games, he started to choke, missing shots and passes. "Suddenly, it was like I couldn't find my feet, like I didn't know exactly where I was going, or where the other guys were."

Roland was a wellness and fitness coach. Though he was intelligent and dedicated, he had trouble stretching his limits and putting himself out there. If an opportunity loomed on the horizon, he would stay up late planning his presentation in minute detail. But when it came to standing up and delivering it, he broke into a sweat and forgot his points. Even thinking about the next deadline caused his back to tighten between his shoulder blades, and he'd slump, his breathing constricted, while his mind went a million miles a minute. If I asked him what was going on, he'd trip over his tongue rattling off a list of pros and cons, concerns and dilemmas.

Lawrence continued to practice breathing. Although he had found some job prospects, none of them were what he wanted to do with his life. A new layer of uncertainty emerged as he became more aware of his patterns. "I don't know what happens when I go in to interviews. Maybe I'm just out of practice. But I kind of fog out and find my mind going off on tangents. Or I talk too much. Or I can't think what it is that *I* want."

All three men needed to learn to ground themselves.

What is Grounding?

Grounding is a real, kinesthetic state, not just a vague notion, even though people now use the term in all sorts of ways. Grounding is what makes it possible for you to be real, really here, really in contact with the present, really safe. It involves connecting with yourself, your energy and also connecting your energy to that of the earth. It is an interchange of energy that provides strong benefits and results.

Taking liberties with high school physics to explain one facet of how it works, imagine yourself existing in a single dimension rather than in three. You are basically a point, no length, no depth. And, nothing else exists except for you, the one point—no stars, no other little points, not really your body or the experience of space, because, there is only your tiny point of awareness. There you are, not in relation to anything. (If you really get into this experiment, you will find that your sense of yourself becomes nebulous, and everything else becomes foggy.)

Okay, now, add one more point, which creates a second dimension— that of line between you and the other point—say, a memory, emotion, belief about yourself, or another person. Nothing exists except you and the other thing. Since there is nothing else but you and the one that is not-you, there is no way to compare it to anything, so you have no way of knowing how big it is. It becomes huge, encompassing all that is not you. (This is the experience of having your worry about something become overwhelming and blot out any reality check. So you find yourself obsessing about the thing and unable to think about anything else.)

What a relief then to add a third point! The third provides a reference, the way a nickel placed next to a new music device shows how tiny it is; or a man is in front of an icicle makes the viewer realize it is forty feet tall. Now the second point—the feeling or other person—slides into its proper proportion, because the third point offers us the ability to compare it to something neutral. Connecting with the earth allows us to regain perspective. If an emotion has ballooned out of all proportion, with awareness of our contact with the earth, the feeling shrinks. Grounding helps us navigate painful feelings by reminding us that they are not as all-consuming as we feared, and by keeping us connected with reality in the present. (As well, we will see in chapter seven that grounding helps you stay with the emotion-releasing function long enough that emotions can be alleviated.)

From a medical perspective, grounding helps you stop stress reactions by calming your autonomic nervous system, reducing the production of cortisol and other crisis hormones, thereby lowering blood pressure and heart rate, softening muscles, easing the breath, redistributing blood throughout the extremities, reengaging systems that have shut down to focus on a crisis.

Being grounded is being related

Being grounded is also an experience of relationship in two significant ways. The first involves being more alive and aware in your body. Being alive in your body means that you are not shutting yourself down or existing only in your head. If you are aware throughout your body, your system relaxes, and the stress hormones abate. You are not holed up in your mind with your shoulders clenched, or held in a fight-or-flight reaction. You are able to access different kinds of information and realizations that come to you through your gut, emotions, or awareness of your body in space, or that comes through moving. You have more options if your system is more relaxed. You can see a wider perspective, a bigger picture, and so may see correlations that you'd missed if you stayed in crisis-mode tunnel vision. You are more able to choose a different response, one based on seeing the situation as not quite as dire as it looked when you were ungrounded.

The second way in which you relate through being grounded is with the earth beneath your feet. Being connected down through your legs and into to the earth keeps you safely rooted and able to receive energy from your surroundings. It makes it possible for you to be nourished, to recover from feeling overwhelmed or exhausted, and to feel stable. It allows you to live calmly and to be fine in an on-going way, rather than going from one crisis to the next.

Awareness of connection with the earth brings you into an interaction with the extremely large energy field of the planet. Any time you are in relationship, there is an interplay of energy in which each being affects the other, offers benefits to (or detracts from) the other, reacts and responds to the other. The earth is a living system, as are we. Its energy affects the beings that live upon and within it. These effects vary, depending on where on its surface you are (which is why different parts of the world feel different). When you open to the earth's energy, you establish a bond as well as an energy exchange. (A vivid example of this bond is the phenomenon that occurs if you mistakenly touch a live electrical wire. If the current is strong enough, you can't move, because you have become part of the current.) The bond between you and the earth's electrical/energetic field is less forceful than that of a cattle fence, but it is still a palpable connection. You can use that bond to receive energy that augments your own, that helps you be safe and settled, and that keeps you from being thrown by people or by events.

The perfect example is the martial arts master. Often in movies he is depicted as a small, wizened, old man who works, say, in a Chinese restaurant as a dishwasher. Unbeknownst to the owner and others who, from the audience's viewpoint, ought to know better, the gentle man is a top-notch practitioner of some martial art. One evening, into the restaurant crash three or four thugs, bent on revenge against the restaurateur. The old man is in their way. They try to shove him aside. They cannot. They get madder and shove harder. They cannot budge the old man, who is now looking feeble but focused. They try to pick him up. They try to yank his arm. They cannot get past him. They look perplexed and then scared.

The old master-in-disguise makes himself immovable by grounding himself. He has his own energy blended so strongly with the earth's that when he applies his mind to being as firm as a tree, he *is* as firm as a tree. He not only sends roots down into the ground, he draws strength from it and is fed by that immense energy source.

Even without vanquishing bad guys, connecting with the earth's energy keeps you solidly placed, so that you don't feel buffeted or thrown off. This is a boon when giving speeches, when making dinner for a passel of tired children, when your boss wants fourteen things at once, or when the news makes the world sound like a scary place. When you are grounded, the earth becomes the third point—perspective.

Connie desperately needed to learn to ground. Terror and flashbacks caught her at all sorts of times. She'd panic, heart racing and body shaking, sure that danger was coming at her right now, and find herself moving before she even knew where or why. Her energy would set way up high—around her arms and head—and throwing itself wildly in her body's attempt to protect itself from something that was not happening. She felt like a car veering and skidding in a chase scene.

A major hurdle for rape victims is to risk being in touch with their bodies. Connie treated hers as if it had betrayed her by becoming the location of the terrible violation. She felt as if she had been injected with incomprehensible levels of hostility and horror by the attacker. (This is true of all victims of rape and other violent crimes. They add insult to their own injuries, however, when they start seeing their bodies as the actual enemy. It's only a short hop to blaming themselves for the attack and seeing themselves as vile, rather than as violated.)

Her hypervigilance also kept her attention constantly on the lookout for danger everywhere. The more she did so, the more locked in terror she became. It was imperative to undo this cycle of self blame and fear of others. The most definitive way to undo the whole pattern was to release the horrific sensations (which we'll get to in the BWITSY chapter), the beliefs that came out of it (chapter ten), and the protective patterns she had developed that were holding her hostage in the traumatic memory (the chapter on APEPs). Then she would be able gradually to come back to herself. Grounding was the vehicle for finding safe haven within herself and working through all the steps to free her.

Connie's practicing the witness started the process of connecting with herself, but she had further to go to be able to be in her body without triggering kinesthetic flashbacks of being attacked, helpless, and harmed. Because there are two aspects to grounding, we came at it through building her connection with the actual ground first. First she paid attention to her breath in order to settle a bit. Then she focused on her feet contacting the earth. As we practiced, she began to be aware of safety, solidity, and comfort that come from being connected to the earth. We played with how that led to feeling a bit more firmly in herself, a bit more able to see the world around her in the present, rather than through the filter of the rape.

It took a while for her to learn to settle her energy into her body and connect with the earth. We started with the areas that she could be aware of without panicking. After settling in those, she gradually extended to area around those parts. If she ran into a place she couldn't go, or started to breathe too quickly, I'd guide her to another, coming from a different direction into herself. Since grounding from the belly down didn't work for her, we started from the ground and worked up. When there was a troublesome spot, I had her imagine warm, calm energy filling up the parts next to it. Over time, she gradually could feel it seep into the traumatized areas, and she was able to reclaim more parts of her body. Eventually, she could ground into all of herself as a unified whole.

Learning to ground and connect with her body physically helped Connie see a way to address feelings. Her physical healing also improved as she freed the energy, part by part.

How do you know you are grounded?

When you ground, rather than being scattered or too focused on others or on your own self-criticism, you engage with yourself. You turn on the lights in each part and move into your body more completely. Rather than zoning out, or trying to get away, or tightening up to only a tiny part of yourself (your mind, maybe?), you inhabit all of yourself. You settle into what is real in the moment, connecting inwardly in order to connect outwardly more safely and with more accurate perception. Grounding enables you to see what is around you and your place in it.

When you are grounded, you also can access many kinds of knowing. When you occupy your body consciously, you can then receive the many other types of information that your whole self is capable of providing, beyond that of your thinking mind. Other aspects of you, such as your emotions, or your gut, or your bodily sensations, are tuned to different types of awareness and thereby can offer insight from their different perspectives. Being grounded provides structure and foundation for your experience of yourself in the world, as well as an energy exchange.

When Roland started learning to ground, he was surprised at how much of his agitation was a smokescreen keeping him from being here now with whatever project was in front of him and keeping him worked-up rather than facing the tasks involved. He saw that his pattern actually made much more trouble for him, as it wasted energy without getting him very far. He started to practice grounding and slowing himself down and attending to the task more quietly. He had to focus on breathing and reminding himself to stay with it. Gradually he found that he could stay in contact with himself during presentations, and so they went much better.

What does grounding have to do with joy?

Grounding changed Lawrence's life. He described it this way, "I see now that I've gone through my life as if I were trying to duck and slide through. I've always felt connected with other people, but I think I have been leaving myself out of the group in some subtle way. And of course the more I've done that, the more my needs seem to make things chaotic. It's so much easier to be optimistic when I feel connected. It's as if I'm safe in some way I didn't realize was missing before."

Quite soon after learning to ground himself, Lawrence was offered a job at a non-profit training company in which his people skills would be prized.

Grounding enables us to be in the present. It awakens us to our interior universe, increases awareness, intuition, healing, safety, and calm. And the secret to experiencing joy is that it is only by being in the present, deeply connected and awake within, that it is possible to tap into the joy lurking beneath our baggage. Efforts to stay away from that backlog of old stuff keeps the baggage stuck and us disconnected from the peace and freedom that are possible. We end up trapped in the very pain we've been trying to avoid.

The question then is, how do we release the pain and return to ourselves? Grounding and centering are two vital steps in the answer. Used together, we can increase our body's ability to heal, our energy to realign and work out the physical effects of old patterns. We can then resolve and release trauma and lay to rest hurts and losses.

As you practice grounding over time, your awareness and responses change. You build new internal and experiential structure. Over time, your neuro-receptors actually change as you build a new foundation for yourself. This neural re-wiring can lead to emotional and physical healing, to feeling more authentic, and confident. Spiritual paths that focus on training the mind aim for this very thing that. When rituals focus on developing a sense of being in which followers are less swayed by or cut off from feelings or drives, and when practitioners work on being in touch with and connected to themselves and their surroundings in a planned way, they are less disrupted by either inner or outer storms.

Grounding makes you more effective when using your intuition. Participants in Energy Dynamics classes invariably become excited as they see an increase in their intuition that piggy-backs on their increased self-awareness and self-empowerment.

What happens if you don't?

The stresses that Bobby faced when on his own for the first time, away from his support systems and with higher stakes placed on his basketball skills, all combined to arouse his nervous system past the point of optimal playing. He was too worked-up, so his system did what systems do when it goes past "excited" and reaches "crisis." It started shutting down functions to focus on what he'd need if he were being chased by a tiger. His heart rate sped up to 165 beats per minute, his hearing closed off, and his vision tunneled. His thought process was truncated and his hand coordination dropped. Because he did not have experience with this level of arousal, he did not know how to reconnect with himself and settle his system down, in order to make use of the energy and play well.

As he learned to ground himself, he learned to lower his heart rate quickly to 120 or so and to steady his breathing. It gave his system a chance to rest momentarily, so he could lower the crisis response and reconnect with his body. Gradually he learned to play primarily in an optimal range of 115 and 145 heartbeats per minute.[1]

When people carry loads of pain that they don't know what to do with, the last place they want to be is where the pain is. When events have flattened us, our first instinct is to get away from or subdue their unbearable aftermath. Because humans have an urgent need to make sense of things, we also try to find reasons for and meaning in what happened, in an effort to make it tolerable. We scramble to get back to our old lives, as if that's possible. All our efforts to control the pain only keep us away from ourselves. We don't realize that we fight ourselves when we fight against the hurt. The conflict against the pain, being at odds with it, is the locked door that keeps it stuck. As much as we try to turn away, the automatic reaction of body and brain holds us in the place in which the feelings, by definition, are overwhelming. No matter what we do, there we still are, elsewhere and elsewhen, in an endless feedback loop that makes old pain recur again and again. It seems as if our entire life is ruled by those most hated events.

If we don't ground ourselves, our immune systems are undermined, because they will be much more likely to remain in a state of chronic crisis alert. Our stress hormones, including adrenalin and cortisol, continue to be triggered, so we perceive present situations as more stressful than they may actually be. The longer our bodies read everything as a perpetual danger, the more overloaded with cortisol our systems become. Chronically elevated levels of stress hormones break down healthy bone and muscle tissue. They retard healing and cell regeneration. While the body thinks it is under siege, it limits digestives processes. Eventually, the adrenals can no longer create optimal amounts when we really need to respond quickly. Other hormones, including progesterone, melatonin, serotonin, and estrogen, are depleted, because when our bodies make more stress hormones, they are choosing not to make other hormones that support normal functioning. Endorphins, the neuro-transmitters that are present in calm, happy states and reduce depression, anxiety, and anger, become seriously depleted. So, squelching or evading old pain undermines our immune systems chemically, neurologically, and energetically. In the long term, these reactions can lead to serious disorders, such as heart disease, elevated blood pressure and cholesterol, auto-immune diseases, cancer, ulcers, skin disorders, and depression.

Then there is the issue of physical pain. Many people have painful health issues after trauma (which certainly adds injury to insult!). In an effort to manage trauma, we close off, tighten up. When we do so, pain occurs more and more often, due to the stagnation our constriction causes, either of energy or some fluid or chemical process. Consequently, both the emotional and physical pain from trauma stay stuck in our bodies.[2]

Also, when we are not grounded, we cannot be clear about the accuracy of what we perceive. We cannot know for certain where the stimulus originates or with what aspect of our own experience we are picking it up. The world looks like an increasingly hostile place when so much of the present is actually perceived through the lens of old shocks. Other people appear more damaging, more malicious than they really are. Any empathy for their preoccupations and motives is lost to us as our own struggle takes over. For this reason, not being grounded keeps us stuck in the trance of trauma, numbed out, desperate to get away, or raw and hurting. We freeze so as not to feel anything, or we hide by tightening ourselves into the smallest possible space.

Being ungrounded, and thereby disconnected from our feelings, also affects the choices we make. If we are too scattered or shut down to pick up cues, how can we know what is the best decision for us at this time? The question then is, are the emotions with which we are weighing our options reactive ones from being blinded by hurt, or are they ones we have in response to the present choices, based on what is true now?

There were several foci at the beginning of Lawrence's work: his "dithering" as he called it, his physical habits that were draining his energy, and his pain and low spirits. Lawrence had trouble at first with the notion that he had to slow down and look at himself to get somewhere.

How do we become ungrounded?

The single thing that everyone does most in order to get away from pain, is we stiffen our diaphragm, (as we have seen in the chapter on breathing). What starts as a rush of energy to the upper body to prepare for danger becomes a defense mechanism of cutting our minds off from any awareness of our bodies. We then feel like a helium balloon that got away—there it goes! It got away! Zip! Bounce! All over the room, until it splats on the floor, spent. All that energy in the head has neither foundation nor checks-and-balances. We then often find ourselves engaged in the same old patterns of behavior that continue to make us unhappy.

Before learning to ground, Roland's thoughts zipped around like that helium balloon on speed. His body looked somewhat like a crumpled wrapper—disregarded, with not enough energy to make it look fully inhabited. He could not access any strength or balance because he had no awareness of his own physical body. He had no energy engaged anywhere except in his head.

When Roland learned to ground, he became aware of his body for the first time. He'd never noticed his back, legs, feet, or parts of his torso before. Becoming aware of his energy opened him to a bigger, fuller relationship with his own body and the space it occupied. He spent quite a bit of time entranced with simply walking, breathing, sitting, lying down. As he became more self-aware, he felt options open up for him in many situations. Speaking became less stressful as he concentrated on being more fully present, rather than on imagining what the audience was thinking about him and criticizing him for. Consequently his reviews improved.

As counterintuitive as it seems, moving toward ourselves is the answer to releasing the pain and finding joy. Being grounded is necessary in order to perceive accurately and to have a clear perspective, both in the present and when processing the ferocious feelings from past events. When Bobby learned to ground and practiced enough to be able to do it on the basketball court, he learned that he could calm his system and reduce its crisis response. But before he could get there, he had to address some of his other stressors. He had to curtail his partying and develop some support systems, so that he wouldn't feel so alone. He joined a church and a literary discussion group, which gave him the chance to meet thoughtful students. As he gained some control over his stress levels, he then learned to slow his heart rate, find his feet, feel his muscles, settle his awareness in his body as he played ball. His vision then opened back up so that he could see other players, orient himself, and have a split second to plan his move. The coach was much happier as his performance greatly improved.

Grounding is a practice-able technique, and what follows are extensive and clear directions with which to deepen your skills. Afterward, you'll find a discussion of different types of grounding that are appropriate for use in various situations.

At the end of the chapter, you will find exercises that will help you develop the ability to be grounded even in trying circumstances. You will also find them on my CD's, so that you can practice without having to read at the same time.

There are different types of grounding for varying needs
Eventually the goal is to be grounded no matter what you are doing—walking or driving, in a contentious meeting, with fussy babies, or writing a book. There are several ways to ground. Each meets a different purpose and involves your attention a bit differently. Some are best to use in specific circumstances. There are the ones that build your self-awareness and bring you back to being stably located within yourself, and then there are the ones that help you navigate in the world. We will go into these in much more detail in the CDs, but here is an overview.

Internal Grounding: This is the most essential one and is what we've been talking about the most. This one brings you home into your body and your energy, as well as connecting you to the earth in such a way that you are stable and safe. All of you is included in your energy, all the way to your feet. Your attention stays mostly inside your body, making sure your energy is able to flow through your legs as well as your upper body, and is not cut off at your diaphragm or even higher, in your neck (if you tend to live in your head).

Replenishing Ground: In this one, you include the earth's energy with yours. You don't stop your awareness of energy at the edge of your skin. All that energy beneath your feet is available, just waiting for you to invite it to mingle with yours. When you connect with the earth's electro-magnetic field consciously, you allow much more energy into your own electro-magnetic field to heal and balance what ails you. As a practice, you could sit with this type of grounding every day. Notice, after a week or two, how it is to be in your body. Do your nerves, your breathing, your emotions and thoughts seem more settled or less tight?

Meditative Ground: Meditative ground is similar to Internal, in that you inhabit your own energy system as fully as possible, and you ground yourself to the earth, but without sinking into it, as you would with replenishing ground. Then, whatever the focus of your meditation is, you can attend to it without losing your sense of yourself. If, for example, you meditate on your breath, then the meditative ground closely resembles an internal ground. If you focus on a mantra, notice the effect on your energy. If you are connecting with beings outside you, as one does when practicing *tonglen* or other lovingkindness meditation techniques, include the object of your compassion, but without merging with him or her. Feel the grounding as a base for your sitting. Let it provide a foundation so that, wherever your consciousness goes, your base is clearly located within you.

You would also use meditative ground if you were doing energy work on another person, or exploring different aspects of consciousness.

The next ones are for use when you are engaged with the world. There is an important distinction between them and the more internally focused ones.

External Ground: This one is extremely useful. Have you ever had a time when you went from meditation, prayer, or quiet sitting straight into activities then wondered why, if meditation and prayer are supposed to be so spiritually uplifting, you have a shorter fuse right after? When you are still wrapped up in your internal experience, you may find other people's behavior or your surroundings more grating. The reason is that you have not allowed your system to make the shift from being very internal to being ready to engage externally. Your energy is involved within, focused differently, and with less firm boundaries. If you transit out of your internal experience without giving yourself a chance to adjust, the outside world seems more bothersome than it would if you were on its wavelength.

External ground is the way to shift. Before you open your eyes at the end of a session, remind yourself to stay grounded both in you and to the earth. Give yourself the cue that you are about to move into world before you open your eyes. Imagine opening your eyes and engaging in your daily affairs. Give your system a moment to shift and watch what it does to accommodate that shift. Once you feel yourself getting ready to get on with your day, slowly open your eyes, remembering to stay connected with your feet. You may notice that your system has firmed up your sense of your boundaries and structure.

Now you have the chance to practice being grounded as you go through your day. Here is where you will really experience the value of being grounded! Notice if you feel less likely to be blown away by events, or if you have less need to armor yourself.

There is an enjoyable and very clear way to tell if you are grounded when your eyes are open. Your vision will go into sync. Once people experience this, they notice a new clarity in their vision. It is as if a scene is slightly out of focus and then, *kachunk,* it falls back into focus. When you are ungrounded, your vision will not be as clear as when you are grounded. Larry, a coach, expressed it this way: "Everything became fluid and movable in replenishing ground, until I moved my awareness back into my body. When I opened my eyes, everything became very stable, solid, and every detail was remarkably crisp, very colorful."

Stabilizing Ground: This last one is the one used by martial arts masters, athletes, experienced police officers, dancers—anyone who is clearly "in their body" and so moves with a connected sense of force and release, staying firmly connected within themselves even during extreme stress. This is External Ground with an added conscious investment in feeling firmly fixed, so that you are safely located within yourself and can trust your body. You are connected all the way through your body and can risk taking a chance. As well as having to deal with thugs in kung fu situations, moving as one with a horse, or throwing yourself to one side and then pirouetting in the opposite direction, Stabilizing Ground is very effective if you want to feel firm in situations in which there is much stimulation around you, or when the kids are acting out the last scene of 'High School Musical' while you're trying to make dinner—any time you feel like a leaf in the wind. With practice, your roots will become more and more solid and strong and more like a part of your body.

The primary benefit of grounding is that it moves you out of your head, out of your spiraling thoughts, and into a sensory awareness of your body in your surroundings. It is quite easy to tell when you are grounded. Your vision seems to clear, colors are more intense, edges are sharper. Your sense of yourself is fuller, more substantive and alive, even as you are involved in activities. Being in your body gives you access to a whole new experience of the world, if you have tended to spend too much time in your mind. The more you experience being grounded, the more quickly you will notice when you've become ungrounded—a bit frenetic, a little wispy, or pressed, constricted, and tense.

Now that you have a deeper sense of grounding, in the next chapter we'll combine it with being centered.

Exercises for Grounding

In the audio instructions, I'll go into more detail as to how to do each of the exercises and practices in this chapter. Here is an overview, so you can get a sense of what we'll be doing, and so you can start to practice.

How to ground

We will work first on moving from being mostly caught up in your mind, or in events going on around you, to inhabiting your body more fully and thereby reconnecting with more of your energy. Start by sitting upright in a chair, both feet on the floor, with your thighs parallel to the floor and your calves perpendicular to it. Keep your back straight, and your head and neck aligned with your spine.[3]

Important! Never have your ankles crossed when you're doing any kind of Energy Work. Western medicine agrees with this. In operating rooms, the first thing the surgical nurse does once patients are under anesthesia is to uncross their ankles. Crossing your ankles confounds your energy bilaterally.

🙶 Take several deep breaths in the way you learned in chapter four. Breathe into your belly, so that your diaphragm is free to bell down as you inhale. As you take deep breaths, let your attention turn inward to focus gently on the way that your belly, sacrum, sides, and ribs move when you breathe. Allow some time for this, breathing and sighing through your mouth, so that you release tension as your awareness turns to your kinesthetic experience. As you move your attention into your body and away from the outside world, and you are becoming more aware of the movements within, exhale gently through your nose.

🙶 Imagine that you are breathing down your legs and out your feet. This will help you to expand your focus from your breathing to encompass a kinesthetic awareness of your hips, seat, thighs, knees, calves, ankles, and then your feet. Feel what it is to be aware of your legs from the inside. Sense the substance of them, maybe the energy moving within them. Can you feel your feet on the floor? As you devote more attention to them, you may notice a slight tingling. Gently let your attention plump up your sense of occupying three dimensions—the back part of your legs, the sides of each area, as well as the front—filled in and alive. Feel as if your awareness, your eyes, are settled in the lower part of your body, so that the body parts that seem extra are above you (rather than the usual state of having our lower body dangling "down there" somewhere). Feel the mass above the area you are focusing on and living in, as if there are extra floors in the house above you.

🍂 When you have that sense of being more awake in your lower body, expand that awareness into your pelvic bowl, your abdomen, solar plexus, lower back, sides, rib cage, back, upper arms, shoulders, arms, hands. Then on up into your upper chest and upper back, your neck and head, simply as parts of your body. Bring your attention to your backbone, so that it feels more supple and fluid, more juicy, rather than brittle and hard. Give it more space.

As you are turning on the lights and moving into each area, and feeling as if you are inhabiting yourself as much as you can, take note of any part that is harder to move into, or that your attention slips past. Is it that tight area in the back of your neck?—or the leg that you hurt snowboarding? These are the spots in which energy has become stagnated. You know those places. They are the ones that grumble louder and louder until they take up much of your attention—your chronic aches and pains.

Go back to it. Right now, see if you can continue to move your awareness into that area as an alternative to fighting it. Do not try to change any of the sensations you have in any area. If some muscle feels tight, let it feel tight. If it hurts, acknowledge that it is sore. If you do not pay attention when they speak, then you will find yourself reacting against them all day. By evening, you will be trying to pop your neck, or making an appointment with the chiropractor or for a massage, or wondering if you should call your physician for some pain medication.

Stages of grounding

Now that you have become more aware inside yourself, try developing a deeper connection with the earth. Keeping your awareness as fully throughout your body as you can, return your attention to your feet. There are two images that are helpful for the next part. The first is of roots. This one works well for feeling solid and safe, especially for earthy people.

Imagine that your energy continues to expand past the soles of your feet down into the earth, as the roots of a tree would. Feel your energy continue from the top of your head down through these roots. This is what the martial arts master does. Imagine that the roots act just as do those of a tree—you receive nourishment and energy through them, feeding you, so that you can relax into feeling supported. And they also keep you sturdy and solid, withstanding winds and storms. Feel how having your energy continue down beyond your feet lessens the sense of having limits on your energy. Rather than being like an object placed on a counter that can be easily pushed off, you are an active personification of the energy of the earth, so there could not even be a notion of being easily pushed around.

The second image, which may be more helpful for more fluid people, is that of water.[4] Lawrence had some trouble learning to ground until we talked about his love of the ocean. When he imagined that he was in the water, with it moving on his skin and its pressure holding him, he could settle into awareness of his inner space and feel connected with the earth's energy. This was also the best way for Lawrence to remind himself to relax and know that he was all right.

You know when you see a lake that the surface looks somewhat like a really shiny floor? Most people interact with the top of the water as if it is the barrier, the dividing line. They are up here. The fish and the monsters are down there. You're on the shore, or in a boat, or swimming with your head out of the water, and you can make yourself scared of the teeth aiming at your toes.

When you put your head under and open your eyes, you see that there is a whole other world under the surface, and you are within it. Now the surface of the water is the top of your world, and you are exploring all the life and sensations within this reality. (For some of us, this is more exhilarating than being on the surface.)

Grounding may be like swimming underwater for you. When you open your awareness to the energy of the planet, there are all sorts of experiences to explore. You can play within it. For example, what is the makeup of the land under your feet? Don't answer by what you know, but what you pick up. Is it sandy? Are you running into rock? Is it loam? Ledge? Play with becoming aware of what earth is like, where you are.

🐾 Next, feel what it feels like to be fluidly interacting with this larger energetic source. How does it make your body feel? How does it change your awareness of yourself? Of your surroundings? Of other people? Feel your senses spread out. Notice how, when you are open to the energy of the earth and feel yourself to be within that energy, as if in water, it keeps you safe, because you are part of the much larger source.

When you open to energy of the earth, you also are fed. (She's not called Mother Earth for nothing!) Most of us are not aware, most of the time, that the earth is radiating energy into our bodies. When you are stressed and constrict your energy, you restrict the energy exchange. If you become aware of the earth's energy (the electromagnetic field within and surrounding the planet, including the atmosphere, stratosphere, ionosphere) you open the channel and can receive healing and nourishing energy that helps rebalance your body, even if you're not doing specific exercises. Get a sense of what it feels like to be nourished through your feet, and then gradually through your entire body by the Earth's electromagnetic field. Breathe into the place you are, right now. What is the sensation? When you feel more aliveness in your body, does it sparkle, or hum, or roll in waves? Or something else?

Practices that further develop grounding
I'll go into this in more detail in the CD, which you can listen to while practicing. Here I'll give you an overview of some important components for developing your skills.

۶. First, practice Internal Ground with your eyes closed. Become aware of your body with the intention of being as wholly present in yourself as possible. Find all the little places that are protecting themselves by staying hidden or closed off from your awareness. Jane said of this practice: "I had thought that I was aware of my feet. When I did this exercise, I realized that, in fact, I wasn't feeling my whole foot. Now, they feel broader, stronger, and I can feel all my toes."

۶. You can feel internally grounded without your feet on the floor. Experiment in different positions and situations until you can feel aware of your entire body and it feels whole and connected, in various postures.

۶. Move from being as aware as possible of being in your body to relating to the earth's energy. Remember that grounding is a relationship. Feel the benefits of Replenishing Ground. Notice if your energy field seems more expansive and less limited by your skin. Allow yourself to feel nourished by the energy entering your sphere. Feel the safety of your energy being rooted in the earth's energy. Ramorrah said,

"I thought my feet felt like blocks at first, but now I'm circling way down deep into the earth and then back to my feet and around, and I feel free and solid at the same time." Ming noticed, "The tension in my shoulders totally disappeared as my feet went into the dirt."

🐾 When meditating, praying, or practicing intuition, try starting by establishing yourself firmly in your body and settled on the earth. Sense your connection with the earth, yet keep your energy in your body, so you're fully within your skin, rather than more fluidly swimming with the earth's energy. Maintain that meditative ground while you connect with or explore the focus of your practice. How does that affect your prayer or meditation?

🐾 Before opening your eyes, give yourself the cue to make the transition to engaging with the room around you. Once your body has responded to that notion, gently open your eyes. Notice if anything shifts. Feel what is different about External Ground. If you are not able to sense the shift, see what it feels like to thrust yourself back into the land of the active without preparing yourself. Try opening your eyes before giving yourself the cue.

🐾 Practice grounding while standing. While staying connected with your feet, the insides of your legs, your hips, belly, and back, try standing up. You could try Stabilizing Ground. Sylvie said, "The energy of my feet is merged with energy of earth and I'm a tree."

🐾 Then try walking, while staying firmly engaged with your feet and with the earth.

🐾 Then try talking! See in how many situations you can remember to ground while being active.

🌢 Play with what's it feel like to be grounded during other activities, while swimming, running, dancing, driving, in a plane. Play with it.

🌢 Look at trees and imagine how it would feel to be one. Watch an animal and see if you can sense how they ground. A bird grounds differently from a deer, yet all animals stay very connected. Watch children playing, running, climbing. Are they in their bodies? If so, how does it feel?

Endnotes

1 As Malcolm Gladwell notes in his book *Blink*, "Dave Grossman, a former army lieutenant colonel and the author of *On Killing: The Psychological Cost of Learning to Kill in War and Society*, argues that the optimal state of arousal—the range in which stress improves performance—is when our heart rate is between 115 and 145 beats per minute...Most of us, under pressure, get too aroused, and past a certain point, our bodies begin shutting down so many sources of information that we start to become useless (and make really bad decisions). "After 145," Grossman says, "bad things begin to happen. Complex motor skills start to break down. Doing something with one hand and not the other becomes very difficult...At 175, we begin to see an absolute breakdown of cognitive processing...The forebrain shuts down, and the mid-brain—the part of your brain that is the same as your dog's (all mammals have that part of the brain)—reaches up and hijacks the forebrain. Have you ever tried to have a discussion with an angry or frightened human being? You can't do it...You might as well try to argue with your dog. Vision becomes even more restricted. Behavior becomes inappropriately aggressive."

2 Later, in chapter eight, we will look more specifically at how to release pain. With Energy Dynamics, those places that hurt will become places that offer you the most opportunity for change. Why are they wanting attention in the first place? Is some emotion stored there that is causing you to contract muscles? Does that area remember something that you forget? Inhabiting yourself fully, and more fully with practice, enables you to release ages-old pain, both emotional and physical. It is possible to release old karma, old self-defeating beliefs, by truly being with them and allowing them to tell you what you need to know. It is not that they are being a problem. They are being truly helpful. It is we who do not want to listen, so we hold ourselves back. Our bodies can become our greatest teacher and truest support.

3 The importance of alignment can be seen in what I call the **Gargoyle Syndrome.** People often sit with their head dropped forward as they look down on themselves (in both senses). In this position, their body seems way down there because the collapsing of the spine and bending of the neck disconnect them from their

body and energy, and sets up this sitting in judgement against themselves. Their viewpoint is like the gargoyles glowering from the heights of cathedrals in Europe, as if to say, "Beware, you unacceptable little creatures below!" Having your head dropped forward applies a neck-lock to the flow of energy and can worsen depressive symptoms. Make sure your head is upright, aligned with your spine. Let it float above your shoulders. If your back is straight, the weight of your head is evenly balanced, so the bones are carrying most of the weight, rather than straining your shoulder and back muscles.

4 Grounding can be quite complex. I've known individuals who need the image of flying with strong wings in order to ground themselves. They need that particular sense of movement and strength. People are different, and it is important to use the image and sensation that supports your particular experience of being a human in your body.

Photo © 2006 Terrence Keeney

Here. Right here, right now...
Let there be no ulterior motive
in this moment but to be.

—Donna Foulds

Centering 6

WENDY AND HER husband, Ronald, spent years trying to get pregnant. When he said no to adoption, she felt her dreams die. A year later, he left her for a woman who had adopted a child who called him daddy, which meant he'd been involved for a while. Reeling, Wendy had a difficult time moving on with her life. She unconsciously made it harder for herself by believing that, if she became happy and focused on her own future, he'd be off the hook and it would mean that she condoned not only his cheating, but also his lying. Every day she rehearsed her grievances with her friends, feeling victimized and rejected all over again.

Tony is a powerful, behind-the-scenes man in Washington, D.C. He'd been a strategic advisor for several senators and then became a project consultant. His wife threatened to divorce him because of all his business travel. It was he who had wanted children, and now he was hardly home, she said. When he became ill, she was unsympathetic. While he struggled to be home more and help with the kids, he felt torn about the jobs he turned down, and worried about how she'd act when he did travel.

Tony had moved often as an army brat growing up. He had not been abused or tormented, but, like many people with similar backgrounds, the beliefs that he developed about life led him to act as if had no say in how things went; that he had to put up and shut

111

up; that he had to keep his head down, work hard, and toe the line. He learned to shut off awareness of his aches and pains, fatigue or worry, and to keep on keeping on. Since his dad was gone so much, and they barely had time to get to know their neighbors, his mother turned to him for help and emotional support. Because his wife was career-oriented and assertive about her needs, he had thought she was the opposite of his mother. But as so often happens, the superficial difference screened the women's underlying similarities. He found himself acquiescing to and appeasing his wife just as he'd done with his mother.

Tony was worried that his career; his kids were suffering; and he had no idea how to ease the situation. He mentioned in passing that he had had a few accidents—a fender-bender that left him with whiplash, he'd cut himself badly while fixing a drawer, and he'd fallen down the basement stairs. He did not draw a connection between being accident-prone and the stress he was under.

What Wendy and Tony had in common, besides their unhappy marriages, was that they were unable to remain settled in themselves so that their perspective could stay congruent with their own points of view. They needed to learn to center.

What is centering, really?

Your center is the place in which you are aware of your being—your sense of your true self that is deeper and more permanent than is your self-concept, your thoughts or even your emotions. It is where you contact your essence. Your center has a location in your body, in your energy body, and in your nervous system. It can be developed, with practice, as more neural synapses are trained. (This correlates with the Tibetan monks' brain activities described in chapter three.) When you are centered, the sense of simply being becomes completely satisfying. It becomes the axle around which is organized the rest of your multi-faceted self. In fact, the more you practice, the more organized—re-aligned and settled—the rest of your experience and awareness can become.

When we center, we are literally in the eye of the storm, the hub of the wheel of life.

Say that, during the course of a day, you find yourself puzzling repeatedly over an upset with your boss, a family member, a concern about a friend, or having an old wound reopened when the past is triggered. These thoughts, memories, and feelings are located somewhere on the spokes of the wheel of your experience. External events that impact you occur beyond the rim, but your reaction, or the extent to which you get pulled into them, draws that event into the spokes. Even deep pains and flashbacks are on the spokes. They are not at the core of who you are. If they feel as if they are, you are not centered in the axle, and your attention has been drawn into their location. Your attention and energy investment are somewhere in the spokes or rim of the wheel. As the wheel spins, or the maelstrom hurls itself around, your sense of self swirls with the events on which your attention is caught. This feels chaotic and overly-arousing and so you may find yourself tending either to hustle or hide, swept up by the chaos of events without having a clear reference point or sense of being settled. When you're spinning around, it is much easier to become unbalanced or to lose your objectivity or not see you own reactions clearly. While you're out there, you'll tend to feel more at the mercy of outside events or of feelings from the past, as well as knocked about by the other stuff banging around with you. You may feel victimized by others as your power is washed away. You may try to block your feelings and grab control, reasserting some sense of control. Either way, many people spend a lot of their lives as if they are in the cyclone with Dorothy in *The Wizard of Oz*.

When you can settle your awareness in the axle, the wheel of experience can spin all it wants. The axle remains still and oriented. The storm may rage around you, but you can still be serene. This is the still point that is at the center of all things. When you arrive there consciously, greater nourishment, and tranquility, and creativity grows. You can see the cyclone of life whirling around you—look! There goes a cow! There's Dorothy's house!—all while in the rocking chair of your being. Or, you may get pulled back into the maelstrom by latching onto some idea or feeling that flashes by. The devil is in the cyclone. That's where you are when you turn against yourself and judge yourself harshly and think you are bad.

As Connie got better at grounding, she became aware that, while she was more present in her body, she was still hyper-vigilant, constantly looking out for danger. Her attention was scattered. When I asked her to locate her sense of self, she couldn't. She said she didn't know who she was anymore. It was as if she were pretending to be a cohesive and viable person. She still felt overly affected by things that happened around her, swept up in larger fight-or-flight reactions than present situations warranted. She was afraid that she was permanently and completely damaged and so was racing to try to catch up with something, she knew not what. To reclaim a sense of herself as whole, she needed to develop a sense of herself that organized her experience in a new way. She was describing her need for a center.

It was imperative that she learn to center. Centering would give her that private place in which to settle, so that her awareness of her true self could develop. We began working on it in sessions.

It takes practice to stay centered. That is what Buddhism and Taoism talk about when they train people in the phases of mind and spirit development in the practice of meditation. Christian and Sufi mystics have found the same place. Centering is at the core of spiritual practice.

There is immense freedom and empowerment (and relief!) in being in the still point in the middle. Simply seeing that feelings in fact are not at the core of who you are and do not define you frees you to relate to them differently. It is then possible not to drown in them or have to stave them off. They can be experienced, watched with curiosity, and released. (We'll go into the technique for doing so in the next chapter.)

Decisions can be clearer when you don't feel yanked by opposing sides. Relationships become smoother and more beautiful. You won't feel swallowed up or distanced from in the same way. When centered, you have more space to see others clearly, empathize with them, and choose how you want to respond. It is more possible to re-center when you have gotten too caught up in events, either internal or external. When you know how to center and to trust being in your center, you can release habits and old patterns. Centering allows your energies to realign, so that they become more balanced, which leads to some illnesses being able to be resolved.

Your center is also that still place in which your joy becomes apparent, where you feel fine and peaceful, safe and un-threatened. It is where you connect with the Divine, if your beliefs and experience tend in that direction. Clarity about intuitions can be determined by centering. Being settled and strong in your center makes child rearing, business goals, life's craziness, much more do-able and enjoyable. Centering equals coalescing one's sense of self in the present.

Why people are afraid of being centered

When Connie first was learning to center, she would only practice in my office, fearing that if she tried it on her own, "all the crap will snag me and I won't get there." Her desire to avoid the trauma warred with the thing that would make it easier to resolve, but that was okay. She needed the safety of my providing a holding environment for her and guiding her through it until her center became more real to her.

When anyone learns a new skill, they are not perfectly competent at first. It's vital to allow yourself (and others) to fall down when you're learning to walk, yell when you're learning to express your anger, send onions skipping across the floor when learning to chop vegetables, and to be fierce when learning to assert yourself. Only after that can the fine-tuning come. Knowing that you can return to yourself by re-grounding if you fall down enables you to have a base for developing more finesse.

Doubts about self-worth seem to be at the base of so many people's fear of settling in their center. They often stay disconnected from themselves either because they can't believe that they have the right to take up space and treat themselves as if they matter, or because they have invested heavily in their outer shell—their constructed persona—and use it to maintain power as a way of avoiding raw feelings. When abusive people or events have treated you as if you don't matter, then treating yourself well, or softening into yourself can cause anxiety.

So much of our psychological and social turmoil is the result of trying to avoid feelings. Usually during the course of growing up, people develop mechanisms with which to push pain away, an out-of-sight-out-of-mind philosophy. Unfortunately, "out-of-mind" does not equal "evaporated." Feelings we push away stay stuffed in our personal holding tanks, whichever we use—stomach, shoulders—(where is your trouble spot? That's where some are stored). Add trauma or abuse to the usual load of being human, and the pain overflows the tanks. Maintaining a cohesive sense of self is overwhelmed by violation or by the destruction of our assumption of safety and of our right to move freely in the world. Hurt and trauma cause us to be at odds with ourselves. If we are not centered, it's virtually impossible to have appropriate boundaries, to be clear about what is okay with us and limit others' access and their effects on us.

When we feel overwhelmed and we lose our center as a result, we become dislodged from our mooring. We're then flying around in the maelstrom of painful feelings. Add some pain-avoidance behaviors and the hurt then appears to be in the core of ourselves, in further than we are. When we are not centered, the notion of dealing with old stored emotions is akin to feeling as if we are perched outside on the rim of a pit of darkness that will drown us if we drop into it. We teeter on the edge and then back away. Who in their right mind would voluntarily spend time in that pit? It looks like seething, overwhelming chaos, no hope of taming it or coming out the other side, our own personal inferno. If we are uncentered, the pain feels as if it is who we are, as if it is what defines us, that there is no self but the hurt. So we unconsciously decide to avoid pain by staying away from our insides, by doing whatever we can to distract ourselves from our core in order to "protect ourselves" from all that gunk.

Only when we are centered can we see that the pain is not who we are and is not an integral part of our core selves. When we ground and center, we can allow emotions to run their course, because we have a stable foundation and can learn not to be thrown by them. There is immense freedom in not being afraid of our own feelings. If one needs to surface and be resolved, we can stand as the firm earth and rock riverbed, watch it flow by, or through, and not have our sense of self swept away.

Connie's first experience of her center led her to exclaim that it felt like a haven. Rather than being lost in the scary thoughts and feelings, she found the core within her that was unharmed and whole. Hope resurfaced when she actually felt that there was a calm place at the hub of her being. While centered, the traumatic memories and sensations were more peripheral. When they didn't occupy center-stage, Connie could glimpse a reality in which she was no longer ruled by the rape.

Connie remarked, "This is an amazing example of the power of practicing. When I studied violin, I couldn't really tell if it helped me get better, maybe because I was little and Mom always made me do it. But I can feel, as we do centering, how it gets stronger and more real. I get better at moving into it." After a few more sessions, she said, "I can't believe it, but I feel just now as if I'm fine. At this moment, I feel happy and that I'm all right, and that things will be all right."

As Connie worked, she was gradually able to re-own her body more quickly as she became clearer that the trauma was perpetrated by the attacker, not by her body. She began to develop a fondness and a protective attitude toward herself, which then developed into a drive to "clean out all his crap and refuse to let him ruin my life."

The more she "cleaned out," the more she began using her new fierceness to take ownership of her life in other areas—how she interacted with friends and teachers, questioning the limitations she'd set for herself including those from childhood. In this way she actually began to have a fuller, more empowered sense of her life than she had ever had.

She began to sleep better. She tried walking to class. She told people to back off, putting self-care before politeness.

What frees us from pain and uncovers joy is a paradox. The pit looks unfathomable and intolerable when we are outside ourselves. Fighting the pain is what disconnects us from our own core self. It is only by risking moving into our center that we find out that it is actually the place in which stillness, love, joy, and the connection with all-that-is resides within us. When we learn to perceive the real nature of our true selves, and settle into our center, the view changes completely.

Centering makes it possible to process feelings, so that they don't stay stuck and stored

When Wendy practiced centering in my office, she was surprised to notice that she was okay, even as the hurt ran its course. Sooner than she'd imagined, the wave would subside and she'd find that she felt strong enough to face the future, at least for the moment. She'd breathe, notice the quiet as the noise of all those feelings receded, and be a little tired. (It takes effort to hold all those feelings down.) A sense of peace would arise, and then she'd experience her center, which had become a bit fuller. Over time, the sensation would bud into a sweet contentedness in her chest and midsection, (which is joy beginning to blossom). The problem was, when she wasn't in my office, she kept going back to the thought that allowing herself to feel settled meant that he'd won and that he was off the hook. So she refused to ground and center when on her own. So her progress stalled.

The paradox is that staying present with pain enables you to grow joy. Being centered aids in resolving feelings, patterns and beliefs. You can build a new, real sense of yourself in your own life, and a new internal structure. Then you can realize that they are not fundamental to who you are, that you are not bad, but that bad things happened, *and there is still a core YOU that is whole, healthy, and connected.*

Centering helps you pull yourself together. Firming up your core sense of self makes it possible to release the headlock that trauma has on you, so that you experience pain as more peripheral.

Centering negates self-criticism

When something has gone wrong, there occurs both the awful feeling of the problem itself, and also all the crap from the past that it reminds you of. Sometimes it seems as if you're falling into an altered state if the stress is great enough to make you regress into old patterns. When Tani was younger, her fallback coping mode was to criticize herself mercilessly and make herself responsible for wildly improbable things.

Self-flagellation was her heavy artillery of choice. As Mark Epstein said in his book *Open to Desire*, "We take too much responsibility for our emotions, blaming ourselves rather than seeing they are the results of the past." And she didn't stick to blaming herself for her feelings. She blamed herself for the fact that it happened, how it affected others, you name it. It took her years to see that all that criticism was just a way of protecting her from the fallout of childhood experiences. Then it took her longer actually to stop it. Through grounding, centering, and BWITSY (see next chapter), she finally was able not only to see that self-blame and anticipation of hatred from others were not necessary, and also that she could stop it when it started. (Other necessary components for releasing that old pattern are covered in other chapters, especially in chapter sixteen.)

It is ironic, and a huge blessing, that self-blame is impossible when you are centered. Self-criticism used to be described as "turning on yourself," and it is literally that. To criticize yourself you have to step out of your core, turn around, and shake your finger in your face. Criticism is by its very nature disconnection from present reality as you channel some past learned diatribe and paste it on the now. The way to stop habitual self-blame is to risk the "pit," by moving into yourself, and giving yourself a chance to find that the blame and the scary inferno can all dissipate.

Centering keeps you from being thrown by others' views

Claire, a class participant said, "I follow what goes on with people. When Jack talked about his tense shoulders, I found mine tensing." Lulu added, "When a friend's child was diagnosed with a serious illness, I felt so bad for her. And then I found myself panicking about my own kids."

The line between self and others can be tricky to perceive if you're sensitive, empathic, or you've been trained to worry about others' feelings. Claire may have simply had her attention directed to her own tension, or she may have started feeling pain where none had been through her sympathetic reaction to Jack.[1] Sensitive and empathic people have to learn how not to get sucked in too far. They then lose not only their objectivity but also their own sense of well-being, as they are thrown by so many other people's situations.

Centering keeps you located in your own world view, so you can take better care of and protect yourself. You will be clear whose feelings are whose, and not confuse your reactions with another's.

In the same class, Ramorrah said "When I'd get tense, I'd tense up in my mind. I'd go into my head, and try to figure things out. Now I have this wonderful tool to notice faster when I'm off, and then release the tension and reconnect with myself! Centering makes it possible to become aware sooner of what's happening while I'm listening. Then I feel everything come together, rather than being trapped in some pattern or thought. If we notice what happens in our bodies specifically when we get tense, then we can undo it."

Finding your feet when your sense of self seems unfamiliar

When survivors work through old material and toward building joy, a stumbling block often occurs. When they notice they are feeling some calmness and happiness more consistently, panic sometimes sets in. It often is quite severe. Is the other shoe going to drop? Their past experience trained them to believe that happiness cannot last. When they break the old rules and move forward in a more positive and empowered way, they often find themselves feeling chaotic, with lots of anticipation of impending doom. When I went against the edicts of my upbringing and insisted on living my way, it felt as if a hurricane were hitting. I'd then yell at myself that whatever I thought was going so well was a huge mistake and I'd better knock it off pronto. This was an effort to get my internal confusion to calm down. Many people report a similar experience. The sensations can be upsetting and scary, because they feel so palpable.

When people move into a new state-of-being, grow new skills, and start to act on them, they have moved beyond their old, familiar sense of who they are and their place in the world. Living well may be the best revenge, but it can also involve breaking some big taboos, the kind we talked about in chapter two. They know what it feels like to be who they are when in coping-with-trauma-mode, or when maintaining the drilled-in messages not to make waves, not to want anything, or only to meet others' needs. They are experts at putting out fires, handling the rapid shift to crisis mode. They have much less experience maintaining a calm, contented lifestyle. It takes work and a different set of skills to get used to a happier self, and to learn to locate themselves in a life in which good things happen, calm occurs most of the time, and crises are rare. It is interesting how many people first define "calm" as "boring" when they reach this point. Actually, they are in uncharted territory and don't know how to settle into being okay when calm.

Wendy continued to equate feeling better with letting her ex-husband off the hook, not only because that meant that she gave him the seal of approval, but also because she was invested in her identity as the wronged person. Much of her socializing with friends revolved around complaining about how badly their men treated them. She was not ready to give that up and find new friends. So she backed off from the new feelings of strength and calm that she'd glimpsed. She just didn't know if she could be that person or even who that person was.

When people ask, "How do I know who I am now?" they are asking in a state of agitation, yet the question marks an opportunity to take a large spiritual leap forward. Asking "Who am I?" requires looking at what you think defines you; who you think, or feel, or believe you are; who you were told you are; who you were told to be; and what defines you as valuable.

Just below the level of awareness, people constantly check their experience against an internal set of assumptions of what constitutes normal. Getting to the point of asking, "How do I know who I am" means that you have succeeded in growing out of what you-defined-by-others toward increased well-being. Voicing this existential dilemma means that your sense of yourself has been shaken up enough that you are not settling for old (and inaccurate, because too limited) answers. You are attending to an internal experience that is so new and raw that the landscape is not yet filled in. New landmarks must be built. By being centered, you build awareness of your true Self, one kinesthetic experience at a time. You build internal structure, changing the old ways of perceiving and holding yourself neurologically, physically, emotionally, and psychologically. When folks build this new internal structure by practicing centering, I have seen people clear up old health issues and release negative results of their previous experiences. They can burn away old trauma, rewrite old history (in the sense that the hold that it had on their lives is changed), and thereby release karma.

Center is a noun and a verb, also a location and an action

Your center is a real place within you that your nervous system responds to and supports. The more you center, the more your center becomes furnished. It gains more reality, more substance. It becomes a refuge that you can settle into more and more easily.

Dedicating yourself to centering starts you toward feeling whole, full, unblemished, healed, fine, and in the present, with the hurts becoming more peripheral and more integrated into the past. It becomes easier to return to being centered and, over time, to stay connected in your core sense of yourself. The types of sensations that occur can become the signposts you watch to make sure you've arrived. You will also notice more readily what it feels like when you're uncentered, so that you notice more quickly when it has occurred. The sensations that you recognize as you center will guide you as your come back after having gotten caught again out in the whirlwind. For example, when I center, I feel a gathering of particles, as in the show *Star Trek* when someone travels by transporter. I also get a sense of what pushed me off as I re-gather. Sometimes the entire left side of my body feels as if it is coming into more of a partnership with the right, which says to me that I have been somewhat disconnected from my more spatial, receptive side. Or it might be that I feel a shoring up under my midsection, as if I could use more structural support for myself and my spirit.

When he started working with me, Tony was not aware of his patterns. Fundamental to our work together was uncovering his way of relating to himself as well as to the important women in his life. In order to figure out what to do to make his life better, he needed to learn to listen to himself and value his feelings and needs.

As Tony practiced grounding and centering, he noticed that his vision cleared, actually and metaphorically, as he also perceived his situation more realistically than before. He saw some old beliefs that were holding him in self-defeating patterns and was eager to clear them and replace them with healthier ones. He was most excited about feeling more supportive of himself.

Being centered removes chaos and organizes our perceptions. Centering invites great self-love. Grounding and centering make it possible to brave our feelings, and by doing so, we become free. This is one of the most powerful paradoxes in our experience as humans: that when we dare to be with ourselves as fully as possible, when we can settle into ourselves just as we are right now, we release old shackles. When we are within the essence of who we are, we reach a stillness, the same pearl of stillness that is at the heart of everything. We are then one with all-that-is. Our center is where our spirit resides in us, and where Spirit also enlivens and resides in us, and where we can contact It. If we can learn to risk facing in a constructive, effective way the old feelings and memories that we have stored in ourselves, then the possibilities for freedom and joy are endless.

In the next chapter, we will apply what we have learned so far to releasing hurt, so that we can uncover joy.

Exercises for Centering

How to Center:

Let's get down to the nuts and bolts. The first step is to start with the breathing and grounding exercises. Make sure that your spine is straight so that energy can flow optimally. Keep both feet on the floor without crossing your ankles. Breathe into your stomach, freeing your diaphragm. Notice as your awareness becomes more internal that you sense the movement of your breath in your back and sides as well. Allow your awareness to expand down through your pelvis, hips, thighs, knees, calves, ankles, into your feet. Check throughout your lower body, so that you inhabit it more fully. Can you feel tingling in your feet? That is a sign that you are more aware of your energy, so it's flowing more. Notice if your awareness extends to the earth. Gradually check in through your torso—your back, sides, front, shoulders, arms, hands, neck, and head.

Try to breathe into any tight, tense, or painful places, so that they can be part of your body too. When you feel fully awake in yourself and connected with the ground, make sure that the posterior part of your ribs, your kidney area, is included in your awareness. Invite energy into your backbone so that you sense it as more juicy, rather than simply as brittle bone.

Now, imagine that there is a clear, crystal column that runs from the crown of your head all the way to down to your perineum, in front of the spine, which places right down the middle of your body vertically. This cylinder equates with the influx of nourishment and connectedness from Universal energy cycling with the energy flowing in from the earth. Somewhere in the column is your center—the location of your sense of Being. This is the place where you settle, where you feel yourself simply being, rather than thinking or even having emotions, where you rest when you are peaceful. It is also where you connect with Spirit.

Direct your intention—ask to become aware, within the clear column, where your true center is. Notice the first place that occurs to you. This is not a hard and fast rule, but it is often true that women's centers are higher, somewhere from the heart to the diaphragm, while men's centers tend to be lower, anywhere from the diaphragm to the area below the navel known as the *dan t'ian*, or "Sea of Qi." This lower place is the physical power center and is very important in both genders. It is not the same point as the center that we are talking about here. Here, we want to locate not the physical center but the spiritual.

Some people first say that their center is in their head. That occurs when the energy you are most aware of is your thinking-mind energy. See if you can settle more into your kinesthetic sense of your body and rest in your breath a bit more. Then look again. (You may, however, be noticing your crown chakra, where Universal energy is entering your body. That is still different from your center.)

If you are under a lot of stress right now, where you hold that stress may affect your awareness of your center. When Mavis learned about centering, she was in the midst of a battle with her landlord who was trying to kick her out of her rent-controlled apartment. She could not notice anything in her rib cage area, because her heart felt agitated and constricted. She tried settling somewhat lower. When she was able to breathe and simply be in the lower spot, she said that the agitation around her heart was reduced within a few minutes by about thirty percent. Months later, after the lawsuit was over, her sense of her center moved up to the base of her ribs.

People have varying sensations as they center

Notice what happens when you give yourself the suggestion to center yourself. Notice what sensations you have. Does your vision get a little sharper? Do you breathe a little more deeply? Is your belly softening? Or your back feeling firmer? Do you feel tingling? Where? Warmth? Coolness? Opening? Notice what is happening with you.

People tend to hold themselves too small or tightly often begin to feel more relaxed and open, with more room to breathe. Others who tend to scatter and distract themselves speak of feeling themselves coalesce, as if the pieces are fitting together into a whole.

Your center may seem empty or tiny at first. This is a good sign! It means that you have succeeded in moving into it, into the still point, and the storminess you're used to seeing inside just isn't there. The rest of your body may feel a bit heavy or as if you can't move. This often happens when you have been disconnected from your body, and then settle in, or when your awareness has gone deeper into an awareness of your spirit. It can happen in meditation as well. It is simply a kinesthetic experience. Nothing is wrong.

Practice: Feel what it's like to be present in your environment while being grounded and centered at the same time. Notice any change in how you feel in the room, as well as in yourself.

Practice: Practice first at home with your eyes closed. Then gradually try other situations—in the restroom at work. (I firmly believe that restrooms are hidden assets! You can go in a stall and breathe, ground and center, really let down and rest for a minute, collect yourself, practice a speech, or vent silently. Then you can emerge and pick up with your day a bit recharged.)

Practice: Remember about Internal and External Grounding. *Before* you open your eyes, cue yourself by thinking that you are about to reenter the world. Allow your system to make the transition for you, redefining your attention, firming your boundaries, and shifting your ground. When you do open your eyes, notice what it's like to be grounded and centered while aware of the world. Take a few moments to look around. How do plants look? Your room? Your dog? How do you feel? What are you aware of? Continue to feel your feet on the floor. Notice the energy circulating in your body, especially in your feet.

Endnotes

1 Sympathy, by the way, is identifying with someone else's situation and sharing it, so that your boundaries are blurred as you take their experience on and feel it as if it were your own. Empathy, on the other hand, occurs when you perceive, or even feel, the other's feelings and understand the validity of it for them, given what you know about their world view. The difference between the two is that, when sympathizing, you lose your own perspective and merge with theirs. When empathizing, you validate and honor theirs as theirs, being clear that it is not yours, even if you have had similar experiences. Empathy gives you greater insight into the unique view of the other person.

Emotions, no matter how powerful, are not overwhelming if given room to breathe.

—Mark Epstein

BWITSY: a silly name for a crucial concept—Be With It, Then Soothe Yourself

7.

HEIDI WAS THE second-in-command in a community-service organization. She was being groomed for the top position by her CEO and mentor, who wanted to retire. But Heidi was worried about being in a leadership position. She felt that, for years, she had held herself back from realizing her full potential. Especially, she needed to lead more effectively and smoothly, become less mired in various factions' fuss with each other, and increase her positive outcome and production figures.

But Heidi had a secret, and it took her a while to see the connection between it and her work performance difficulties. Heidi had been bulimic for years.

Eating disorders are notoriously difficult to interrupt, as they involve something we have to do every day in order to sustain life. It's not as if she could just stop eating. Heidi was upset that she had been throwing up for so long, and had tried so many times to stop, that by the time she came to me, she was sure that nothing would work. She had quite a bit of insight into the patterns in childhood that had led to her starting a binge/purge cycle in adolescence. She didn't know what kept her habit in place or what it would take to get unstuck. In the meantime, she found herself continuing a behavior that not only ate away at her teeth, GI tract, and self-esteem, but robbed her of energy and attention and undermined her ability to work through emotional issues constructively. Right when she should have been at the top, she felt that she was hitting rock bottom.

So much of our psychological, physical, and social turmoil comes as a result of trying to avoid feelings. Usually during the course of growing up, people develop mechanisms with which to push pain away, an out-of-sight-out-of-mind philosophy. Unfortunately, out-of-mind does not equal "evaporated." Feelings we push away stay stuffed in our personal holding tanks, whichever we use (stomach, shoulders—where is your trouble spot? That's where some are stored). Add trauma or abuse to the usual load of being human, and the pain overloads the tanks. We may then have trouble maintaining a healthy sense of self. Hurt and trauma cause us to be at odds with ourselves. If we are not centered, it's virtually impossible to have appropriate boundaries, to be clear about what is unacceptable and limit others' effects on us.

If it were possible to reach self-acceptance without facing excruciating stuff, I'd be all for it! After all, why hurt if there is no point? But there is a huge point. The goal of releasing trauma is to have your own life rather than being frozen in an endless argument with the past. And the only way out is through.

The question is, how do we learn to resolve and integrate painful material so that it does not have so much power over us? The problem, as we know, is that facing *really* tumultuous feelings is scary, especially with all the visuals that come with them. And it is not only the emotions. There are the bodily sensations, the flashbacks, the physical triggers that make up the really frozen encoding of trauma. The things we do to protect ourselves from the overwhelming nature of those feelings and experiences—the self-punishment, self-criticism, compulsive, or out-of-control habits and addictions—*those are the very things that hold us IN the pain, and hold the pain in us.*

Trying to push away discomfort never works. We tend to become more dissatisfied, which leads us to push them away more. Pleasures engaged in to fill a void of emptiness or loneliness, habits indulged as a way to distract from pain, can never really work. If we are trying to fill the void with indulgences in the present, we are avoiding the reality, which is, in the past, we didn't get enough, or we were hurt. Indulgences can only mask the old stuff momentarily. We know it's still there. We're so sensitized to it that we have one ear cocked for it all the time.

The war we wage against ourselves

Heidi was good at her job because she really cared about the mission of the non-profit. Even so, her desire to help was not grounded in empathy for people. Her ability to connect with others was limited by her need to stay away from her own emotions. While she was aware of childhood patterns, she had not ever addressed the fear and anxiety that had come from her mother and stepfather's behavior.

Heidi was the middle child of three girls. Her stepfather was a minister who ruled his flock with a fire-and-brimstone approach. At home he believed that sparing the rod spoiled the child. Luckily, Heidi's mother did not agree. She insisted that parenting her daughters be up to her. But she was not much warmer than her husband. She was interested in the girls' activities and studies but more interested in her committees and good works. Given that she was the ignored middle child, Heidi felt especially unnecessary, ignored, and unloved. Locked away inside were beliefs that she could never be good enough, that it must be her fault if no one loved her, that she couldn't count on people, and that she never knew what others would do.

As we identified her beliefs and feelings, it became clear to Heidi that bulimia was a really effective distraction from her pain—effective because it took so much time and planning and led her to spend hours berating herself and feeling like a powerless failure.

People often don't realize that while they are trying to manage or banish pain, they are battling themselves. They are so afraid that they can't tolerate their memories—that they will be washed away forever. The act of fighting to make those feelings go away actually holds their worst nightmares in their bodies—often in a specific location. Eventually the clenching will lead to physical pain.

Emotions are an important and inextricable aspect of who you are, and of your energy system. You can't cut them off without turning against yourself. You set up a conflict in which the energy moving one way—toward expression—is combated by the energy you've deployed to demolish it. Those two forces lock heads and, like sumo wrestlers, stay stuck, sweaty and unmoving, exerting tremendous amounts of force in stasis. Each side fears that if it gives up its wrestling stance, the other will plow over them, and they'll disappear in a flood of torment.

Because they are in a lot of pain, people think that they are working through their material. In fact, they are so acutely sensitive to any sign of sensations getting past their blockade that they mobilize the protective wrestler at the first hint. They don't see that a large percentage of the pain is actually caused by the forces locked in a death grip with each other. The gritted teeth, the dug-in heels, the tight back muscles: the war is physical too.

Gwyneth had lots of emotions from her childhood that she was not yet aware of. These only surfaced as she felt more connected with her body—through her breath and through grounding—and began to access memories.

Gwyneth had a sister and brother, twelve and ten years older than she. Their grandmother had also lived with them. Rather than a warm and homey type, the grandmother showed no interest in Gwyn and would walk right by her yelling at her siblings to deal with her. Since no adults in the household took care of her, the teens just saw her as a pain and left her to her own devices. Gwyn had no space to herself, not even a drawer. She slept on the couch until her brother and sister moved out.

Luckily, she was a feisty little thing. When her grandmother ignored her, Gwyn climbed up on the kitchen table and teased her into playing cards with her. I think that's how she developed her sunny exterior. She persistently chattered and charmed people into interacting with her. She focused on pleasing or entertaining others, or she went off by herself for hours, befriended only by her imagination.

As well as the neglect and hostility in her family, she had felt rejected at school. In kindergarten, she had cried for months, which led to her being badly teased and bullied.

Gwyneth felt unconfident, unable to control circumstances, alone, inadequate, undeserving, unloved, deprived, and afraid. She hid a deep well of shame—that feeling that it was her fault and so did not deserve to be happy. All of her external focus—her trying to please others and to be a good girl—stemmed from these feelings and contributed to making them worse.

Gwyneth had no support during childhood that would have helped her deal with these feelings, so they were bottled up. She had gone through life, so far, with no awareness as to the pressure those bottled-up emotions exerted, and how much they governed her behavior and outlook.

Our emotions and sensations are not the originators of our pain

They give us information about events and try to get our attention so that we will support the process of resolution. Staving them off is similar to being mad at your arm for hurting, rather than going to the doctor and getting it reset because it's broken. The emotions have been there all the time. They are not new, not something we've never seen before. And, they haven't killed us yet.

So many people think they've been working through their trauma for years, when in fact they've been racing around in their endless feedback loops of pain management and distancing strategies. Unfortunately that usually leads to believing that there will be no release and that nothing works. Many people come into therapy only after they've been stuck in this pattern for a long time, and sometimes they don't let themselves try something new, because the belief that it's hopeless is too strong.[1]

The ribbon-on-the-box

Before, whenever Heidi had tried to stop throwing up, something had frustrated her efforts. When the pressure of the compulsion started building, not only would the red flag of anxiety atop her garbage-can of history press her back into her habit, but she'd run into the fear that the stored stuff was too big, and that she was too small to be able to survive working through it. She'd find herself stuffing the feelings back into garbage can by stuffing her face.

Many people run into this problem. The certainty that she was not up to the task originated in childhood when in fact she *had been* too little to tolerate the pain of the bad things that had happened.

Unless children are helped to deal with traumatic events, they do not have much choice but to stuff their reactions down into their systems to be dealt with when they have grown. Their certainty then acts as a ribbon on the holding tank of buried feelings. On the ribbon is printed in glaring neon letters, *"Danger! You can't handle these! You are too small, and they are too huge and overpowering! Back away from the toxic waste!"*

Because they were three, or five, or twelve, they *were* overwhelmed by events, so the ribbon was accurate when it was written and the tank was buried. But now, it's an old garbage can with a really old, tattered ribbon. There is no need to believe the writing on it anymore. Yet it takes braving a reality check, when the tank bobs up showing the ribbon, to then risk moving forward anyway, and then discover that, as adults, they are no longer so helpless. Now they can drive, do their own laundry, earn money, walk away from strangers, and so maybe they risk using new skills to process old feelings.

Gwyneth shut down when she was upset. She moved very fast, both physically and mentally, keeping herself busy to the point of overwhelm in order to stay away from unresolved feelings that terrified her. She had no idea how to work through them, and she believed she could not contain them—that they'd be too much for her and she wouldn't survive them.

When people keep themselves running really fast and so heavily focused on their work or on the demands of others, they have no energy leftover to focus on themselves (which is, of course, the point). But they pay other costs as well. As successful as Gwyneth was in business, it was because she met challenges put upon her by others. She was not proactive, looking at the big picture of her life and planning what she wanted in a mate or a career. As she said, she did not have a sense of who she was. Consequently, no matter how much money she made or how many promotions she received, she did not feel she had any stability in life. Deep down, she knew she was adrift in life and awash in old feelings.

Be With It, Then Soothe Yourself

The most important factor in freeing ourselves and moving to joy is to release pain, and to do so we have to stop trying to protect ourselves from our own past by setting up these battles with ourselves. There is a more effective way to deal with feelings. The only way to release a painful feeling, to have it lose some of its intensity and not define us anymore, is to **Be With It, Then Soothe Yourself** (BWITSY). In the past, we were hurt. Now we must make sure that we are not the ones fighting against ourselves. Our feelings and our history, even the most excruciating, have to stop being seen as the enemy.

Being with it then soothing yourself is the polar opposite of feeling washed away by your own history or having to squash yourself in order to seem like a together person. BWITSY makes it possible to release the pent-up feelings and the power they hold over you. Then they can be integrated as a section of the fabric of your life. Only then can the incidents recede into the past (not vanished, but at least not pasted on your face) rather a part of what made you who you are. You will be reminded of the memories and feelings sometimes. But enough studies have shown that what alters one's experience of life most effectively is to allow one to Be With the pain, and then turn to the present and plan for a better future. There are several benefits here. One is that you're grounded when you experience the pain, putting it in perspective by reconnecting with the present, in which you are whole, adult, safe, strong, and in your living room; you have friends, skills to take care of yourself, the ability to get yourself where you want to go.

Another benefit is that soothing yourself gives you practice at a new attitude toward yourself. Simply having the notion that you deserve soothing gradually builds a more positive outlook and better outcomes.

BWITSY leads to several key benefits

❧ You do not get lost in the automatic reactions your reptilian brain—that primitive danger/survival system that has you reacting in the ways that you really wish you wouldn't. (Not to say you won't react, hey, you wouldn't be human if you didn't. I just want you to be able, over time, to find yourself reacting less often and less extremely.) You maintain awareness of yourself, so you can counter those reactions by engaging your pre-frontal cortex, your ability to think, observe, and assess. You build on your adult, empowered sense of yourself, rather than finding yourself ricocheting back into your childhood or traumatized view of yourself. The process and the outcome change dramatically when you have yourself available to witness what is going on.

❧ You stay in your body and maintain your connection with yourself, rather than being overwhelmed. You experience kinesthetically that you continue exist. If you pause and check in, you find that you are okay. You give yourself a place to stand and feel that you still exist kinesthetically. You can then tolerate finding out that letting the feelings wash on through is less painful than is tensing against them. Moving through them while being grounded and centered proves to you that you are not lost. You remain safe and connected enough to tolerate those unsafe feelings.

❧ You stay in touch with your internal resources—your energy and ability to think, your values, toughness, compassion, all your strengths—which makes it possible to process the past and to investigate new choices for the future with a full toolbox. You can be nourished, supported, and held by the energy of the earth, and of Spirit, when you stay connected with yourself.

❦ What ultimately frees you is to *be aware of you while feeling those feelings,* committing to staying present until they subside. When you are centered, you find that you don't have to be afraid of your emotions or sensations, because you experience your core surviving. If you can notice that, you experience first-hand that the pain does not define you. You give yourself a chance to find that you can survive them. Having feelings abate while still being present allows them actually to be released. It also gives you profound new messages. By experiencing their attenuation first-hand, you come to know that old pain does not have the same power to disrupt your life. Change *is* possible, because you just watched it occur!

❦ You learn to experience your reality clearly, in present time. Not only are you being with your pain, you learn to be with the actuality of life after pain. You gradually get used to being calm, restful, and soothed by your own compassion and self-care. You provide the love and safety that makes it possible both to be with the feelings and to notice that your situation is better now. You find yourself in the present, washed clean after the feelings subside, settled into a place in which there is no need to strive or struggle, in which you can simply *be* and find that restful, if not downright delicious.

❦ You will free yourself, and a tremendous amount of energy, when you gather your courage to stop fighting against your emotions. By doing so, you will also allow the natural processes that we have for processing emotion to do their job. You'll stop blocking the river. And, because you thereby give up the war against yourself, there is an odd kind of peace in being with what is truly present at this moment, even if it hurts. You free the natural process of healing, which enables the hurts to subside.

Chunking the memories

Prior to engaging in Energy Dynamics, Connie had been absolutely positive that she could not tolerate the feelings stored in her body from being raped. Until we started working, she had thought that her only option was to distance from it and pave it over with emotional scabs. The more that she tried to control her pain with willpower, the more on edge she became around men. Connie needed to work through her feelings productively. In her situation she clearly needed to BWITSY, especially the Soothe Yourself part. A large barrier to recovery is that victims of violence or abuse feeling overwhelmed by the avalanche of bodily memories, images, and emotions. What works is to chunk them into manageable bits and work through them in a way that doesn't make you disconnect from your self or your body.

Connie gradually learned to ground and center first, so she could see that the feelings were not central to her core. Then it was more possible to allow the feelings to surface without being swept away by them. She'd go through the memory, staying with the feelings and pictures as much as she could. When it seemed that her system was about to be overwhelmed, I'd stop her and direct her back to her body in the present, breathing, re-grounding, and thus learning to settle her nervous system. Included in this were exercises focusing on the parts of her body that were not particularly tense, settling those first and bringing them to her awareness. We also developed calming phrases and images that helped her re-gather herself as okay in the moment.

Chunk by chunk we went through the memory, several times, until its charge was reduced and Connie could stay grounded while she remembered the incident. Returning over and over to the here-and-now broke the mesmerizing quality of the traumatic memory. Over time, it also dismantled the automatic flashback that would make her body think it was back into the alley.

In the process, the concept of soothing herself became much more important. Connie became dedicated to her own well-being as she never had before. She'd check in to see how she was doing in everyday circumstances and take a moment to calm her nervous system, now that she knew it was possible and knew how to do it.

It is freeing in many seemingly unrelated areas to realize that one can manage and resolve intense feelings, rather than drown in them.

How to clear feelings

Be With It:

First, make sure you are in a location in which you feel safe and in which you will not be interrupted. Give yourself half-an-hour to an hour for the whole thing.

- **Be:** First, you be in yourself by being grounded and centered, and thereby present and self-attentive. Throughout the process, you continue to focus on being located inside your skin and in your core. You maintain this awareness steadily. You refuse to lose your sense of self.

- **It:** You allow the feeling or sensation—the object of your attention, the It—to be present. You acknowledge that it exists. The pain needs some recognition. It deserves to be respected enough to be listened to. And, you honor yourself by doing so. You deserve to *feel* hurt, if you were hurt. If you didn't feel hurt, that would be as if what had happened was okay and so you shouldn't have a reaction to it.

- **With:** You allow the feeling to be in your vicinity, without overwhelming you, and without its being squashed or annihilated by you. You *Be* in relation to *It*. You let yourself stand still without struggling, with a certain amount of tolerance, and curiosity if you can muster it, to find out what it wants to say. You continue to *Be* while it surges, or rages, or lurches through. The feelings will ebb eventually. After a while, when they surface, the waves will be smaller.

- **Be, again:** With post-traumatic symptoms, in order to successfully reduce the power that the memories have, it is imperative to break the process into manageable chunks. The focus needs to be on keeping your sense of self stable. If you try to clear it all at once, you will feel overwhelmed and thereby re-traumatize yourself. Be with a piece of it, maybe even a single moment, and then *before* you are washed away by it, **breathe.** Check in with each part of your body and make sure that you are grounded and centered. Reestablish your connection with each part of your body, in your present reality, the substance and energy of your body, an adult, in your own room, door locked, arms fine—check, feet fully on the earth—check, stomach calming down—check, no one else here—check. Then rest. Once you have re-established your sense of yourself as okay in the moment, you can decide if you're ready to be with another chunk of the past. If not right now, move to the next phase.

If you can't seem to control the chunk sizes, and the memory takes over and hits you over the head, *insist on not being overwhelmed and find a good therapist who can coach you through it, act as referee, and contain the process.* This is not failure or hiding. It is making sure you succeed. The point is keep yourself from being overwhelmed, which, remember, is what led to trauma in the first place. The key is to allow yourself to relive just as much of the past as you can manage without disappearing or shutting down, and then you return to paying attention to your body, your breathing, and staying present with yourself. If you lose your sense of yourself, the pain will not be reduced. It needs to travel through *you*, not over your head or behind your back. Feeling your body in the present is key to restoring a kinesthetic, real sense of yourself, so that you can be clear that you are no longer in the traumatic moment.

As you do make your way through each chunk of the whole, you will be transforming the experience from a) trauma—i.e., overwhelming; more than you can deal with—to b) an experience that you *have* been able to deal with, that you have gone through. You will be teaching yourself that you *are* in charge, that you *are* able to limit the present task to the amount that you can handle. This message in itself erodes the trauma. It puts you back in the driver's seat of your own process. (As a matter of fact, any time that memories or feelings intrude on your being in the present is a time to pause, breathe, and ground yourself in your body and to the earth.) If you become vigilant in interrupting the physiological arousal of those memories, and the habits that may have grown out of them, you will build a sense of mastery where before you felt out-of-control.

When you Be With It, you may see other parts of the picture that you may have missed before. You can be clearer about what happened and then have the chance to counter any self-punishing decisions or disempowered perceptions you may be saddled with.

When Heidi was able to be with the pain that she had carried most of her life, she released the pressure that had led to and locked in her eating disorder. Gradually she saw that she could tolerate those feelings, and they no longer scared her into harming herself. At that point, she was able to stop her bulimia cold turkey. (In this, she was unusual. Bulimia is very difficult to stop.)

Then, Soothe Yourself

Honor yourself enough to take breaks and to be compassionate toward yourself. No matter whether the memory you're working with is run-of-the-mill, jumbo-sized, or gargantuan, the next step is to care for yourself and make sure that you have a sweet, gentle experience coming back to present-day reality. Your system needs to experience kindness from you, especially from you. This was key for Connie whose 'scabbing' maneuver had involved getting harsher and harsher with herself. She had been treating herself cruelly, more as the attacker did than as a caring friend would. After being all stirred up by painful emotions, your body may be on high alert. It may have to take some time to return to the present. Don't abuse yourself for having a brain stem! Many folks I've worked have been angry at themselves for having fearful reactions, as if they ought to be "all over that." If you really want to change the way your life feels, change the way you treat yourself. At first it will be hard, because softening to yourself will allow the emotions to flow. But this is what will release them.

🐾 Notice the parts of your body that do NOT feel riled up. Connect with them. Gradually expand that sense of being okay to other parts of your body. Feel your energy as warmth, or light, or warm water, gently and gradually seeping into the freaked out parts, until your sense of your body is whole and unified again.

🐾 Settle yourself wherever your body, and your reptilian brain, will feel safe, uninterrupted, and cozy. Give yourself what you need. Maybe that is walking around to remove any sense of being frozen. Moving is a great way to snap yourself out of a state. Breathe, ground, and center. Treat yourself lovingly, as you would a child who had just been through a storm of weeping. Try not to go for the ice cream right away, which is a masking device. Know that anyone needs time to integrate a piece of work like that. Wrap yourself in a blanket, pillow your head. Allow yourself time to rest. Scan through your body and gently reassure each part. Say to yourself, verbally or kinesthetically, nice toes, thank you, feet, mmm—heels, warm ankles, and so on. Use a warm, soft tone as you would with your pet or child.

🐾 Then say to yourself, "Good work, I did it. That's enough for now. If some more needs to come up later, I'll deal with it then. For now, I've succeeded! I'm so _____!" (Name a positive characteristic that helped you Be With the difficult emotion, such as persevering/curious/brave/dedicated).

🐾 "Now I'm home, at rest."

🐾 Feel the fullness, the quieting of your energy that comes with grounding and centering in the present after a big job.

🐾 Next, choose one kind thing you will do for yourself sometime today. It could be a bubble bath, or buying a new lip gloss, or stealing a few minutes to read an escape novel, browsing in an art store, or making time to meditate— anything that makes your heart sigh with pleasure. Be clear what it is and when you will do it. Then do! Don't break faith with yourself.

Inculcating pleasure into your life is an important job. I want you to take it seriously! Okay, not so much tension. What would happen if you practiced being nice to yourself and enjoying yourself and your own company, every day? Just a thought.

Of course, it is much easier for me to write a few paragraphs about it than to go through the process. But it really is much easier and more effective to BWITSY than to flail, try to shut it off, be lost, wallow, or spin around, caught in the maelstrom. I've done both, and I know.

For Gwyneth, her first breakthrough occurred when she considered the notion of self-dates. I asked her to schedule a block of time—at least four hours—each week to spend with herself. The goal was to get to know herself, as she'd get to know a new date, and also to enjoy unstructured time. That idea was entirely foreign to her.

It took a few weeks to take the plunge, but then Gwyneth got into it. She'd set aside an afternoon on the weekend, go out her front door with no plans, and follow her nose. She'd wander into a park, have iced tea sitting at an outdoor café, wander into an poster store, then walk by a lake. Sometimes, she'd simply turn off the phone and sit on the couch with tea and a book. It was an entirely new concept to relax rather than constantly committing herself to household projects or to the wishes of other people.

When I saw her next, she was excited by how enriching and fun it was being in her own company. She was learning to be with herself, to settle in and become aware of the present moment and her place in it. By taking time just to be, she was learning to enjoy life. She saw that soothing herself had much larger impact than just calming down after being upset. It increased her commitment to deal with old pain, as she found that she could comfort and renew herself. She wanted to stand up for herself better around others and craft her career on her own terms.

If your history was particularly hairy and this process seems too good to be true, by all means engage a competent therapist. That's what they are for. My advice is to make sure you find one that knows how to take you *through* the pain *and then to continue on into your strengths and into new ways to address the future.*²

To reiterate; the purpose of feelings is to provide us with information regarding our experiences. Our sensory and emotional centers have the job of gathering data and reactions about the outside world, about our inner experience, and how the two come together. Our thought processes are designed to assess that information and weigh it against what we already know. We know that something is bad for us because we have uncomfortable feelings. Say we find that we're angry. We then use our thought processes to look to see what caused the anger to arise and then to assess the situation to see if it is a present threat or reminds us of something in the past. We think about possible courses of action, and we choose (since we haven't gone screaming off on automatic pilot) what response seems likely to bring us the outcome best suited to us.

Sometimes there is a big rock in the river of emotions. We cannot always see when a sudden wave is going to be thrown up in our face. It is important to understand that rocks and unforeseen waves do not mean that we are bad or that things are out of control. Having a painful feeling does not mean that there is something wrong with us or with our process. It just means that more information is incoming, or that something buried is now working its way to the surface, probably due to our having done such good work at releasing what was on top of it. All we need to do, once again, is to Be With It while this new wave surges and then goes on by. Eventually the water level *will* subside.

Pain of any variety indicates that we need to bring our attention to something. Something magical happens when we take the point of view that there is wisdom in listening to what feelings have to say. When we ground, center, and Be With them, we become able to find the breathing room to take a more interested and benevolent stance toward even the most painful memories. We can begin to take a curious interest in them and treat them as if they are on a par with an interesting dream that we want to understand. Or, perhaps it's similar to going to the dentist—we don't like to, but we go, because getting that tooth fixed is better than avoiding it and then having it rot. We then can ask the presence of the feeling some questions:

"What do you want me to see that I haven't?"

"What do you want me to hear about this?"

"Is there another way to look at what you are showing me?" even,

"What is your name?" or

"What do you want me to know about myself?" or

"What do you want me to know about another person or event?"

If we can take this curious attitude, the past can lead us to epiphanies of insight. We may find that we learn much more about the situation. We may then be able to soften toward our own nature as we integrate deeper learning into the narrative of our lives, where it can develop into wisdom.

In the following chapters, we will build on the base we've established with breathing, grounding, centering, and being with our feelings, and develop the skills that will make it possible to move into a more positive and satisfying experience of life. First, let's apply them to the stubborn issues of physical pain and anxiety.

Endnotes

1 The Buddha's teachings state that human experience is defined by four noble truths. The first noble truth states that suffering and discontent are universal, meaning that while it is not possible to avoid pain in one's life, everyone adds suffering to that pain. Suffering comes from our attitudes and interpretations. The suffering can be eliminated, even if the pain cannot. Getting to the root of our suffering and seeing it clearly is the beginning of freedom.

2 Psychologists doing research on the efficacy of different therapy modalities were surprised to find that those that had the best success rates (defined as increased happiness, optimism, and successful future behavior) used processes that didn't stop at helping people face their old pain and work through it until it eased up.

When clients also worked on changing their outlook, were guided to plan their lives and take positive steps, and looked at how to use new tools to change their experience in many areas of life, they got over old depression and anxiety, were healthier physically then control groups, and were happier. (*Peterson, Seligman*)

Part III

Don't stop there!
Further Applications

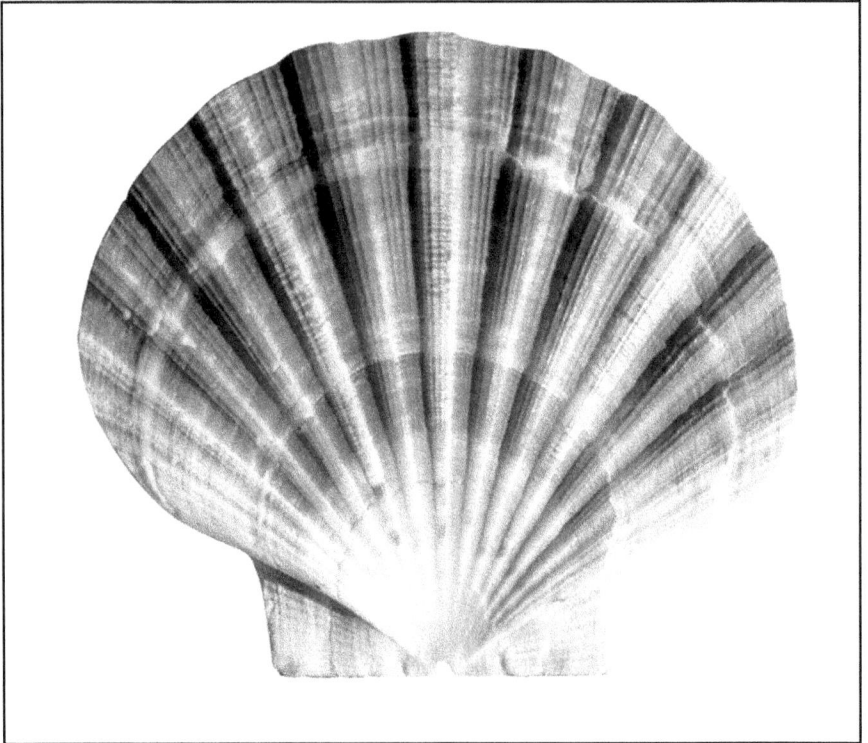

What people call "pain" is actually a combination of pain and resistance.

—Shinzen Young

Release Physical Pain   8

JANE CARRIED A lot of tension in her shoulders, so when under stress, she'd find herself rubbing them, trying to make the soreness go away.

GLADYS'S GALL-BLADDER SURGERY was successful, but every two months since, she experienced shooting pains in her side that lasted for several hours.

SAM HAD SEVERAL old ski injuries that acted up from time to time. Marisol's jaw hurt from clenching her teeth, something she'd done since childhood.

Pain was one of the original issues that Lawrence came in to deal with. I asked him if he saw a connection between it and his intensity. The question surprised him. It was time to take the next step, from beginning to be aware of his body and the world around him, to finding out where his patterns came from and what held them in place. Lawrence slouched in an effort to blend in with the general population. Like many tall people, he was uncomfortable standing out—literally. He was also quite lanky. Added to that, to succeed in his career thus far, he'd developed a tense, hunched way of attacking work that went against his warm and effusive nature and affected him physically and mentally. It was as if he had tried to force himself to be someone else in order to meet the needs of the corporate culture of his old job. When he did exercise, he gravitated to hiking and yoga, which were excellent for his nature but not his physicality. His upper body didn't get enough workout to provide adequate strength with which to support his spine and be toned. Old injuries in his knee and elbow also caused him trouble.

Physical pain

We all have some. I've had my share. I've been injured several times, starting at two, so I've had chronic neck and back pain, as well as knee and ankle injuries from sports. Pain relief is a multi-billion-dollar business. It is a difficult area for doctors to address as there often are no direct correlations between the state of the body and the experience of pain. People are different in what triggers pain for them, what their threshold is, and how they react to it. Often, what works for one person will not help someone else. Western science does not fully understand what relieves pain, why some occur, and what makes certain conditions excruciating for some people and tolerable for others.

It is important to talk here about pain abatement when working on releasing trauma, because many of us have injuries from abuse or physical effects from emotional overwhelm. The ways we try to manage or minimize those emotions often lead to physical pain, and eventually that affects the immune system.

As with emotional hurt, the things we do to hold pain away are the very things that hold us in the pain and hold the pain in us. The most common is unconsciously to try to cut out the parts of our bodies that carry the effects of old events. By doing so we send disapproving or even hate-filled messages to our own bodies.

In the last few decades, more practitioners in many disciplines have been looking at the mind-body connection when it comes to pain. Researchers are investigating the effects of patients' attitudes and emotional states on the lessening of pain. Some healers teach patients concentration and positive visualization exercises, which often help manage discomfort more effectively than does medication. Some research is looking into the effects of patients' attitudes and meditative practices on enhanced and accelerated healing.

Whether they know it or not, these practitioners are often using forms of Energy Medicine. Let's discuss why they work and then learn a very effective technique for reducing pain, both the kinds that you've had for a long time and the more circumstantial. The technique that I'll show you helps alleviate pain resulting from simple injury, disease, surgery, or stress.

Pain is your body alerting you to something you need to hear

There are beneficial reasons why we hurt—not enjoyable, just valuable and necessary. The first purpose is to get our attention when some injury or illness occurs. Pain also triggers bodily systems to limit movement and initiate healing.

But what about the nagging kind? What about the sore shoulders, the cranky neck, the aching lower back, the gimpy knee? These also are trying to get our attention. They may be the result of a chronic condition or the outcome of habits of hunching, or clenching. Okay, but why do we do those things? Are we just lazy and saggy? Or do we hunch as a hold-over from feeling criticized a lot, or because we feel overburdened? Do we slouch because we were teased or nagged? Does our back hurt because we are pulling back from anticipated irritation, rejection, or hostility?

In Chinese medical theory, pain is caused by the occurrence of stagnation of any kind, whether of fluids, from the buildup of mass, of stagnant energy, or of other pathogens. If blood or other fluids are not moving the way they should, it hurts. If there is a bottleneck somewhere, it hurts. If some muscles are too tight or overworked, it hurts.

When we hide painful memories, wherever we store them (and these are real locations in our bodies: they don't disappear when we push them out of our minds), we obstruct the flow of energy, which causes stagnation. When we tighten in one area, some other place does not get enough energy, so it becomes sluggish, or vacuous—empty of energy, or under-toned. So, other discomfort is generated by the dissonance between tightness and deficiency of neighboring or opposing areas. If we either clench or under-inhabit long enough, it starts affecting the function of joints, muscles, and organs.

Over time, we develop tunnel vision about the causes. But we can't change something that we can't see. Even so, it is a radical idea to turn toward the messenger, rather than trying to kill it off, and listen to and investigate the message.

The importance of looking clearly at your own story

Maybe you have had the experience of getting a massage and having some memory pop into your head when a massage therapist really works on a certain muscle. Your body stores memories in the places that were affected. In order to release old, chronic pain, it is necessary to be able to tolerate your own memories. You can gain a deeper understanding of your own story through what your symptoms can tell you. Sometimes the insights are surprising. If you listen, your body can show you aspects of the hurt that may be the key to resolving the issue that the pain is trying to highlight in the first place.

Something magical happens if you can change the way you interact with pain. If you take the point of view that pain is your body's and your being's way of trying to get your attention, your experience of the discomfort can shift. It is the simple but profound step of turning toward it with curiosity, rather than gritting our teeth against it. Eventually this allows it to reduce. You can then see how shoulder aches have built up over time, and about the irritability in your GI tract. You can expand your view by not grabbing onto or wrestling with it as the pain releases. Stopping the resistance to it reduces the amount of stagnation, because you are not building up more tension.

As we remove the fight against pain, insights often arise. We can see where we have turned against ourselves, interpreted our normal reactions as a reason to hate ourselves. We can map our story more fully. We may simply come face-to-face with the pain and emotions associated with it, as we stop our attempts to manage it. Or we may get a chance to view old events in a larger perspective.

An example of this shift in focus comes from my own story. Years ago, when I received bodywork regularly (those were the days!), I found that my Aston Patterner (a type of bodywork) noticed a phenomenon that I also had become aware of when working energetically with clients. We found that many women who have been sexually abused have pain on the posterior crest of their pelvic bone, about half-way between their spine and their hip. For me it flared when I felt assaulted by events in the present. If I fell into self-criticism, that specific spot would hurt terribly. Shame increases pain, because blaming yourself turns you against yourself (remember from Chapter Two) and makes you freeze. The pain showed me how much I had clenched into my back, and how little I inhabited my front. As I looked more deeply, I found that the brittle holding was an effort to stop feeling pummeled by events. The hidden benefit to being too sensitive to tolerate most pain relievers (and being stubborn—uh, persevering) was that I then discovered the pain protocol in this chapter. It softened my grip and allowed the pain to ease and often to disappear.

In working with your own pain you may not need to relive any specific memory. Releasing hurts requires a willingness to allow them to come up if they need to, as well as becoming aware of any coping mechanisms that have built up on top of the memories. Remember that you have survived this long with those same memories. Most often there is not some big secret that is completely unexpected. Mostly those old beliefs saying that you can't handle it (remember the ribbon on the box?) are what keep you from releasing the pain. It is the stance of being willing and not fighting against the pain that is important. The willingness is often enough.

How to clear physical pain energetically

Besides softening your grip, this energetic pain reduction method allows you to re-inhabit the blocked-off parts of your body. As you move your energy into the place that hurts, you'll open more room in your body and allow energy, blood, and fluids to move more easily. To do this, you must be centered. Let's look at the actual how-to's of relieving pain.

Note: Have someone read this section to you. Or, listen to the CD on Releasing Pain as you practice.

Breathe: As always, start with paying attention to your breathing. For this protocol, begin by taking air into your entire body with big, open-mouthed breathing. Make sighing noises when exhaling, and draw out sighs on several exhales—big "hunnnnnhs." While inhaling, spread your arms wide. Then while exhaling, wrap your arms across your chest and around to your back. Bow your back and collapse your chest to push out as much stale air as possible. Repeat several times. Feel your torso loosen up any tension as you breathe. Notice your ribs moving, even your lower back, your sides. You may feel the movement that your breath causes all the way into your sitz bones. This exercise should feel really good.

Ground: Let that feeling extend down through your legs to your feet, so you become aware of them from the inside. Notice if you feel some tingling in your feet. If it helps, stand up and bend your knees, or clench different muscles, to move more attention into your legs. Then relax the muscles and notice the solidity and energy of your legs, just as they are right now. Don't try to change how they feel, at this point. As you move down through your thighs, knees, calves, ankles, and get to your feet, say hello to the ground. Feel connected to it, but don't wander down into earth too far, as you would if practicing internal grounding. Just make sure you're really connected throughout your own body. The way to know that you are in all of your body is that your feet do not feel as if they are "way down there," but rather you are "here" in them, as well as "here" in your elbows, or the back of your neck - everywhere. When you feel fully in your legs and feet, and solidly grounded to the earth, include your upper body.

Turn the lights on throughout your pelvic bowl, abdomen, torso. Feel your shoulders, arms, and hands. Then include your upper back, upper chest, neck, and head just as parts of your body. Take another deep breath when you get to your neck and head. Feel yourself occupying all of your body. Let your head float like the flower on a stem nodding in the breeze. Your spine is the stem that everything else rests on, with your hips and legs providing the foundation and connection, so that your spine can rise lightly. (Here's why good posture is so important.

If you are sitting or standing straight, your muscles do not have to work hard to hold up the weight of your bones. If your bones are stacked, the energy can flow smoothly up and down, and you can feel the sensation of your bones resting and floating.)

Center: Now, ask yourself to center. Sense your awareness settling in the place where you simply be. Feel the adjustment that happens when you do so. Do you feel a gathering together? Do you open up and establish a bigger place for yourself? Do you settle down? Straighten to be more upright?

Release Pain: Now, notice where you feel some pain. If you don't have any, be thankful! You can pick a place that feels tight, if you want to practice this protocol.

Breath is energy, as are warmth and light. Staying grounded and centered, allow yourself to breathe around the place that hurts. Imagine the energy moving around the painful place until it is surrounded by the soft movement of the breath, the warmth of it, like warm water. If you prefer, see your energy as light moving around the area. As you be near it, sense the light and warmth seeping into it. Feel your awareness gently move into the area rather than holding it separate from the rest of yourself, as if sliding into a warm bath. Gradually intend that the warm water feeling spread into the pain place. Include that place by thinking, "This is my body, part of my being. I'm going to be in here, as well as in the rest of me. I'm not going to cut off a part of myself." Simply be there, breathing, opening space, allowing light in and energy in. Keep breathing into that place, so that your breath goes from tight there to taking up more room. It will naturally create more actual movement in your body.

Feel it gradually be re-owned and become part of your body. Settle into that place that used to be separate, as well as in the area around it. Let the boundaries of the pain dissolve, so that there is no distinction between it and the area around it, and the area is whole. Include your feet. Remind yourself to stay grounded, to remain attentive in all of your body. You don't want to become ungrounded and have your attention constricted back to tunnel-vision, or you may reestablish the pain. (Remember that with pain, the usual fear is that we will be swallowed up by it, that we will be lost in it and it will never end. When we fight pain and fear, we solidify those fears. We lose ourselves in them by becoming ungrounded, leaving us unaware of the ways in which we are fine, and of our connection to the world around us.)

Marisol said, "There's something about the way you talk about including pain. When other practitioners teach pain relief, either emotional or physical, and say breathe, relax, and let go, it's always felt like they're asking you to make an effort to push it away, as if letting go of the pain means it should leave. When you say to breathe into it and include it in yourself, I find that I stop fighting it. It gives you an accepting message, takes you out of conflict with yourself."

Samir said, "I'm used to isolating and blocking off pains, rather than including them. When you initially said the words, I found myself bucking your suggestions. Then I stopped fighting it and was able to do it."

It is natural to pull away from pain. It is counter-intuitive to go into it. But try it, and see what happens. Your mindfulness will awaken the painful spot from its endless feedback loop of neural firing and allow it the chance to change the chemical impulses in the synapses, letting those nerve axons close. If the pain or tightness melts, focus on feeling your body as a whole, without that area cordoned off, so that your energy flows smoothly throughout your entire body. Then, staying grounded and centered, notice your surroundings. Spend a minute feeling yourself as you are now, within yourself and with a place in the world around you. Breathe. Rest. Relax.

As Lawrence learned to use his breath to become more in tune with his body, we worked on his alignment. He quickly became aware that he sagged into his lower back, making it arch at the same time as he slumped his shoulders. This posture denied his chest and shoulders the support they needed and increased his depression. As he became more aware, he could hear each body part broadcasting the pain it held. Grounding and breathing, he moved his energy gently into old injuries and hung out, or rather hung in, with himself there. He learned not to pull away from the soreness but to move into it gently and stay with it. To his relief, the pain eased, and each part gradually was included in that sense of watery fullness that he identified as his grounded energy. He felt more alive and present. He straightened his pelvis and breathed more into his kidney area, filling in his back to join with and support the front of his torso. Then we worked on his moving awareness into the area between his shoulder blades and connecting that to the center of his chest, as well as to the front of his shoulders. His head came up, taking the strain off his neck and upper back.

The longer I practice Energy Medicine and Energy Dynamics, the more it looks as though suffering comes from having cut ourselves off from our own energy through resistance to feelings. Tension so often is exacerbated as a result of holding ourselves up away from the ground. Because we disconnect our upper half from the lower, we carry ourselves as if our upper body is unsupported and dangling in space. It makes our energy systems feel as if they have no foundation, that there is nothing they can count on.

If you can feel your hips, legs and feet as the base of a pyramid, and your pelvis as a nest, you can build each layer on the support of what is below. You will lose much upper body tension if you let your torso settle onto what's below and rest. The minute you can get your shoulders or heart to rest on the huge foundation of energy and structure that supports it, the minute you can feel it nested, tension disappears. The upper functions related to the chakras—caring, reaching out, communicating, etc, gain the sensation of being supported. But, since it is automatic to react by stiffening the diaphragm, many people don't realize that they are walking around as if they are balloons with no string attaching them to solid ground.

Practice: So, try visualizing your legs and feet being the base of a pyramid, on which rests your pelvic area, on which rests your abdomen, on which rests your rib cage, in which is nested your heart and lungs, then your shoulders, air passages, and mind settle on that. See what happens and how it feels.

What happened with Jane, Gladys, and Marisol? When they learned this technique, Marisol noted that her jaw pain went away completely within five minutes.

Jane's shoulders loosened as the tightness felt as if it was dissolving. "The pain exercise was so cool! I'm really enjoying noticing where energy is and where I feel it, and centering, especially when in sessions with other people. I am doing a lot of breathing in my own work with clients."

Gladys was able to relax while we were practicing, but since her pain came from adhesions caused by surgery, it was necessary to do a healing session on her to reconnect still-severed meridians (the pathways noted in Chinese Medicine are cut by surgery when the physical body is) and then balance and redirect the energy. After that session, she never had the adhesion pains again.

Sam got better at interrupting the pain cycle that his old injuries triggered, leading him to feel comfortable much more quickly. In the process of practicing, he became more a fan of relaxing than he had been before. He noticed when he tended to drive himself too hard and started interrupting that as well. Over time, he found that his old injuries didn't flare as much as they used to.

Lawrence felt his body as a whole for the first time as his torso became more upright, and his energy and breath could flow more freely throughout. One day he called me, excited that he'd been able to release pain in his back on his own for the first time. He felt he'd taken charge of his body, and his own comfort was under his control. He felt he could also be more in charge of his presence in the world. His natural enthusiasm blossomed again and he figured he was able to stop working with me and focus on his new job.

Some extra notes on pain and healing

When you ask yourself to center, you may become aware of work crews springing into action within you. When you center consciously, your energy has the chance to release physical, emotional, energetic issues, as well as pain. When you bring your attention inside and remove resistance, more cleaning out and construction can happen.

You may become aware that some issues are being worked through without your struggling with them.

The indication that this is occurring is that sensations may claim your attention out of the blue. They might be passing tensions, or they might be old topics taking the opportunity to get be worked out. Aligning your energy with your attention enables the energy to work through stuck places where previously it hadn't been able to travel smoothly. See if you can allow these events to happen. If you notice an area, be with it. Give it light and intend that the work will happen. See the light or warmth spread a bit within you, so it isn't clamped down on. You can follow it around. Watch as the energy moves. Notice any gaps, thickness, congestion, lack of energy that may be trying to even out. If you find energy really wanting to be in an area, it will draw your attention there to be with it. Imagine your attention as a light, and give it the permission and intention to do what it needs. Intend the light to spread, so that your energy gets the idea to move more smoothly and not be stuck.

There are more advanced techniques for addressing more complex pain issues, yet those outlined here will give you a good start and will help you release or reduce many types of discomfort. The most valuable aspect of pain management with Energy Dynamics is that, with practice, you will develop the ability to reduce the suffering that goes along with it.

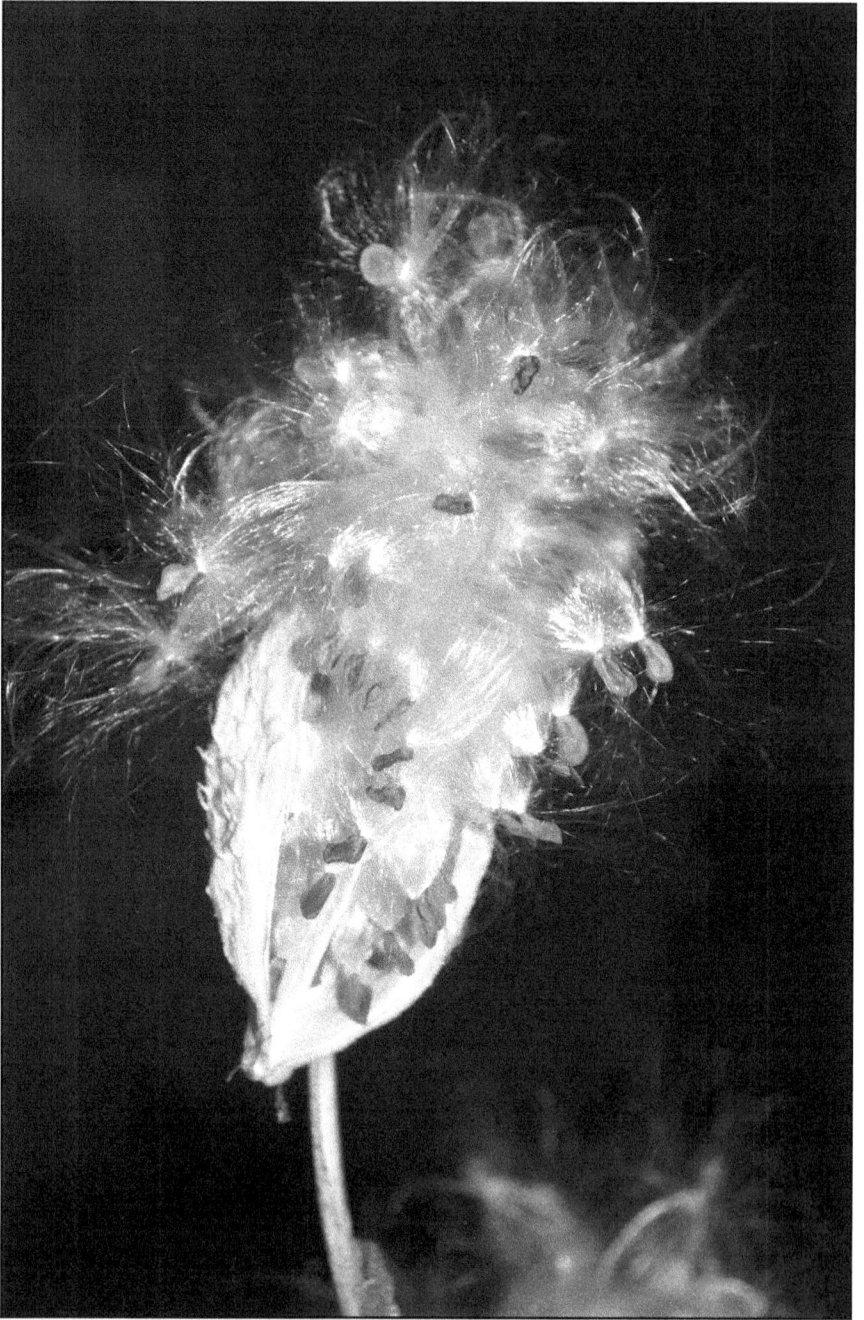

This we can all bear witness to, living as we do plagued by unremitting anxiety. It becomes more and more imperative that the life of the spirit be avowed as the only firm basis upon which to establish happiness and peace.

—The 14th Dalai Lama

Release Anxiety 9

SANDY WAS AN anxious child. The second of three, she idolized her older brother, alert to his every whim and change of expression. But she was not protected from him. He hit her, blamed her for everything, and treated her like his servant. Their mother had no idea what to do. As Sandy grew, she seemed uncertain of her place in the world and couldn't focus on her own interests. She developed nighttime incontinence, dissolved into tears at the least sign of stress, and was terribly anxious at doctor visits or school interviews. She got to the point of refusing to comply with medical practitioners at all, hunching into a ball and sobbing until taken out of the office.

Sylvie called in to one of my teleclasses feeling quite worried. Her husband was unhappy with their move to a new town, and they were fighting a lot. Sylvie did not feel that he was taking on enough of the parenting responsibilities with their two-year-old twin boys. He was frustrated with her medical problems, stemming from the birth, which limited her ability to work. She felt overwhelmed trying to juggle work, kids, and her health, and was worried that he would leave her.

Lawrence had stopped working with me when he took his new job, but later on I heard from him again. In his six-month review, his boss expressed concern about Lawrence's disorganization, his getting lost in details, and his sometimes missing deadlines. His office was a mess. Jobs that should have been completed months ago were under the pile somewhere. Lawrence said he was overwhelmed with the workload. He couldn't keep track of things, and he was flummoxed as to where to start. He felt unfocused and unmotivated, as if he had a short-term memory problem. He worried that his worrying made him appear less competent. He spent time on little things and didn't get to the big things. He went to meetings unprepared, even when he was to lead them. He wanted to learn to prioritize, to be more efficient, and to communicate more effectively.

So what had happened since I'd seen him last? The stress of his new job, and some pressures at home due to the proximity of his wife's family, had led to his reverting to his old ways of being scattered. Also, his new job was a lot less structured than was his old one. He was expected to see the big picture as well as manage the creative efforts of a group of people. As we talked, he realized that he felt anxious, and that he'd actually been anxious often in his life without recognizing what it was. He had often doubted his abilities and been hard on himself.

How had this worry and anxiety affected his life? Lawrence needed to become aware how his unresolved past issues kept taking over and dictating his reactions when the chips were down. The sense of self he'd developed through grounding and centering was real. But he hadn't completed the work of developing a solid foundation for his new, fuller sense of self. That is to say, there were still old issues that had to be dealt with before he could experience life on his own terms, based on new perceptions of himself and the world. Anxiety and some depression had been hiding under his habitual, controlled coping mechanisms.

In his previous job, he'd had to be "perfectionistic," his definition being that he had to keep track of lots of details. That had served him well when he could control everything he focused on, but it wasn't working so well now. As we got down to work again, it took several sessions for him to begin to talk about his childhood. He was the second youngest of eight children, with an alcoholic father and an overwhelmed mother. Lawrence was still close to one sister, but the rest of the family had gone their separate ways. As is often true in alcoholic households, their father's drinking made everything unpredictable and chaotic, so no one knew when a bomb was going to drop or what state mom or dad would be in. They felt they had no control over their lives. Lawrence managed details now as his mother had when he was little—trying to control little things, when actually both felt powerless in their situations.

There are lots of causes of anxiety—the state of the economy, government decisions, stress, and feeling overwhelmed by circumstances in our lives. There is also anxiety we carry as a result of buried emotions, which often leads to worry in the present moment as our reactions are locked in old patterns.

Free-floating anxiety

If we are anxious about an upcoming presentation, or because the kids are downtown on their own for the first time, at least we know what is worrying us! But many people are anxious for no reason that they can discern. If we find ourselves with muscle tension, a palpitating heart, short, tight, panting breaths, and we don't know why, then the sweating starts. This is known as free-floating anxiety, which can be really scary, because it seems to happen out of the blue.

Free-floating anxiety is only floating freely because we've cut the tether of awareness. When we disconnect from our feelings and from our bodies, we do not receive signals. It may be that we are so good at shutting down that we don't see the connection to our upcoming job interview, or that our new neighbor resembles the boy who assaulted us years ago. Often, though, free-floating anxiety is a sign that our buried time-capsule of unresolved emotions is starting to move due to some triggering event in the present. We may not even know what is prodding at it because, again, we have cut ourselves off.

Remember the ribbon-on-the-box from chapter seven? That was the particular anxiety that pokes up first and makes us believe that we are not big enough to tolerate the emotion that is trying to surface behind it. So we disconnect from our feelings, push them down, and around we go again.

Anxiety is a useful tool

Then there's the Red Flag from chapter two. As Gwyneth got better at identifying her feelings, she became aware that she had a red flag of anxiety when she first woke up in the morning. This happens to lots of people. As they first float out of sleep, feelings are near the surface, because the person's shields are not yet in place. Anxiety is often the first that they are aware of, as its job is to signal that there are feelings that need attention. Given all the emotions Gwyneth had shut away, it was no wonder that she started each day with a cold dose of worry.

Anxiety has an adaptive function in that it notifies us when we need to pay attention to something surfacing or about to happen. If we can see red flag as helpful and are willing to look at a situation or surfacing emotion, then anxiety won't throw us for a loop. Instead it is a useful tool. We pay attention, attend to something when we need to, and then we won't panic. We'll feel more in control of our lives and empowered to be in the moment and keep moving forward toward our goals.

The summer that I was sixteen, I went to Lake Champlain with a close friend to her family's summer place. One morning, before dawn, her younger brother and I went out in a dinghy to fish for bass. It was an idyllic morning. The as-yet un-risen sun stained pink and shell-orange the mist rising from the water. A nearby island was vague, and the distant shore was lost in the soft, watery air.

We rowed out until we could barely see the house, baited our hooks and dropped them overboard to dangle in the water as we relaxed. Now, I am not making any of this up: first Ricky felt a tug. Our somnolence evaporated as he excitedly pulled it up. Great hunk of seaweed. Or should I say lakeweed. Back to dozing. Then I felt a tug. Huge reeling-in effort with lashings of masculine advice. (He was the age of one of my brothers, so that was not easy to take.) A boot, I swear. Tossed it overboard, not so relaxed. Then Ricky pulled in a little (and I mean tiny) fish. Back it went. The mist started to melt away as the sun came up. We talked about getting hungry—should we give up and go back for breakfast?

Suddenly, I felt a tremendous lurch. This was it! The big one! Ricky couldn't contain himself. He almost capsized us clambering to my end of the boat as I fought the monster. "Play him in! Don't jerk the line!" Ricky bellowed. "Shhh!" I said. "You'll scare him off!"

Now, the thing about lake water is that it is often murky. We could not see down further than a foot. So, the first view was of thrashing movement just below the side of the boat. Eagerly I leaned over, reeling like mad, while Ricky prepared the net to bring it in. My nose was only about a foot away from it when it lurched into view: huge, needle-like teeth in a gaping eight-inch tall mouth on a white, UGLY head. All this in a blink, as it drove up and out of the water straight at my face. Ricky and I both screamed. I shook the line like mad. It broke, and the ugly, scary, three-foot eel sank out of sight, back to the bottom.

I have told this story many times, as it epitomizes an essential facet of our nature as human beings: when an emotion is buried, we can lapse into thinking that it does not exist, simply because it is out of sight. When it starts surfacing, first we are aware of movement, disruption without clear details. Then, if we are committed to Being With It and releasing it, it surfaces in all its hairy ugliness just as it arrives at the surface—the point at which it can be released. So often we react to its appearance by frantically breaking the line and making it sink back down into the pond ooze. Then it is out of sight again— what a relief!—unless we realize that it is still inside us, lurking until next time. If we can only stay grounded and centered and Be With It a little longer it will come into view, break surface, and then dissipate.

So, let's see what makes it possible to stay with it long enough to release both the anxiety and the original emotion or situation.

What works in responding to anxiety

Here are the steps
First, think of a type of situation, or a specific time that made you feel anxious. Recall your reaction. What are the characteristics of anxiety for you? Notice where in your body you feel it. At first you may believe that it is everywhere. As your attention moves inward and you look with curiosity, notice that, most likely, you feel it in some part of you torso. It is helpful to give yourself the chance to see that it is not as widespread as you thought.

Next, identify the shape it has. If it is not in all of your torso, is it a round area, a crescent from your throat to your lower back? Edward felt it as a diamond encompassing his chest to navel. For Donna, it seemed like a circle that was constricting around the agitation within it. The more detail you can clarify, the more it will alter, because you are really paying attention to it.

Now, notice what the actual sensations are. Lawrence perceived it not as clear or solid but as a spongy area. Mine feels like a mini-sandstorm in my chest with tightness at the base of my throat, and my lower torso disappearing. Sylvie felt it as a fist squeezing through her heart. She said, "There's a band of tension dividing my body in half. The upper part feels active, but the lower half feels very small and far away. My feet seem teeny! There's not much connection to the ground." Sylvie had noticed that her usual reaction to anxiety led to her being ungrounded. And in that fact lies the solution with which to counter anxiety and panic.

Breathe and ground: Now, set aside the anxiety. Turn to connecting with your breath. Allow some time for this, breathing and sighing through your mouth at first, to help you release tension. Once you have belly breathing going, sense your awareness moving further through your body. Take deep breaths, exhale through your nose, and move your attention down through hips seat, thighs, knees, calves, ankles, feet, so you enliven yourself, moving in to live in yourself. Let your energy connect to the earth. Relax your feet. Feel them spread. Press different parts of them onto the ground— notice your toes, your metatarsal arches, the outside ridge, the front of your heels. Press your toes flat to the floor, so that the base of them is wide and flat, more so than the tips of them.

When you feel grounded, include the upper half of your body. Let your awareness enliven your back, sides, front, all through your torso; your shoulders, arms, and hands; then into your upper back, your upper chest, your neck and head, to the back of your ears, the bridge of your nose, the top of your skull.

Are you still aware of the bottom half of your body? Make sure you have depth, and the back part of yourself, fuller, filled in. Make sure you feel full in your pelvic bowl, and expand that feeling into abdomen.

Special Note: Sometimes people have a hard time connecting to their bottom half, to their feet and to earth, when they are anxious or otherwise stirred up. If, after you have given it that old college try, don't fight to get there. Don't set up that kind of conflict. Be wily as an aikido master and go around the problem. Sidle your attention out and around to the ground, and then build your connection from the bottom up. Have the energy of the earth fill, as if it is warm, sunny liquid, the bottom of your feet, then up through and into your ankles, up your legs...you get the idea. Build your base, and move more awareness into areas that may have been cut off for quite a while.

Center: Now, give yourself the direction to settle in your center. Make sure your center includes the back of the space in which you sense it. Get a more substantial sense of the size and depth of your backbone. Give it country to live in.

Re-introduce the feeling: Staying grounded and centered, re-include the feeling of anxiety. When becoming aware of it while you are grounded and centered, what happens to it? Does it alter? Does your perception of the precipitating event change? Keeping your feet and your connection with the earth, what has happened to the texture and shape of the anxious place? Many times, simply by bringing attention and energy into the area, the holding of the anxiety will soften and ease.

If it is still present as a form distinct from the rest of your body, breathe light and warmth around it. Gradually allow the energy and breath to move into the shape, into the sensation. Intend that the sensation release and your body become free and unified in that area. Just notice what happens when you intend for it to be altered by your attention and energy. Let it change in the way it needs to. Do not limit it by holding some preconceived notion as to the way it ought to disappear. What do you notice?

Special Note: Sometimes, when you pay attention to pain or anxiety, it tends to seem to intensify at first. Actually, you are becoming more aware of it. If you continue to stay with the experience of your body, the anxiety will lessen. Sylvie's anxiety cleared quite easily. "Instead of a circle, there's flow," she said. But Edward felt that his anxiety held on as a hard diamond shape, until, when he surrounded it with his breath, it became a smooth column rather than having sharp points and edges, and then it became smaller.

Lawrence was having trouble with his anxiety. He felt the sensation in his chest give way and move to his throat. "Now it is like trying to remove a glob in water. I'm chasing it around to break it up." He had gotten caught by being too focused on the glob chase and losing the rest of him, so he became ungrounded, wondering why the globby feeling was not going away. I asked him to back off and simply be with sensations in that area. He then noticed that warmth began spreading through him. Looking at what was occurring in his energy, I suggested that he connect his head (which was strategizing and insisting on being busy) with the base of his spine and sitz-bones, so that his head could feel supported by his base, and his eyes and mind wouldn't be way up there by themselves. Breathing into his seat, his eyes then could feel as though they had a foundation to support them. With that, the glob of anxiety softened, and the pressure went away.

Remember the situation that triggered the anxiety in first place. How does it appear to you now? Imagine being in that situation now while awake in your body, and with the area in which you felt the anxiety-shape no longer separated from the rest of you, but rather having a more unified and flowing sense of your energy.

Imagine going through that event while in this state. Do you feel freer, with your energy flowing more smoothly? Do you have a bigger sense of connection with yourself and with your surroundings? Sense whatever it feels like now. It is fine if your experience is different from what I am describing. Just notice what it is, and be with it.

At this stage in the work with Lawrence, we combined coaching with energy work. He learned to organize, prioritize, and delegate while we also worked on the source of the underlying anxiety. So, on the one hand we were talking about how to distinguish between tasks that were important in the big picture and those that yelled loudest but were not vital, and on the other hand we looked at the ways in which the new responsibilities, new boss and colleagues, and lack of familiar supports, triggered the sense that he couldn't count on anything and the fear and hurt that had been hallmarks of his early years.

As Lawrence looked at the historical fear and chaos that fueled his present anxiety, he noticed when he stopped breathing and became ungrounded. That early fear was the signal for disconnecting from himself whenever it was triggered. The more he noticed it, the sooner he reestablished his breathing and grounding. As he practiced gently insisting that he be connected with his body and energy, it was easier to work through the anxiety and the past memories. Gradually his breathing deepened. He learned to recognize the purpose of the anxiety—to notify him that a situation was activating past memories and beliefs—and he tried giving his system some attention and respect in the moment, rather than becoming frazzled. A small amount of time spent on the real issue greatly reduced the amount of time wrapped up in being overwhelmed. He was able to be kinder to himself. He found that his depression (which largely had been the result of feeling out-of-control and helpless) was alleviated as well. He also noticed that his lack of exercise was not self-supportive, and he again scheduled hikes and yoga classes into his week. The yoga also helped him get in touch with himself and balance the physical workout aspect with the relaxation and breathing exercises. His body hurt less due to his exercising more. He still needed to get more upper body strength and to have some harder workouts, so he could develop stamina and work his big body as it needed.

At this point in the exercise, Lawrence said, "Whatever energy I need will be there. What a shift from the tension I felt before!" He applied what he'd learned to his job, focusing on grounding and centering at the beginning of his work day and before meetings. He found that he felt more confident and able to think on his feet. He paid more attention to his thought patterns, bringing himself back to a positive and clear place when he found himself saying pessimistic things. At his next review, his boss was thrilled with his more relaxed and confident demeanor, as well as with his improved management skills. "Lawrence is working on all cylinders—contributing more, getting more done."

Even with all these changes, Lawrence said that what mattered most to him was that he was treating himself with more understanding and compassion.

Gwyneth quite quickly was able to release the early morning pattern of anxiety using the centering and mindfulness practice first thing. Subsequently, she caught herself worrying mainly when up against decisions or changes in her life. She worried a lot about the future. She described herself as "risk-averse," a trait learned from her mother. Her mother was extremely controlling as a way of avoiding dealing with her own fears. Mom wouldn't let Gwyn ride a bike to a friend's house or play ball. Everything was "too hard, don't do that," including going to college or applying for a new job. So Gwyn said the same to herself. The idea of a new job or a new relationship scared her—what if it went wrong?

The problem was that Gwyneth was not really assessing the new situation. She was projecting her fears onto the future possibility as a way of deflecting attention from what had already happened in the past. As we saw with Connie, this is a natural, instinctual defense technique, but it must be made conscious, so that the actual, already-occurred hurt can be resolved. Otherwise, people become more and more limited by fear.

In order to make headway on that, Gwyneth needed to look at the hidden beliefs about herself that she carried. (We'll look at how she did this in chapter eleven.) She also needed to learn to be compassionate toward herself and remember where the panic, fear, and self-criticism came from. She needed to learn to put her arms around herself rather than attack herself.

As Gwyn learned to alleviate anxiety, she became more aware how much it had ruled her life. Feeling in control of it now felt empowering. She wanted to consider taking planned risks. We identified specific tasks with which to explore new directions for her career and broke them down into individual steps to take, so that she could stay grounded while moving in the direction that her heart and interests dictated. Gwyn also considered dating again.

What about panic?

Sandy was seven when I saw her, so I cleared the beliefs and the way her body held onto the trauma of being attacked by her brother. (I also had the chance to work on her brother.) Since she was so young, I gave Sandy's new belief to her mother, so she could reinforce it with her in quiet moments. Then I walked Sandy through the grounding exercise in an abbreviated version. She didn't have to comply. Her nervous system took note. A few weeks later, her father wrote to say, "I took Sandy to two medical appointments today, one at the dentist, and one at the eye doctor. She was very calm at both, a real change from previous appointments. She seems to have no fear of the medical world anymore. Thanks for your help in getting her past her anxieties."

This technique can be of help with panic attacks, which are closely linked with anxiety. From an energetic standpoint, panic attacks are caused by sufferers' being so disconnected from their own feelings, and so much trying to avoid painful and scary material, that their reactions come to them as through a thick fog, seemingly out of nowhere. It becomes panic when people react by becoming anxious or fearful of the anxiety or fear, thereby having put another layer of distance between their conscious mind and the precipitating memories, and when they react by losing themselves even further, so that they feel out-of-control. When their bodies are reminded by something that happens around them, they cannot even see the trigger, let alone the connection between it and their emotional or physiological reaction.

Working through this protocol will help you, or your clients if you work in a healing profession. If you have children, doing the exercise with them will help them feel that they have another option than fleeing from their experience. When people discover that it is possible to alter their reactions, their outlook often changes dramatically. If they are willing to stop and be with themselves, they find that their panic episodes subside. The empowerment that they feel when they see a solution that they can perform themselves often provides enough motivation to start turning to face the old, unresolved issues. Even children can experience gradually being more in charge of themselves rather than feeling and acting out-of-control and tantrum-y.

This energetic approach is a very kind way of working with difficult emotions within ourselves, our children, and our clients. We do not judge them as toxic, throwing them away or cutting them off. We honor our feelings and the messages they bring. We are helping them heal and transform into something useful and enriching. So we do not set up another level of conflict.

Other uses

Have you ever found yourself in a meeting or a conversation and notice that you are focusing on your own worries rather than on the topic? Besides the possibility of boredom, it often happens when we are riled up by the prospect of speaking or by something that has happened. Performance anxiety often occurs in these settings. In those situations, where are you located? In your head, cut off from your body, except for the thumpa-thump of your heart revving up to meet the challenge, whatever it perceives it to be. Being able to ground and center frees your focus so that you can access your creativity, your great ideas, or your strategic awareness.

When you need to show up as spontaneous and enthused, then getting out of your headlock is a definite plus. You can access more information from other perceptual centers in your system and stay focused, connected, and safely located. Otherwise you may push to closure, push your ideas, push the dynamic.

The beauty of using Energy Dynamics to change your state is that the method provides the magic: by focusing your attention inside your body, you move it from the thoughts racing around and around like rats in your head, or from stunned fixation on something, to practicing being settled and connected and thereby able to move, respond, and see more objectively and from a larger view.

Special Note: A sure way to know that you are more connected and settled in your energy system is to notice a change in your perceptions. Your vision will be clearer, your sense of your location in your skin and in space will feel firmer, your hearing and sense of touch may be more vibrant. Your senses become more vivid and more in sync. It feels like waking up to a clearer day.

Part IV

Safety, Freedom, and Empowerment

I do not at all understand the mystery of Grace, only that it meets us where we are but does not leave us where it found us.

—Anne Lamott

Using Intention to Move from Hurt to Joy (or, how do you make these techniques work anyway?) 10

WHEN I WAS learning psychic skills, I met with a group once a month for a day or a weekend. This was before there were any acupuncture schools in the United States, let alone any recognition for consciousness work. There was a surge of interest in alternative medicine, eastern religions, and spiritual topics but no structure for them and no acceptance by the culture at large. Back then, we didn't talk in terms of laws of intention or attraction. In the group, we explored expanding our perceptual abilities, experiencing different states, transmitting them to each other, and checking veracity and accuracy.

One early exercise to learn to affect energy and reality was to create parking spaces. For the month, our homework was to open up parking spaces before we'd arrive at a destination and would need one. Mind you, we were in the greater New York City area, where many folks don't own cars, if only so they won't have to find and pay for parking spaces!

I learned as much from hearing the different ways that people approached it as from the assignment itself. One friend was Sammi, a high-powered and assertive executive in international marketing who was very clear about who she was and comfortable wielding power.

Another group member was Bridget, mother of six children who had just gone through a very nasty divorce. She hated her job because it demanded that she be high-profile and persuasive. She was much more comfortable in roles in which she provided support and advice, and she could make amazing things happen from behind the scenes.

Then there I was. I was in New York dancing and trying to figure out a structure for using my clairvoyant and healing gifts. I was aware of all this energy and perception that was pressing to be used, but felt stuck. At at the same time, I was struggling with old abuse issues, so I tended to be harshly self-critical.

When we came back after the month, the leader asked us to describe what we actually did to create the parking places. Sammi said that at first she was sure she could assertively open a space by putting the force of her will into it to carve out space for her car. It didn't work. When she asked the Cosmos, 'If it is in my best interest and in the best interests of those around me, could I please have a parking place?'—she'd find one.

I looked at her in amusement and said, "That's so funny, because I thought I should do the polite thing—ask carefully, be respectful, but it never worked." I drove around for hours and never found one. It wasn't until I went into my center and toughened up and fiercely demanded it, saying, "I want it, I deserve it, and so show up NOW!"—that I'd find a space. I could even swear. All that mattered was that I be forceful and bingo, there it was. I was so confused by that, because I thought it wasn't spiritual enough, not the way one should interact with "higher powers."

Sammi was so assertive that her energy was limited in the ways it could interact, due to the force with which she was planted in herself. She could not take the energy of situations or other people into account until she softened and stepped back. Creating the parking space pushed her to be more aware of her relation to others.

At that time, I, on the other hand, walked through life not taking up enough room. So I had to move into the experience of deserving a parking place in order to open one for myself, rather than unconsciously emitting the intention that there was no room for me.

Bridget's method still makes me chuckle because it was such an illustration of the nature of her gifts and energy. She psychically sent out a note to whoever was near where she wanted to park. "I'd call to all those people who were hemming and hawing, standing on one foot and then the other, not able to say good-bye, and I'd help them make the decision to leave. I just reassured them that it was okay to go now, told them to get in their cars and stop messing about. Then I could have their parking place."

This story is a good illustration because intention is a function that requires that you align yourself, be willing to be precise about what you want, to ask for it clearly, and to open space for the thing to appear. You can learn a lot about yourself by working on your technique. There is a specific area to identify in your body in which your intention consolidates. To become adept at using it successfully, it is helpful to know the energetic steps needed to create through intention.

Intention is not just about creating parking spaces or Maseratis to put in them. It is also used in Energy Dynamics to move your awareness to new levels of complexity, to increase your perception, to develop new internal abilities and states. The reason why I am including a chapter on intention is that, in the skills you will learn in the following chapters, it will be necessary to focus yourself in order to create the specific energy discussed, or to become aware of some aspect of the skill, or to move into a new area. Energy practitioners and intuitives use their intention all the time to ask for information and see the "unseeable." All sorts of people use intention to achieve goals.

What is Intention?

Intention is the organizing force that focuses and directs energy to transform a desire into accomplishment. Intending is action-oriented. It aligns, clarifies, and hones your asking and your focus. It involves clarifying a goal, your desire to achieve it, and marshalling your energy to go for it. To be an intention, rather than a vague wish, there must be a decision, a commitment, and a clear statement to yourself and to the powers-that-be of what you want. Some people look at it as a prayer, as it also requires opening to the levels of Being that assist with creation. Intention combines clarity, concentration, determination and perseverance with an allowing and being open to receiving.

Every object and action is first created on the energetic level before manifesting as an occurrence of some kind. Whether you want a physical object, an event, or a new way of responding, bringing something into existence requires creating the energy of it first. The concept and the energy inherent in it make up the seed out of which that manifestation blossoms. Intention is the focusing agent that increases the likelihood that the energy of the idea will coalesce into a reality. Intention organizes your energy, feelings, and thoughts into a clear goal. Intention opens the opportunity for help and opportunities that you can't anticipate.

Intention is the insistence that something occur

The question is what something is going to show up? The intention has to be well-defined and detailed as well as being aligned with your goals and values, or else your subconscious worries, old beliefs, doubts and counter-arguments will undermine the message and you might be surprised at what arrives.

Intention is a combination of a) the functioning of conscious awareness, b) directing it as a laser-focused and aligned energy, moving in concert, and c) the effects of asking, creating a reality, inviting, and receiving.

This is what it means to be creative

As humans, we have the ability to move things from glimmers to ideas, to possibilities, to fleshed-out plans, to events. Everyone who has worked to create something knows that, at first, it seems unlikely that any new notion will ever become solid fact. Others often scoff and have "rational" reasons why it won't work. The reality in which you start to build is, by definition, one in which the item does not yet exist. This present reality is filled to the brim with what is already here. You must carve out room for the thing you are bringing into being. You must also create the energy of the thing itself and then bring it into the physical arena. It takes a lot of attention to get momentum going behind some ideas, to build up the force necessary to change inertia from static to active. (Others may have the energy already aligned for them, so that they manifest quite easily. An example is when I intend to receive information about a client's health. I already have the avenues established, so that once I'm ready to ask, I usually receive the information quickly. Another example is a situation in which you have been contemplating something for a long time, so that when you do ask, some of the energy is already in place.)

You may remember encountering scorn and nay-sayers. They don't have your vision. They are in their own reality, in which your idea is not yet real, and they didn't come up with your idea, so their reality does not even include having the notion of your vision. For this reason, their negative reactions do not prove that your idea is idiotic or unworkable. They only prove that there is no consensus on your vision yet. So, can you see why it is a really bad idea to let others' attitudes and negativity stop you from your dream?

Even though it sometimes takes a lot of work to talk people into your idea, it is your job to help them see your vision in their minds' eye. When they start to envisage it, they build up some energy around it themselves, which creates more energy in the world for it. They then may spark ideas and options that you hadn't thought of, which you can then incorporate in the process of creation, and the thing grows bigger. Eventually, honing your message, getting clearer in order to sell others on it, helps you to flesh out details so that your intention becomes sharper. The former skeptics gradually become engines driving your vision. The image becomes stronger than your doubt or than the nay-sayers' dismissiveness, and it moves through steps to begin construction and eventually takes on a life of its own and manifests in the world.

The same steps apply when an idea only involves you. The scorn and nay-saying simply comes from your own head, from the voices that you have introjected over the years, and from your old, self-defeating beliefs. As Marisol said: "'I don't deserve it'—that's big work. That will stop you from intending."

What gets in the way of successful intention?

What happens when we think that we are intending to attract something we want, and we either don't get it or we get something glaringly different? The Law of Attraction works on the premise that you must be crystal clear about what you want, for what comes to you is greatly determined by what you put out energetically deep down inside. So it is necessary to be congruent with yourself on as many levels as possible and not gloss over hidden pessimistic notions. If the intention is unclarified or is muddied by sneaky backchat—that critical voice casting aspersions in your ear—then what you receive may be the opposite of what you want.

However, if you don't get into medical school, or marry your high school sweetheart, or win a MacArthur genius award, it does not mean that you wanted your dream to fail. People often do receive what is aligned with their subconscious beliefs rather than what they think they intend. When less-than-desirable things arrive instead of that parking place, it may illustrate that you have some assumptions and self-criticisms that need to be brought into the light of day and questioned before you can become truly in sync with your spoken desire. What does arrive may give you valuable information about the nature of your self-doubt. Many a person who has survived awful things carries unconscious beliefs that counter their spoken intentions. Those beliefs are imbued with a truckload of power, and no half-clarified, un-researched intention has a chance against them.

When you identify self-doubts, either because you are paying attention or because an intention that backfired led you to investigate, see them as steps on the way to a clearer intention. Use them as an opportunity to view those beliefs more accurately, so that you can release them and replace them with ones that support a joy-filled life. Take the opportunity to become clearer about them now so that you can work through them and then improve your success rate when making intentions. (We will discuss how to clear self-defeating beliefs using your energy systems in chapter twelve.)

Sometimes, things just happen

While unclear intentions can illuminate subterranean beliefs, I don't agree with well-meaning but inexperienced people who blame sufferers by saying, "You must have wanted to marry a louse/lose your job/get in an accident, or it wouldn't have happened!" In every life, some bad things just happen. It is helpful if you adopt a silver-lining view of life: crises often occur that nudge you in a new direction, one in which you were meant to go. Losing that job may have been the propellant you needed, because you were holding back from risking going for the career that really excites you. It helps you move toward a more joyful life to take a larger view of events and invoke some faith that there may be a reason things happened that you can't see right now; optimism that life can improve; and hope that, as you practice the new skills that you are learning, you are aligning energies that will help you toward the experiences you want. You may be getting practice in supporting yourself even when the chips are down. It is all-important mental and spiritual training to stay with joy and not fall into doubt and despair, to move the locus of your well-being into your own control, into your center, rather than giving too much power to external events.

With all this, it is still true that in every life some rain falls. How we address tough times, how we choose to perceive them and how much we choose to support our own attitude is what matters and ultimately determines our well-being, and to a large extent, our happiness.

Why does intention work? And how?

The way I teach intention involves the Laws of Attention, Intention, and Attraction. Attention focuses your energy and makes the thing seem real in your imagination. Intention fires your energy in the form of your commitment to have it be so. Attraction involves receiving it, inviting it to you and inviting other energies to assist in bringing it into being.

1) Attention

The first step is conscious attention. Bringing awareness to anything brings energy to bear on it. Awareness is a manifestation of energy. This is mindfulness, this Being With the thing on which you focus while staying present in yourself. Because awareness is such a powerful potentiator of energy, when you are mindful, amazing things can happen. Pain lessens, tension eases. Performance is enhanced. When you learn to be conscious of the energy in your body, it actually augments. It flows better. Impediments dissolve. Weak places start to strengthen. As you stay present, you actually build and alter neurological structure to increase the involvement with your focus.

The same happens externally. If you pay attention when walking, you not only notice more birds and colors, your muscles strengthen more quickly. If you breathe automatically, at least you're still in the land of the living. When you attend to your breathing, you can change your hormone levels, your chemistry, and relieve tension and pain, as we have seen. Conscious attention to anything—healing, grounding, centering, intending—augments the energy that occurs. This is one reason why Being-With-It works so well.

As an illustration, if you've ever taken art history (or anatomy, astronomy, wine tasting, fencing, almost anything) during the first classes, you may remember thinking, "Sheesh! The professor is on a trip with herself! What on earth is she talking about with this painting? It's just some dame standing in front of a castle by some woods. What's the big deal? Why wreck it with all this unnecessary stuff—'painterly vs. linear,' dimension, layering, perspective, brush stroke, chiaroscuro? She's just showing off."

But, since you need the grade, you struggle through the homework, and along about week seven, it starts to see what she's been talking about. Those fancy terms start to mean something as you find yourself perceiving more levels of complexity, going more deeply into the technique than you were able to before. You've built more synapses in your visual cortex and links to your pre-frontal cortex as well as to some limbic sites.

Focusing your awareness also activates the energy that will bring your intention into being. You do get what you focus on, circumstances willing. When you really pay attention, you charge the object of your focus, you endeavor to catch as many details and levels of the reality of it as you can, as fully, deeply and broadly as you can.

2) Intention

A) Breathe, ground, and center
Okay, the how-to part: make sure your body is aligned physically. Have your shin bones perpendicular to the floor, your feet lined up

with your hips, so, not too close together or far apart. Take deep breaths into your stomach, so that you are using your diaphragm to breathe. Move your awareness with your breath down through your hips and thighs into your feet.

Include your torso, your tummy, pelvis, rib area, shoulders…you know the drill.

Feel your lower back and on up through your shoulder blades into your neck and head. Ground your awareness fully in your body, and connect with the earth, so that you are settled, connected, and present.

Center in your Being place. Take a moment to notice being grounded and centered at the same time.

B) Clarity

Clarify what you want to have happen. Be as specific and detailed as possible. Flesh out the image in your mind. This takes time and repetition. Becoming very clear and filling in as many details as possible helps to gather your attention and sense of purpose to make your energy laser-like in its focus and aim.

C) The Rightness Place

How do you know this is the right thing for you and congruent with your path in life? When I asked a class how they knew if their intentions were aligned with their goals, they answered that they could feel the rightness of it, a sense of knowing in their heart area, a sense of flow in which the body's energy felt balanced, with an expanded-ness. Sylvie said, "Tightness in the chest often signals that the choice is not the right one. Then it's a good idea to check in and find out what's going on."

Earlier I mentioned the research on pre-frontal cortex injuries which showed that people who had suffered brain damage that disconnected their reasoning process from their emotional centers could not, for the life of them, make any decision at all. It seems that you can only make a decision if you check in with your feelings.

There is a specific sensation that you experience in a particular place in your body which tells you that something is right for you. For me, if I feel tight or stuffy in my head, or a sinking feeling in my chest, that means the answer is no. The "yes" feeling is a full warmth, very small (it never shouts) just above my solar plexus. Do you know where that place is in your body? There really is an exact spot. Locate it in your body. Check that an intention is aligned with your values and goals by turning to that spot and seeing how it responds. The more you practice checking in, the more information you will receive from your felt-sense, because your feelings give you information about the world around you, as well as within you. You will know it's right, even if you don't want to do it or it will be hard. If it feels right, even if not comfortable or easy, continue.

D) How do you know you're doing it? Where's the engine?

Just as there is a place in which you use your felt-sense to become clear about what is right for you, there is specific location in which you power up your intention, somewhere between your waist and heart level. Mine is just below my rightness place. Men's tend to be lower. Identify that place in you, and how far into your body it is. The more you can become aware of it as a specific place, the more you can focus there to rev your engine and build up energy for your intention. You may also use the physical energy in your gut to augment the power and also to keep you grounded. You must stay connected with yourself when you do Energy Work. Working with intention in a grounded way increases your ability to use your mind without getting caught by it or lost in it.

E) Send your intention out

Many people feel that intentions are like prayers, because the crucial step is to ask for (or demand, in some cases!) the thing you want. Once you feel centered and connected to your energy, clear about your intention, and have powered up the engine, now send the message. State consciously, "I intend that this will happen successfully," or "This is now true," or "I want to perceive this now"—whichever fits your circumstance. Feel the laser-like focus. Sit into the place of intention and invest it with energy. Feel yourself powering it up, adding energy and "charge" to your clarity of focus to achieve this thing.

F) Direct your focus and fine-tune your engine

It's not enough to put it out there and then forget about it. For any intention that doesn't appear instantly (namely those that are an asking for awareness in the moment or some such) it is necessary to continue to power up your intention, both to keep focusing on it clearly and to insist or ask enough. If you are like my friend Sammi, then you'll find that you'll need to use energy, yet make sure that you are not pushing so hard that you close the door to possibility.

G) Empower others to help you

This is a magic step. When you ask clearly in such a way that you include the possibility of receiving assistance, you move out of any lingering uncertainty or pessimism about the likelihood of success and wash the entire intention with even more positive energy. Broadcast the message that you mean for this thing to come true, either by telling others or by including your Guides and Higher Power. Ask, demand, or invite. Put it out in the world so that others get a clear sense that you are open to assistance. Give your powers-that-be the clear go-ahead to intercede on your behalf or at least to support your intention. When you do so, imagine yourself giving them energy to help you. Empowering them to aid you in your efforts exponentially increases the energy you receive for the project. In doing so, you clarify the energy to move through you. Also, the intention needs to be created. It's highly likely that your powers-that-be will have a hand in that, along with aspects of yourself besides your conscious mind. Be open to ideas and opportunities that you might not have thought of.

H) Believe that you deserve it!

This is crucial! This is where those sneaky, negative thoughts come in. If you find yourself saying, "Oh, yeah, right, in my dreams!" or "Who'd ever give that to me?" or some other negative message, all this means is that you have work to do before mustering the intention. Take it as an opportunity to expose and resolve lurking beliefs and assumptions. Discovering self-defeating messages while attempting to intend a life-affirming change is actually a valuable part of the process. While hidden, they've been running your life. Doing so will free up a tremendous amount of creative energy and uncover happiness that has been waiting patiently under the weight of those misapprehensions. If they prove stubborn and difficult, it might be the time to find a really good therapist, so that you can work through those issues successfully.

Anyway, if you do have major issues to clean up (well, join the human condition, eh?) in what way does that make you undeserving? If you do believe that you deserve to receive what you want, then spend some time, repeatedly, giving credence to that notion. It opens up space and fertility in the creative realm to radiate positive, affirming, receptive energy around the idea being included in your life.

I) Visualize it as a *fait accompli*

One aspect of the Law of Intention is to have clarified your goal so much that it already is real for you, that you hold it as already existing, already done. When I was in my twenties and in graduate school, I observed this law in action. I had to hunt for jobs to support myself and my schooling. I'd search for weeks while getting low on food and worrying that I wouldn't make the rent. No luck. After a while I noticed that I'd been holding it as—"looking for a job." All that effort had been going into looking. Well, I'd done that task successfully, I realized. It just wasn't what I really wanted. I wanted to find and *have* a job, not look for one. When I switched my internal focus to "find a job," it took less than a week until I was again gainfully employed. It doesn't work this simply every time, but the example points out the value in paying attention to the details.

See your intention as if it already exists. Watch the words you use when you talk to yourself. They matter. Formulate it as a done deal. The more that you see it as real, the more you fill in the picture with details, the more energy you generate to move it from the realm of ideas to a reality.

Every day, or many times a day, stop and focus on what you want to create. Give it attention, so that you can fill in the details, build up the context, gather the energy.

It doesn't have to take ages to bring something into being, although concrete objects may take the longest. Intention can manifest less physical items in a second, if the way is clear. When I do Energy Work,

I use intention all the time to receive information about the person's difficulty and the direction in which it would be best to work. I receive this information quite quickly because I've practiced a lot.

When you use intention to become aware of and create new states of being, as we will be doing in the next chapters, you'll need to clarify for yourself and hold steady the place through which you receive information.

J) Keep focusing

Be willing to wait. Practice keeping your attention on the details, the reality of the intention. If the item is not something such as an answer to a question that you'd receive in a second or two, don't drop the ball. Turning away would be as if it was someone else's job to make your intention happen. If you want it, remember that you must gather the energy to create its arrival. Persist. If it is an intention that will take some time to manifest, keep creating the energy that will bring it into being. Keep your intention clear and active. Avoid sliding into pessimism or old thought patterns of not having it.

3) Attraction

A) Open the space into which your intention can appear

A major aspect of the Law of Attraction is the necessity of inviting. Become receptive. Open the space that will attract your intention. Open to possibility and to allowing. When I intend to receive information, I wait (even if it is only for a split second). I open my arms to it, energetically. Since it is not I who creates the actuality of the thing, even if I am forceful in my asking, I don't want to tighten up and limit room for it to arrive. (The opening and receiving are not only essential in themselves, they may be another step at which negative beliefs rear up, so watch for that too.)

B) What, not How

Remember the joke about the guy who, stranded by a flood, was clinging to his roof? He prayed to his notion of the Divine, "God, God, I've been your faithful servant lo, these many years. Now, prove you believe in me and save me!" He waited and waited. A couple came by in a canoe and offered him a lift. "No! I'm waiting for God to save me! God, I've been a good man, I've tried to live a good life. Prove my faith and save me!"

He waited some more, as the rain pelted down, and the water level rose to his gutters. Some time later, a motor boat came by and offered him a ride. "No! I don't need you! God is going to save me! God, please, please show me that my faith has not been in vain! Create a miracle and save me!"

The rain came down. The water climbed higher up the roof. A helicopter spotted him and hovering, lowered a ladder for him to climb up to safety. "No! he cried. I won't use these worldly ways! God will save me!"

Time passed. The water rose to his feet as he straddled his rooftop. Soon he'd be washed away in the floods. "God! God! Have you forsaken me? What have I done to disappoint you? I thought my belief in You was strong enough that You would send me a miracle!"

Through the downpour, a voice boomed from on high, "FAITH? YOU CALL THAT FAITH?!? YOU WANTED A MIRACLE. I SENT YOU A CANOE, A MOTORBOAT, AND A HELICOPTER! WHAT MORE COULD YOU WANT?!"

The moral of the joke parallels one of the major precepts of the Law of Intention: you can have what you want, if you give up your fantasies about what it should look like and how it should occur.[1]

Why doesn't it work to dictate how things should unfold?

Trying to dictate how something will manifest not only limits your choices and chances of success. It tightens you so that you don't open the space in present reality for the new thing to appear, nor do you open yourself to receiving it. How something will manifest may come from directions and in forms that you wouldn't think of in a million years. You have much more potential than that which is generated by your mind. For starters, there are those great information gatherers and integrity-checkers, your feelings and sensations. As we have seen, you absolutely need your emotions and felt-sense in order to make any decisions whatsoever. There are also the other ways that you perceive and digest information besides your thought processes—if you let yourself access them. For example, your gut energy quickly tells you where you are in space, what is near, what might be dangerous. Your empathy, your internal strengths, the brain functions which assess and compare based on what you've experienced before, all offer you information without your thinking about it.

There is also circumstance and the rest of the world. If you put out an intention, energy will start moving that will send currents to alter events in the world. If you have a strong grip on how something must show up then very likely you will limit the currents that are bringing your intention to you.

Then there is your Higher Self, the totality of who you have been and the guiding hand for your future. And there is the Spirit that resides within you and is manifest through the largest sense of you. There are the teachers and supporters who are on your team, helping with this life. There are also, if you are open to those realms, your disembodied helpers who really know how to use energy planes, so you don't want to limit them in their attempts to assist you. The ineffable aspect of you has access to those realms that your mind may not grasp or function well in. It is essential to the Law of Intention that you allow Energetic Beings to have full scope. You need to allow them to manifest your intent through their own channels as they work from their larger perspective and not limit possibility by dictating how the intended event should unfold. We will visit this again in specific examples when we look at changing beliefs and old protective patterns.

What happens may not be what you anticipate at all. Go along for the ride. It is your job to use your attention and concentration to set the intention. If Lawrence's anxiety moves to his throat, it would be more helpful if he did not try to make it go away by trying to break up the lump he feels there. If he intends clearly to have energy flow freely through the area that's been held apart, then he needs to hand over how it is done. It might melt like chocolate or butter, or soften and expand as a new sponge when you first add water, or it might become clear-sightedness. It might turn into little sparkling particles of light, what I call beam-me-up-Scottie-dots, and then disappear, as the Star Trek personnel did when they went into the transporter. It might pull to the back and swirl around to be used somewhere else as an energy source, or spread up or out. It might shrivel and blow away as dust. There is no way to know, until you watch while holding your Intention.

How do you know you were successful?

The facile answer would be that you'll know when you receive the item. That is not always the case, though. You very well may not receive it for quite a while, even though your intention is aligned and laser-like. Often what manifests is the next step, if you haven't seen some piece of work you need to attend to. It may be that you need to go through some experiences more fully before you can make use of the intention or align yourself with it. Or it may be that some things need to be cleared out or moved around in the world that you are not aware of. This is where perseverance, self-support, and faith come in.

Practice: As an exercise, creating parking spaces is terrific for practicing. You will know without a doubt if you succeed or not, and as the goal is not too important you can feel free to experiment. Don't practice first on creating your dream job or a Maserati, or you might confuse the outcome with unexamined hidden issues.

Intention is not something nebulous or conceptual. People often use the word in the same way that they'd whine, *"But I triiiiied!"* as in, *"Well, I intended to be an honest politician, but things just happened…."* Their use of the word shows that in reality it was not an intention, it was wishful thinking, a rationalization, or a vague idea. What they leave out is the crucial part of true intention—responsibility. You have to make it clear, put it out, and carry through. Wishful thinking is the same as a child's not knowing that the outcome is up to her, not knowing that she has to gather her own initiative.

Intention is on a par with a mature, more evolved stance in which you hone your energies, attention, and emotional truth into a force that produces results. The clearer you can be about how that force works for you, the more you can be aligned with your goal, and your goal with your deepest values. An added benefit will be that practicing intention increases your ability to feel when something is not right. To use intention in your daily life you need to become clear and aligned with your purpose and moral stance.

We will see how all this comes into play in the next chapters involving special skills and uncovering joy.

Endnotes

1 This is so important! There are so many ways that this factor is essential to joy. Relationships are a great example. Give up your fantasy pictures about who your partner should be, and what events should look like in order to mean that you have arrived—events such as weddings, holidays, interactions with your children or your partner. Let go of the preconceived notions that have become tests or requirements for success or love. Stay true to the valuable nugget of what you want—to be loved, as opposed to having it proved with jewelry or what your friends think—and you will end a huge amount of suffering in your life and be much happier.

As we willingly enter each place of fear, each place of deficiency and insecurity in ourselves, we will discover that its walls are made of untruths, of old images of ourselves, of ancient fears, of false ideas of what is pure and what is not.

—Jack Kornfield

Replacing Self-defeating Beliefs with Life-Affirming Ones 11

SASHA, A NURSE, didn't believe in "woo-woo stuff," but after her doctor and her chiropractor both urged her to call me, she figured she had nothing to lose, stark-raving bonkers as she felt. A single mother of a two-and-a-half-year-old son, she hadn't slept enough or brushed her teeth since he'd been born. He couldn't tolerate being at any distance from her. He wouldn't let her leave the room. If by a miracle he fell asleep at nap time, she never made it to the door without his waking up shrieking. He panicked if he was not touching her at all times. He had to sleep with her at night, or he'd scream for hours. All day he clung like a limpet to her clothing, if he couldn't get at her body. She was beside herself.

When I did an energetic work-up of his system, more came to light. It turned out that the birth had turned into a medical crisis, with Sasha in the ICU bleeding practically to death. Nikita had been separated from his mother for the first three days of his life.

Sasha was a good mother and spent as much time with her son as she could. But nothing seemed to reassure him except the clingy physical contact. His first experience of life led him to the belief that mama was not there for him, and once formed in the crucible of that crisis, no later comforting or constancy could dissuade him from that "fact." If he didn't have his body in contact with hers, he was sure that she was gone forever. Any tiny amount of loss triggered that catastrophic abandonment. No amount of *mommy-couldn't-help-it-she-really-loves-you-and-is-here-now-so-calm-down* could counter his locked-in belief.

As humans, we grow by crystallizing our understanding of events and patterns into beliefs about ourselves, our place in the world, and how the world interacts with us. People begin making beliefs about their experience from birth. These protective beliefs then color our whole lives.[1] Whatever happens, we work to explain what, how, and especially, why. To do so, we'll ascribe motive and rationalize away parts of events that don't fit what we "know""already. Humans have a hard time tolerating things not being understandable or occurring for no reason.[2]

It is clear in working with babies energetically that they make decisions based on their experience as early as birth or sometimes even in the womb. A key to releasing trauma in little ones is to be able to identify what those beliefs are by empathizing with an infant's view of events and then checking with his or her Higher Self to make sure I'm on the right track. When I work with babies and small children, I don't teach them directly to be with their anxiety as I do with adults. They can't do that. What makes it easier to clear their beliefs is that they don't have years of solidifying them by rehearsing them over and over. They haven't seen events through its lens, making each experience prove that the belief is true. So it is easier to install a new belief and have the child's life unfold based on it, rather than on the original one.

I identified Nikita's crucial experience and his interpretation of it. Then I cleared the feelings involved in the crisis from his energy field, identified and cleared a belief about being desperately unsafe that he had made in reaction to the medical emergencies that interfered with his birth. Next, I cleared his crucial belief about his mother never being there. The last step was to insert new beliefs that Mom was, in fact, there, that he could count on her, and that life was good. His day-to-day life could then support and be built on those new beliefs.

I don't have small children stay in my office while I do clearings. Once I get a connection to their energy, it is better for them (and for the work) if they relax in the waiting room. I've developed a set of cues that I can say so that their Higher Self and their nervous system join with me energetically in the work, but their minds are not ready to deal with the content. They do hear some of the conversation with the parent that occurs beforehand. So Sasha was skeptical when they left my office that anything had happened. When I didn't hear from her, I checked in. She was relieved beyond measure.

"I don't understand it," she said, sounding puzzled, "but since our session, he has slept, no problem. I'm thrilled to be able to establish some routine. And I can even leave the room when he's playing and come back in a few minutes, and he's fine. I didn't call you, because I don't believe it!"

Beliefs organize our experience. They make it possible for us to adapt to our circumstances, to figure out what to do, to turn toward what seems to work best. They are the shorthand we develop so that we can learn from experience and move onto other things. If we did not develop them, the brain would not have the ability to recognize things we experienced before and put them aside to a certain extent. We'd be stuck in amazement at the most basic things—"Oooh, a leaf!" We wouldn't progress. We'd die very quickly with no notion what hit us, thereby leaving the planet to animals and plants that were able to adapt to their environment.

It is the layering of belief upon belief that builds our view of ourselves, of the world, and of what we expect in the future. If we can recognize something and how it fits with what we already know, then we can put that event aside as already assimilated and move on to other things.

You can watch animals have beliefs as well as people. I had a dog who had been beaten as a puppy. Even after years of happiness as a highly valued member of our family, if he saw a man with a certain ethnicity, he cowered.

Beliefs are created in two basic ways. First the gradual: after living through many similar moments, we get the picture that this is the way things happen, and we make a note. Parents watch small children do this all the time. It is a big relief when we can stop being the voice of experience for them—"If you get your jobs done, you'll be able to play,"

"Mom makes you feel better," "Daddy always comes back"—and see them start to catch on for themselves and provide their own impetus for table-setting, dog walking, and waiting until Grandma wants to give them the gift. Some beliefs clearly are based on positive experiences and foretell good things happening again. Some, based on pain or disappointment, organize us to anticipate negative events. "Mom gets mad when I need her." "Dad only likes me when I'm being entertaining."

Then there's the instantaneous: in response to a very big, very attention-grabbing event, we decide on the spot. This is what happens with victims of trauma and to animals. If the occurrence is shocking enough, attention-grabbing enough, it leads to what is called 'one-trial learning.' No need to repeat that, thanks very much, I got it loud and clear. Daddy coming home means I get a big hug. Amusement parks are a gas. Big black dogs bite. Round black things on the beach blow up, even if they are on Cape Cod (where round black things on the beach are horseshoe crabs, not land mines).

Beliefs are meant to be adaptive and protective, to ensure our survival. It is vital, when wrestling with self-defeating beliefs from the past, to recognize that they *did* help us way back when. Beliefs about ourselves very often are built to help us avoid pain that we think we can't survive. Usually we were pretty accurate about that at the time. Either we were little and dependent on others and didn't have the internal resources to face really bad feelings, or we were in the middle of a crisis, which was not the time to sit with our heads in our hands.

Self-defeating beliefs are adaptive and protective, but outdated. They become self-defeating when we are no longer in those situations yet we behave as if we still are, treating the present as if it is the past, continued *ad infinitum, ad traumatum.* In behavioral psychology they are described as situation-specific, meaning that they originated in reaction to a certain event or interaction, but that we apply them in all sorts of circumstances in which they don't have any relevance. They hold us in old patterns, whether we like them or not—those ones that make us react the same way over and over, even though we've analyzed the originating events to death, even though we hate the way they make us act and feel.

Often, the beliefs that came from our efforts to explain why bad things happened are the very ones that become damagingly limiting. In trying to gain a sense of control over events that made us feel helpless or victimized, we often end up placing the blame on ourselves. After all, if it's our fault, we can do something to stave it off next time, right? "If I hadn't worn that red dress, I wouldn't have been raped. Therefore, to be safe, I must dress in baggy duds." "Mom wouldn't have treated me so badly if I had been a good kid. It must have been my fault then, so it must be my fault now if someone mistreats me." We use self-hatred to try to gain control of the chaos we still feel, as we saw in chapter two.

Beliefs are neurological events that impact the development and structure of our brains. The brains of people with early trauma are different from those without it. Because they are the building blocks of development, beliefs are not meant to be disposable or interchangeable. When we make one, it's supposed to stick, not change with every passing fancy. After all, we made them once it become clear that "that's the way things are"; not while we were still waffling about what things mean or not yet paying attention. Our continued growth uses these beliefs as foundation, so more structure cements them and holds them in place. Further experiences only seem to prove them right.

The nature of our neurology explains why learning can be so fun. If something is new, it is not yet integrated (read, ho-hum), and so it stimulates our brains and nervous systems and calls for our engagement with it. Our systems are more alert when something is new. If we have a belief that learning is fun and interesting, we also enjoy the freshness and look for the new information, connections, and implications that the subject may offer.

In therapy, we try to help clients change beliefs by looking at the old ones, analyzing them to see when and in response to what they were formed, whether they are still true, what outcomes occur when they are used to filter the present. Then clients pay attention to current circumstances and see if the belief is operating, and counter it with a more realistic view. The belief is altered through painstaking building of new experiences based on the new messages.

When I did traditional therapy, the lens through which they viewed life was really hard to alter for clients who'd suffered trauma. It takes work to clear self-defeating beliefs and replace them with self-supporting and life-affirming ones, yet with Energy Dynamics and Energy Medicine, it is usually more quick and profound. This is because physical, emotional, and mental reality is first created on the energetic level. Beliefs are first formed as energetic events, as epiphanies or decisions. If you remember some impactful event, you may remember feeling an almost electric buzz, or a ka-chunk, kind of sitting-down-into-the-realization-type sensation that rooted that moment. In that anchoring, the belief becomes a neurological event, since the nerves are the energy communication pathways in the body.

Then, because they were the underpinnings of experience, it is necessary to replace them with another belief. By doing so, you lay down the nexus for new synaptic connections. As you recognize the foundation the new belief provides, you can return to it and groove in new pathways, rather than going down the old habitual road. As you release enough old ones, it is exciting to note your experience of, and expectations about, life shifting to be based on healthier, more optimistic beliefs that you insert. Change is possible, and what a joy and a relief, not only to release painful feelings, but to affect your outlook for the better!

In getting to this point, Katrina, a young woman who had been repeatedly sexually abused as a child by a neighbor, kept coming up against beliefs that locked her in hopelessness and self-loathing. Katrina talked about those beliefs as her "Katrina-is-broken pile." Her boyfriend made things worse by his oh, so helpfully pointing out what was "wrong" with her and trying to "fix" items in the "Katrina-is-broken pile" by pushing her to get medication.

To grow a healed, whole experience of herself, however, Katrina had to take the risk of blossoming in a new direction. She had to turn away from her "Katrina is broken" pile and label a new area in herself "Katrina is wonderful."

Some beliefs will be obvious to you as you go through the exercises, and you'll be able to release them. As people work through their stored feelings, they have success in clearing old beliefs. But don't get discouraged if things don't seem to be changing. Clearing deeper self-defeating beliefs and replacing them with life-affirming ones can tough to do on your own. They are the matrix for our experience of the world and, as such, are not meant to be altered. It is difficult to nab the really crucial, underlying ones in their exact wording. We are meant to assume that these organizing principles of reality are so true that we don't need to look at them, let alone question them. When I help people identify theirs and we get to the crux of it, they always say, "Oh, yeah, of course! That's been riding me my whole life!" But until then they don't really notice the air they breathe. It just is.

If the crucial beliefs were formulated in reaction to heavy circumstances or seem hard to identify, therapy would be very helpful. The therapeutic relationship is designed to uncover material hard to locate solo. It also provides safe interactions with a person trained to gently explore the effects of your past. That's better than succumbing to acting on a belief that nothing is going to work, that relief is not possible. (Talk about a self-defeating one right there!)

Here are the steps for clearing beliefs, and you can experiment.

How to clear and replace beliefs

First, find the baddies: I'll bet that you are aware of some of these toxic ones. They are the quiet (or maybe insufferably loud) voice in the back of your mind. They are the gremlins that pop up to comment on your behavior, or on that of others, or to generalize about situations. Remember the chapter on self-criticism? Your critical voice is based on toxic beliefs. Don't take the first wording you get, though. If you hear something like, "Well, that wasn't very nice," I'll bet you dollars-to-dillie beans that isn't it. The power-holding belief is the much more judgmental voice beneath that *knows* that you are selfish, or mean, or worthless, or whatever your opposite of "nice" is.

People often find it hard to expose the actual beliefs, because we spend every waking moment trying to prove those voices wrong. "No, no! I'm not selfish/worthless/inadequate/damaging/demanding/stupid!" We've spent years arguing against them and trying to stamp them out. But to release them it takes a cease-fire and letting them show up enough to see them accurately. We have to face the impact of having, deep down in our subconscious, the belief that there is something wrong with us, that we are fundamentally flawed. Slow down and notice what phrases float through the back of your mind, especially when you feel stressed.

If you have trouble identifying one, look at the recurring patterns that make you cringe, since beliefs are the engines that drive our patterns. The disparity between what we try to espouse in our adult, conscious minds and what we actually experience or do when under pressure is the clue that a belief is lurking. Try to put it into words, even if you thought for sure that you'd vanquished that one.

Next, it is important to hone in on the wording. Beliefs are set in very specific language. They become our truth because they land in a core, primitive way. It is necessary to nab the precise wording as well as to understand how to shape new ones, so that they are interpreted by your psyche in the way that you mean, and provide the effect that you intend. You will know that you have it the way it is held in your nervous system when the phrase buzzes with a sense of *"that's it."* Beliefs have a specific structure which affects how we identify them, as well as how we must compose the replacements. Because it is the primitive part of our psyche that encodes these beliefs, they are phrased as universal statements—"always," "never," "all people," "won't ever," and are very direct and potent. It is also the way small children think. When beliefs are created later in life, they often are in response to crisis situations, when adrenalin drives our more primitive minds to be dominant, and they go in as rules in the same way.

Because the belief-encoding function is extremely literal, your most powerful beliefs may actually be in layers. Some may be attempts to explain or resolve deeper ones—a "since that's true, and I can't face that, how about we explain it this way?" It is necessary to identify their relation to each other, how they are put together, and in what order they need to be unraveled. I check to make sure in what order, from which direction, and through what channels clients' beliefs need to be undone.

I also work with people to make sure that we have the replacement belief worded in the way that addresses the issue fundamentally.

Often, when folks aren't successful in using positive affirmations, the reason is that they have not uncovered the way their belief structure organizes itself.[3]

Gwyneth had lots of beliefs from her neglectful childhood, and they weren't far below the surface. They ran her life. Her reactions and assumptions showed that she believed that being emotional meant she was behaving badly, and that any anger at all meant she was exactly as hostile as her mother. Then there was the next layer which said that wanting something for herself meant she was bad, that no one wanted her or would ever really love her, and that she'd be alone forever. Deeper down, she was certain that if someone was upset, it was her fault, and that love wasn't real, because people would use and abuse her if they professed to love her. At the same time (which is not paradoxical, psychologically speaking), she believed that she certainly didn't deserve the kind of care she gave so insistently. At the deepest level, she believed that she had no power to make things happen the way she wanted, so she'd never be stable or secure. The bottom line was she unconsciously believed that she had no right to exist.

If you approach your beliefs in an open way, you'll find that your psyche has its own opinion how it wants to untangle them. Sometimes it's like an onion—from the more surface ones in toward the fundamental ones. Sometimes your Higher Self wants to start at the most crucial and dismantle them in the order in which they formed. Sometimes, it follows a logic of its own, tracing idea threads that become clear only as you unravel them.

Gwyn's Higher Self first picked the belief that she didn't belong and was not accepted, no matter what she did, that she'd always be an outsider. It was a great relief to her to clear it. Since a belief is a building block of one's foundation, it had to be replaced. Gwyn chose, "I am included, accepted, and wanted. I belong."

Next, her system wanted to tackle "I have to please others, or I have no right to exist." That was changed to, "I'm valuable just as I am." Then, there was the layer that included, "It's her responsibility to make things work out"; "If relationships fall apart, it's because she's not doing her job"; "If anything doesn't go well around her, it's her fault"; and, "If she doesn't make things work out, they'll never go well."

You can see the pattern here. Like facets of a smoky crystal, she needed to release each angle at which her psyche held her learned reality. "She can only be happy when everything around her is handled"; because "Others' emotional wellbeing is her responsibility. If they're upset, she's failed." So, "She can't focus on her own needs and reactions and feelings, or she isn't doing her job of taking care of others and will be harmed." Each one was released and replaced with one that built a sense of herself as whole and valuable.

Complete these sentences to jump-start identifying your profound beliefs. There may be lighter ones that are more obvious, but these are a version of prevalent beliefs held by many people. (And it doesn't take away from their huge effect on you that other folks might have the same one. When looking at this level, our experience becomes more simple and universal.):

- Bad things happen to me, because_____.

- It's only when I _____ that people love me.

- If I don't_____, I'll be rejected.

- I must do/be _____, or _____will happen.

- If (the bad thing listed above) happens, I'll disintegrate/ disappear/ die/ explode/ or _____.

- I can never count on_____.

- You can't trust men/women/_____ because_____.

- If I speak up, (bad thing)_____will happen.

- I'm only safe when I_____.

🐾 If I put my needs first, I'll be rejected/punished/
attacked/_____.

🐾 I'm not worthy/loved/talented/smart/_____.

🐾 If only I could _____, then I'd be loved/
not attacked /not rejected/taken care of.

🐾 Because I'm _____, it's my fault that _____
happened.

🐾 I'm always_____.

🐾 I never_____.

🐾 I can't survive my feelings of _____.

🐾 It's my fault that Mom is _____. If I weren't that
way, she'd be better at_____.

🐾 It's my fault that Dad is _____. If I weren't
that way, he'd be better at_____.

🐾 If I show my anger, what will happen is_____.

🐾 If I show weakness or don't stick up for myself, I'll be

_____.

Second, make sure you see it as a belief. The next step is to get a sense
of the impact of the belief you're working with, and also to sense how
your life has been based on it. Your adult mind may argue that it is not
true. That actually means the old one is still there. Your knowing in the
present that it's not *really* true gives you perspective to see it as a belief
that you developed to try to make sense of things, rather than a booming
voice handing down *the truth* from on high. "You're selfish!"—well, no,
intellectually at least, you know that you have the right to get your needs
met, that you care for others and volunteer in your community, and that
your mother accused you of being selfish when she really wanted you to
give up some normal childhood need to meet her expectations. So who
behaved selfishly in this picture?

Now, rather than arguing back and forth between what you know cognitively and what grabs your entrails and says it's true, grounding and centering yourself will help you allow it to surge up, so that you can see all the ways it has run your life.

If you're still emotionally tangled with it to the point that you *know* it's really true, you'll need to wrestle with it a bit longer, to explore it more fully. Journal about it. Investigate it. Imagine if your best friend had that one. How would it look to you then? Or your favorite neighborhood child. What would your suspect about his circumstances if he believed what you believe?

Third, undo the locks holding it in place: When you are ready to release it, here is a simplified, at-home version—a Do-It-Yourself belief-clearing protocol.

* Settle yourself, focus on your breath, then ground and center.

* Now, staying centered, gently include the belief in your attention. You've spent years trying to prove that it isn't true or denying its reality or arguing with it. For now, allow it to be present and feel what it feels like to believe it. If it's stubborn, remember that it's been there for years. Remind yourself that you can tolerate it for ten minutes now, in order to lessen the effect it has on you in the future. If you can't find it, you probably just froze, so your usual mechanisms are keeping it at bay. Breathe and remember what it feels like to believe that. Keep your attention on it throughout the clearing process. The more you can be with the belief, the more the latches can be disrupted.

* Let yourself remember times when it ran the show. What did you feel? What scenes show in your memory? What happened to you? What kinds of results did it lead to? How did it affect your behavior? Be with the feelings that go along with it and that probably led to your forming the belief in the first place. Are they sorrow, grief, anger? Shame, guilt, rejection? How about abandoned, trapped, lost? Hopeless or helpless? Be with whatever those are. In order to clear the belief, it is necessary for you to hold the experience of it in your awareness, along with the related feelings, as much as possible without overwhelming yourself. Suspend what you've learned and figured out over the years and the logical thoughts with which your adult, rational mind counters it. For now, let yourself experience what it's like to be in a world in which it is true. Immerse yourself (that does not mean "drown yourself") in what it feels like. For this ten minutes, let yourself feel the effects of believing such things about yourself and about life.

ॐ Remember the chapter on intention? Here's your chance to practice. While holding those emotions and thoughts, intend to release belief. Be clear that you are going to let go of it now.

ॐ When I clear clients' beliefs, I use a no-touch technique. The way you will get your own nervous system's attention and cue your system to release is by brushing your hands down your body. That's what I do when I clear one of my own. Learn to feel the energy that can extend from your hands. To do so, rub your hands together with quite a bit of pressure, so that friction builds up heat between them. The heat is a form of radiant energy, a feeling similar to holding cotton fluff between your palms. Gradually move them a bit apart, still feeling the energy between them. Feel, or imagine, energy flowing palpably from your hands, even as they move further apart. This is the energy that you are going to use to loosen the latches holding the beliefs in place.

You don't have to be a contortionist to do this. Just reach as much as you can, and intend your energy to reach behind you for the rest. You can aim it from you palms or fingertips. I find in what order the vessels and meridians want to be cleared. The Du/Governing vessel, running down the spine, and the Conception vessel, running down the mid-line of the front of the torso, always go first. See yourself brushing down your spine. Then brush down the center line in front. For this do-it-yourself version, then start at the top of your head and brush down all sides of your head and neck, torso, legs, and arms, ending each stroke on the ground. (You may sit or stand, if you want to get a bit of a tummy workout at the same time, with all this bending over…) Imagine that you are brushing the belief out of the energy lines in your body. Breathe deeply, keep focusing on the feelings, and continue brushing down your body until you feel an easing of the feelings, not as if you've distracted yourself, but as if they're flowing away. Then start at the ground and brush up all sides, ending at the top of your head. Continue until you feel the sensations ease again.

ॐ Next, imagine you are clearing the encoding of this belief from your cells. Intend to do so. Brush your hands down your body again, imagining that you are clearing out your cellular structure, all the cells in your bones, muscles, blood, connective tissue, every cell.

ॐ Finish by intending to clear your energy field as a whole. Hold your right hand (the giving or sending hand) down by your thighs and your left (the receiving one) above the top of your head. Say to yourself, "I clear out any remaining negativity held in my energy field," and imagine or feel energy passing from your right to your left hand through your body. When it feels clear, switch hands, and imagine feeding energy in through the top of your head throughout your giving hand, saying, "I receive all good energy to fill and heal my system." Continue until you feel filled and balanced. When I do it, I know it is enough when the energy stops flowing out and instead gently washes back against my right (giving) hand, showing that the field is full enough.

Fourth, replace them with useful ones: Now, since beliefs are the building blocks of experience, dislodging one means that it needs to be replaced with another. You get to choose what you'd like your life to be based on, and also what you *would have liked* your life to be based on in the past. (The real change in your experience of life comes when you alter the old lens.) Come up with a replacement belief that would set you on a new path and be a strong basis for being happy. One of the first beliefs that showed up for Lola when we started identifying them was that if she relaxed and let go, she'd fall apart. That one was replaced with, "I can relax and move freely as myself, knowing that I'm taken care of by Mother Earth." Another was that being visible put her in danger. She replaced that one with, "I'm safe and supported when I settle into myself and take my rightful place in world."

Here's how to insert the new belief successfully:
Close your eyes and say it again, out loud, with conviction, even if you have to play-act. Imagine the belief as a fine mist that you are now breathing into every cell, every tiny, atomic space in your body. Feel it settle in everywhere. Keep saying it and breathing it in, so that it enters your feet, your back, your creaky right hip, the back of your neck, your fingernails, behind your ears, your tennis elbow, everywhere.

Then, open your eyes and notice how you feel. You'll probably be tired! That's normal. You may also feel relieved, calm, freer, thankful, optimistic. Or not. That's okay. No matter your reaction, give yourself an hour or so to be quiet while your system integrates it.

Rules for creating beliefs

Besides going through the steps because beliefs are neurological beliefs, it is necessary to follow some rules in forming your new ones.

Rule #1: The new belief is not based on your prior experience.
Don't worry that it does not match with your history. You are shaping a new experience of the world. It takes effort to "be the change you want to see," so fly in the face of old evidence here. It is supposed resolve the feelings and beliefs that you had. You want to create a belief that will be a piece of the foundation of your new way of looking at life, from here forward.

Rule #2: It must counter the old belief and its assumptions.

If the old one was, "Mom was never there when I needed her, so no one else will be," then the new one must address your expectations about relating to others. "I meet all my needs and am fine on my own" doesn't cut it with this one. It'd be better to word it more along the lines of, "Mom had her own stuff going on and did the best she could. Other people love being here for me." Or you may be able to go straight to, "Mom loved me and WAS there for me, and others are too." This often is the truth with beliefs formed due to crises in which mom didn't abandon you on purpose.

Rule #3: The unconscious knows no negatives.

Freud was right when he said that. If you word something as a negative—"I will not be scared anymore," it is encoded as, "I will be scared anymore." "No one will attack me" becomes "One will attack me." So, word it in positive terms: "I am brave." "I am protected."

Rule #4: Keep re-wording it until you get that buzzing sensation of "that's it!"

You want it to have the same strong sense of rightness as the old one did.

Rule #5: The way that they are held is completely literal and in the present tense.

If you say, "I will be optimistic," your insides read that as "but I'm not now, so I must actually be pessimistic." Avoid the indefinite future. If you say, "I can assert myself when I need to," it will be read as "yeah, I can, but I don't." So, as much as possible word it as an action you are doing already, a belief that is already in play—"I am doing this now," as in, "I am optimistic," "I am wonderful, safe, and protected around strangers," "People love me just as I am," "Support is here when I need it," and so forth.

Rule #6: Don't reject the new one simply because it hasn't been true for you before, or even if you feel unsure whether it'll be true now.

In the past, events were experienced through the filter of your old beliefs. Of course your memories verify them! Now, you are putting in a *new* base, a new view. (I know I'm repeating myself, but I want to make sure you see that this is important. If I were there in your living room with you, I'd be striding back and forth saying it again too. I can get very enthusiastic, shall we say, to make an important point!)

Rule #7: Adults need to break the habit of chanting the old one.

When I work with children, clearing the belief is pretty much all it takes. But adults have years of having said the old phrase over and over in the back of their minds, reaffirming the filter with every incident. So we need also to break the habit of turning to it to explain what happens in our lives. If you have done all the steps, the belief has now been cleared as a neurological and an energetic event. Write the new one on a small card that you can keep in your pocket. Many people stick the card in their bathroom mirror to look at while they brush their teeth. You could make multiple copies to place on your computer, the dashboard, your ledger. Pull out the card at several times a day and pause to remind yourself of it while feeling it in your body. Any time the old belief is triggered by habit—you know, you always say it when you enter a roomful of strangers, or when your uncle calls, or whatever—say the new one to yourself.

As Gwyn altered her core beliefs, her world started changing. She could much more quickly see that her anxiety was based on old messages from the past. She countered them with her new ones that said that she had the right to be here and have the life she wanted. These led her to support herself more. She grew calmer and more assertive around her family and with dates. Each step was scary, but that wasn't a reason not to take it.

As she dismantled her fear of being abandoned, Gwyn started enjoying being alone for the first time in her life. By doing so, she then uncovered the belief that all relationships were false. Deep down, she thought that even her closest friends didn't really care about her. Her reactions said, "What do you want from me, because you can't really just want to be with me!"

Gwyneth continued to work through her neglect beliefs. As her sense of her true self emerged, she thought carefully about the direction she wanted for her career and her life. She interviewed with several companies before choosing a new job direction. She took her time and turned down some (although she had to wrestle with herself a bit to do so). Gwyn knew that she'd developed a new emotional foundation when she felt confident enough to move to another city for an exciting new job.

Some interesting things surfaced when she uprooted herself. As we talked about her first two weeks on the job, she said that she felt uncomfortable if she was not busy every second of the day. In her old position, she'd been head of her department, so she drove herself until all hours. Now she consulted on projects, so there were times when the director was busy elsewhere. She talked as if her worry was totally common and natural.

Natural, yes, but an issue. What was worrisome? What kept her from relaxing and scoping out the place, meeting people, finding the vending machines?

"If I'm not busy, I get anxious that I won't be seen as productive, and they'll let me go."

"But they wooed you away from your old company! They're ecstatic to have you. It's just taking them a bit to get things in place to best utilize your expertise. You're helping them out even when you're just sitting there and being ready when they need you, rather than their having to go hire you or something. This anxiety seems deeper than the job."

It came out then that Gwyn was certain that they'd reject her if she didn't win them over every moment, and then her biggest fear from infancy would come true. She still had the belief that she was rejected because she was worthless, that she was unlovable and had no value, and so she'd disappear from everyone's attention and fail to survive.

It wasn't about the job at all. Being the new kid and not knowing where she fit in had pushed her into those early childhood experiences. Psychologically, she was back in her parents' house having to meet everyone's needs and be entertaining in order not to be neglected completely. Back then, her emotional and psychological survival depended on her tap dancing as fast as she could to prove her worth. Now, it didn't. Yet she was feeling helpless, inadequate, and not inherently worthy.

Gwyn replaced those beliefs with ones supporting her sense of self as strong and capable, loved and supported. More and more, she was able to see the difference between the past and the present and to question her old reactions when they reappeared. She still got anxious sometimes, but that is normal. She settled herself by grounding, centering, and reminding herself of her new beliefs.

Her life blossomed. Her boyfriend even followed her. Her anxiety at work all but disappeared, and she relaxed into the much more professional atmosphere of her new company. On her days off, she explored her new city, went to the nearby ocean, and walked on the beach. She and her boyfriend were making progress in a much more mature and mutually supportive and responsive way than she had ever experienced in an intimate relationship. A few months later they bought a house together.

One final note: If you find yourself resurrecting the old beliefs and responding as if they're true, several things may be occurring. First, are you centered? Stop, breathe, ground, re-center, then remind yourself of your new one.

It may be that you didn't identify the belief or the wording accurately enough. Or it may be that the structure of the old one is more complex and requires identifying the layers and clearing them one-by-one. Or, there may be a related one that you need to get to that is only able to surface now that you removed the old one. At least you removed a layer of the onion! That's a big piece of work! Or, it may be a troubling enough issue that it'd be better to get some help in dealing with it.

Remember that the goal of life is not to have an absence of feelings. We will have material to work on until we move on to a different playing ground. And there will always be echoes of old events. Changing your beliefs will go a long way to uncovering your innate joy. You've reached success when you have integrated old events into your past, feel more settled about them, and can turn your attention to the present, rather than having them stationed as the prison guard in front of your face telling you how to think and feel.

Practice: Practice your new belief by repeating it in rhythm to your walking until it gets to be the new automatic background voice.

Some examples of positive, life-affirming beliefs:

- Mom is always there when I need her. She loves me very much.

- I take care of my needs first and others support my doing so.

- What happened was due to others' problems. I take excellent care of myself and am supported by the Universe.

- I am wonderful, fine, and free.

- I am valued and valuable.

- I am loved just as I am.

- I protect myself from bad things and receive good things happily and safely.

- I deserve to have a good life and get what I want.

When you alter your beliefs energetically and learn to undo your APEPs, your Automatic Protective Energy Patterns, (which we'll discuss in chapter twelve), that's when your experience of yourself and of life will improve to the hopeful, optimistic, able-to-work-toward-your-own-goals perception of life that you want.

Endnotes

1 Often these babies are seen as colicky, have digestive trouble, or difficulty being soothed or sleeping, or they panic at any change in routine, or they can't tolerate being alone, even for a moment.

It is possible to clear babies' and small children's early decisions about life, if they can be accurately recognized. It's also very satisfying! (Think about saving them 40 years of therapy for their self-blame!) Often one or two sessions identifying the meaning they gave events and helping their systems to clear them, can lead to a removal of those disruptive and painful patterns. Babies are so new to life that they don't have years of accrued habit of interpreting events through the filter of their belief, so that it is easy to see when they are cleared successfully. The crying, or panic, or sleeplessness, or anxiety at the doctor's, stops.

2 In psychology, this involves several concepts, including resolving cognitive dissonance, accommodation, and assimilation.

3 Alfred Korzybski, in his book *Science and Sanity: an introduction to non-Aristotelian systems and general semantics*, called these layers (as well as each thought we have in reacting to an experience) "orders of abstraction." Each takes us further from the direct experience itself. His point was that, as we add meaning, we actually remove ourselves from the experience and not only misinterpret it but cease to experience it. What we are then going through is the result of a construct in our head. He wanted people to recognize their assumptions and interpretations and learn to push them aside and experience events directly. Buddhists agree, saying that it is our interpretation that adds suffering to direct experience. Pain is painful. Thinking that it means that we are bad, deserved it, or will never be cared for, adds suffering.

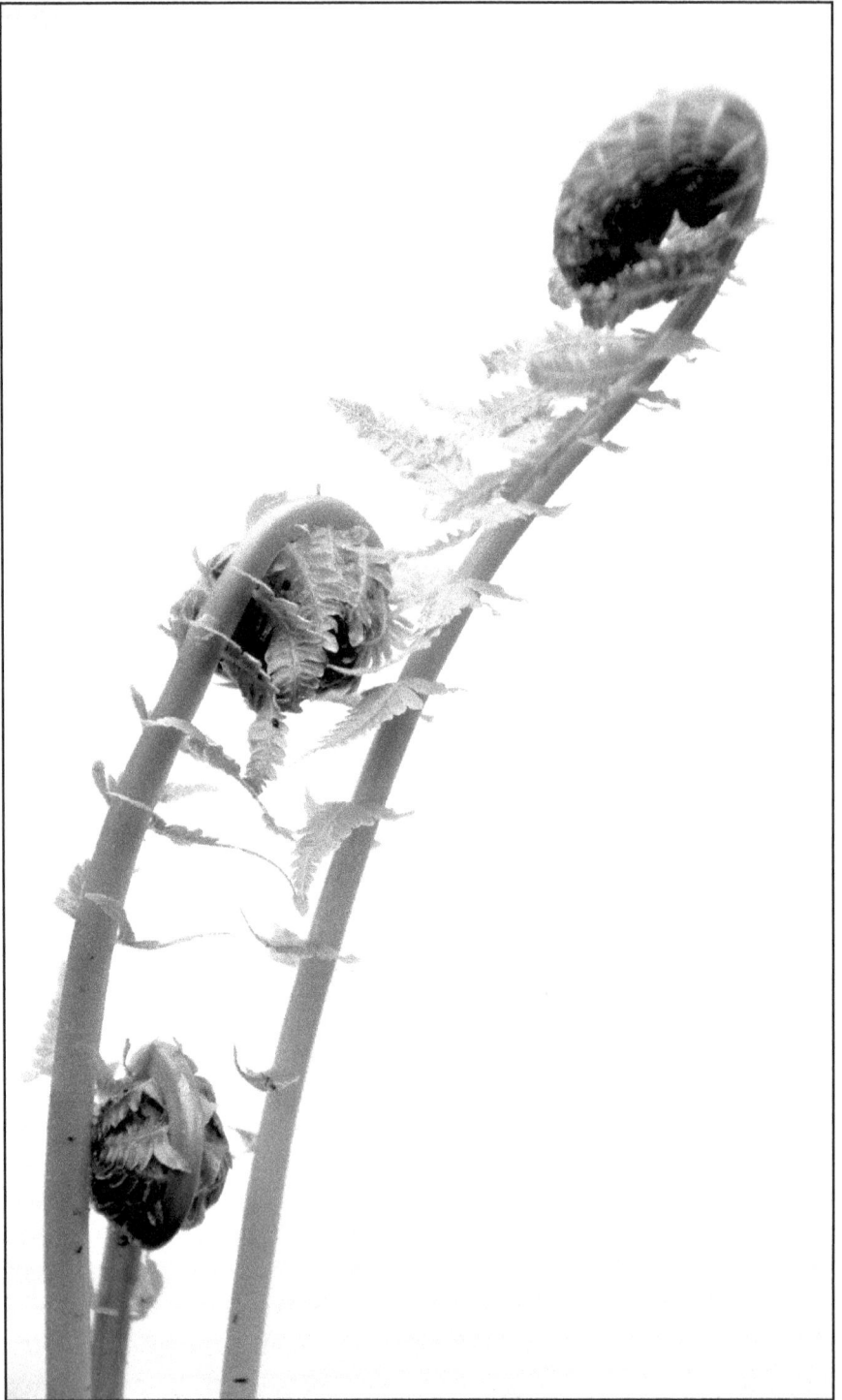

*It is a fundamental aspect of maturity to be able to redirect one's own focus,
rather than being caught by stimuli: to have the internal, central control
to manage one's attention. This shows up in psychological literature from
behaviorism through ego psychology as an underlying theme, even if it is not
directly articulated.*

—Terrence Keeney, professor, Lesley University

APEPs—Automatic Protective Energy Patterns: releasing your locked-up energy

12

A LARGE VAN blocked Tani's view when she wanted to leave a parking spot. As she backed out cautiously, a truck careened around the corner and almost hit her. The driver swore violently at her before he drove off. She sat and shook for a moment and then went her way. Later that day, she noticed that she'd been scattered, forgetful, and had dropped things ever since.

Ming turned in a big project at work only to be called into his boss's office a short time later and read the riot act. Hank accused Ming of not doing enough research, of being sloppy and late, none of which were true. What was clear was that Hank hadn't actually read the report. Everyone knew that he'd been chewed out for poor performance by the president. Ming's wife was pregnant. The last thing he could afford was to lose his job. For the rest of the week, Ming had indigestion and looked a bit caved in, with his shoulders rolled forward and his back slumped. He didn't speak up in meetings. When he did talk to colleagues, his voice sounded pinched.

Rajani was at her wits' end about her dissertation. It seemed that, no matter how she altered it she couldn't seem to satisfy her committee.

The tension in her thoughts was only surpassed by the tension in her shoulders. She had a neck pain that, on its own, was applying for status as an instrument of torture. She could understand why her shoulders hurt so, but what was the deal with her rib cage? It didn't make sense that the front of her chest hurt to the touch.

We all have the right to protect ourselves, and everyone has protective mechanisms. We all have idiosyncratic patterns that our systems snap into when feeling threatened. Automatic Protective Energy Patterns—APEPs (to give them their own handle)—are specifically what our bodies do in reaction to perceived danger. What happens inside us before we use that adrenaline to fight or flee (or gather and nurture, as it has been found that many women tend to do in response to stress)?

Say you're concentrating, head down, focused on your project, and someone suddenly appears behind you. You're startled, your diaphragm freezes, and you fly into hyper-alert, energy and breath yanked upward. Unbeknownst to you, your body has also gone into an Automatic Protective Energy Pattern. It has locked energy in an effort to save you from the tiger/murderer/practical joker who has crept up on you. You jerk around and see that the "intruder" is your office manager/clumsy, teenaged son/absent-minded neighbor. If you're a saint, you laugh shakily. If you're like me, you yell, "Don't sneak up on me like that! What are you trying to do? Give me a heart attack?!?" You start breathing again, but you may not reconnect with your body to reground, much less undo the protective pattern the energy has locked into.

Because APEPs happen way below the level of awareness (hence the "automatic"), they often are not released when the hairy situation is over. If, say, a baby reacts to stress and then mama soothes her, then the APEP lets go. However, unless the unconscious assumptions that go along with it are unraveled, adults' and older kids' systems stay frozen in their protective pattern.

The effects of staying stuck in an automatic pattern are far-reaching. Stress or threat reactions are chemical, neurological, muscular and energetic. Even after the threat is over, the body continues to generate stress hormones—cortisol, epinephrine, and norepinephrine.

To whatever extent we don't undo the pattern, our systems assume that the tiger is still about to pounce, so we unconsciously stay in our own energetic version of a low crouch. That on-guard position warns our system that it better keep putting out stress hormones, and voila, we're caught in an endless feedback loop of fear and trepidation. This is a primary reason that we keep running around on the hamster wheel of our old memories and patterns. Over time, some our most damaging beliefs are built on this chronic state with its biased view of reality. We become certain that we are not safe or worthy or (fill in your yucky belief here).

Not only do we stay in a sad, fearful view of life that strangles our outlook and emotions, it also affects our health. Chronic reactions tie up our energy, tire us out, and compromise our immune systems. They drain our adrenal glands, which can lead to severe imbalances and eventually to illness and injury. As we unconsciously freeze in our clench or run-for-the-hills posture, we are also training our muscles into holding patterns that slow down reaction time and affect our posture and functioning. Since it's automatic, we're surprised when we become irritable and tired, have trouble sleeping, misjudge things, fly off the handle at small events. Down the road, there is much more possibility of heart problems, auto-immune disorders, reduced ability to heal from injury, obesity, relational difficulties, in short, all the ills of modern society. (This is not an exaggeration. Check out the medical research on chronic stress-hormone outlay. More than anything, it points to the necessity to balance our lives with relaxation, meditation and prayer, fun, and creativity. We also need to take time to enjoy the amazing planet on which we live, as well as enjoying each other and connecting deeply within ourselves, so that we, at the very least, release our muscles and hormonal triggers.)

What happened with Ming was that he took his tension into his stomach, clenching it into a tight ball as if he could hide his essential self from the attacks of his boss. He couldn't think very well during this period, didn't speak up much, and looked worried and drained. He also locked himself into feeling helpless, with no options. The continued triggering of cortisol and stomach acids led to an ulcer.

Lawrence became aware of his APEPs in this way: as he continued with sessions, two things happened. He did better at work, and he became more moody. As he resolved the surface layers, his deeply buried feelings were pushing their way to the surface. For a while, he stopped coming to sessions, but his job suffered and he became depressed. In his habitual manner, he was hiding from emotions that needed to be worked through.

When he came back, he was sure that there was no way to change the pattern of moodiness and helplessness that routinely came up after a spell of high functioning. He had taken antidepressants for years, yet he didn't present the same clinical picture as someone who has a genetic chemical imbalance. It was clear that something hidden needed some air time. Something was pushing at him. When I asked when the moodiness showed up, and what triggered it, and what he assumed it meant, he gradually revealed a further historical occurrence. His eldest brother had beaten and tortured him and his siblings for years, delighting in terrifying them.

Finally we had gotten to the root of Lawrence's entire pattern. Whenever he felt helpless or overwhelmed in the present, his old terror was revived. His physical habits of slouching and caving in his chest formed an APEP that tried to protect him from blows and fearful anticipation. His terror had been hidden away in his body through this APEP, which sapped his energy and covertly controlled a large percentage of his decisions and reactions. It was natural that his system tried to hold itself together however it could, but his hiding from his feelings kept the beliefs of the small child locked in his body.

When I used only traditional psychotherapy I often found it frustrating because, while some people could resolve difficulties, those who had lived through trauma, and arguably needed relief the most, had a much harder time changing. They could gain quite a bit of insight, and could alter behaviors, but profoundly changing the way they felt about themselves and what they expected from the world was nigh-on impossible, due to the way that traumatic memory is held captive in the brain. But, when clients released old beliefs and learned to undo APEPs, they then began experiencing life differently. They were able to build on a foundation of new beliefs and learn to stay in the present more of the time and realize that they were safe and competent.

Not only were they then triggered into old terrors less often, over time, they started to notice when they'd gone into their APEP again in reaction to some present crisis: say, a car speeding at them, or their flowered-housecoat-and-curlers-clad neighbor aiming a shovel at their pet wallaby, Binky. They undo the pattern more quickly, thereby cutting short their burgeoning panic at the sight of curlers.

Recognizing and working with APEPs is unique to my form of Energy Medicine. Because I see energy visually, as well as perceive it kinesthetically, the protective patterns appear to me as shapes in which energy has been held. Once identified, I then teach clients how to undo them. This is one of those turning-point moments for many people. It is only when they accurately undo the energy patterns (and alter their beliefs) that their experience of reality begins to transform. It is then that they can see first-hand that their old view of reality is not indisputable fact but is actually a construct which can dissipate, with time and attention.

Over time, your system gets used to having stress hormones triggered less often. You then find that you don't see threats as often, because your system is not mis-defining events as crises as much. Over time, you notice when your APEPs is about to be triggered and have a gap in which to choose not to go there. You stay whole in yourself and come up with a more constructive solution to the situation than spraying your nemesis with a garden hose.

What APEPs look like

In working with thousands of clients over the years, I have identified at least a hundred or so APEP shapes. While people have their own patterns when it comes to reacting automatically, there do tend to be some general categories of pattern. For example, many start with a crunched-in-and-hiding kind, while others do an I'm-outta-here-until-the-threat-is-over kind. These two are quite common, so I will describe them and give you steps for undoing them, if they seem to relate to you. You will know which one applies when you read the description and you find yourself saying, "Oh yeah, that's it. It's been there in the background all along! That explains the knot in my gut/ spacey way I get/pain in my neck/orangutan jumping in my chest."

Splitting out: The first is "splitting out." This one turns out to be the same as the phenomenon that shamans call "soul-splitting." They use shamanic journeying to retrieve parts of the person's soul from the past event in which it is caught. Rather than something that only happened in the past, I see it as a function that people do habitually and continue to do if they do not become aware of it. It is possible to split out in small, subtle ways as well as in much bigger ones.

As I see splitting out, people leave their bodies (when it's an extreme event—think all the movies you've seen of people watching from the ceiling as something's happening to their body on the floor or operating table) or more commonly send some element of their essential Self away on the premise that anywhere-but-here would be safer. It's as if a dimension of your awareness, your power, or your dynamism flies away and hides at a safe distance from your physical body. The problem is, it then is caught in time, stuck in that painful moment. That wisp of you does not know that time continues. It holds a permanent link to the past event, so then side-effects develop—you start believing that life is constantly threatening, you subconsciously try to manage the feeling of threat by believing you're to blame/that you'll never be free of it/that the world is out to get you.

It also affects the energy in your body, which can include feeling like Swiss cheese—not quite all there, not totally able to handle things, less able to cope. People who have split out often become a bit scattered, more distracted, and often a bit more easily overwhelmed. As people learn to re-integrate split-out aspects, they talk about a feeling of recognition, saying to the wisp that's coming back, "Oh, there you are!" and recognizing the bit of their nature that's been missing. They comment on only then noticing that they've been a little holey (we're aiming for the other kind) now that they feel the difference. When you resolve the split, the energy that went out is re-integrated into who you are now and is thereby able to release that aspect of the old hurt.

No one makes a conscious choice which APEP to use, but each of us reacts in our own way, based on our energetic type, history, and psychological makeup. Splitting is my body's most-used APEP. When I first learned to recognize splits (people often have a quite a few built up from pains gone by. You could be walking around right this very minute with several orbiting around you like space dust around an asteroid) and learned to bring them back in, I could sense that they'd been formed during tumultuous moments in my life. But it didn't end there. Since my history led me to be on the lookout for danger, I continued to split out when things happened in the present—a car lurching out of its lane at me, money trouble, anticipating a confrontation (big trigger), or a hefty case of party remorse (that's when you come home from a soiree moaning about what you can't believe you said or did in a moment of high spirits. It's a way of second-guessing and not supporting yourself). Once I knew how it felt to split out, and had pulled in enough of them that I knew how "all present and accounted for" truly felt, I found that I could catch myself when I'd just done it again and thereby undo it more quickly, so that the beliefs that came from it didn't get activated. On down the road, I learned to sense triggering situations before I split out and could then choose to stay present and use my energy differently to resolve the situation, or simply take care of myself until it was over (think, intense and long-winded meeting. Huge benefit.)[1]

Jamming In: The other APEP I will describe here is "jamming in." Ming and Rajani both jammed in. This was Connie's pattern as well. When she was attacked, her APEP went into high gear, trying to lock away her essential self so it couldn't be damaged. The problem was, since Connie didn't know she jammed in, she couldn't then release her energy to feel whole again. So the APEP inadvertently kept her in the very place she didn't want to be—that of still being attacked.

When Connie had first come to treatment, she was so tense that she looked half her size. I happened to see her on the street one day, and she was practically invisible. It was no coincidence that lately she'd been bumped into quite often by others hurrying on their way, which did nothing to help her feel safe. In fact, each time it happened, it re-traumatized her because it seemed as if she couldn't control her own space or take care of herself. It was happening because her energy body was still holding onto hiding in as small a space as possible.

Often it is very hard to release a locked-down-tight hold. It's as if our bodies are certain that we'll be annihilated if we pry our fingers loose, relax the tension just a tiny bit, open up enough to breathe. It takes bravery to face that primal fear and trust that releasing the frozen tightness will actually be more protective and healing than is staying clenched. It's such a conundrum: our bodies tighten to protect themselves, then the tightness keeps it locked in the experience of trauma.

Jamming in involves closing a part of your essential self into a tight and tiny ball and hiding it far inside, so that bad guys can't get at it. Unfortunately, neither can you. You may come to believe you must stifle yourself to be safe. The constriction becomes a part of your body that you do not inhabit. Its tightness may lead to pains or digestive problems. It can act like a small rock impeding flow, or like a black hole—so dense that it pulls other negative energies to it. Also, the energy used to jam in is no longer available to you. Often, but not always, those who have jammed in become subdued and guarded. They look less vibrant and more cautious, as if they are holding themselves down, which they are.

Releasing and re-integrating her APEPs was a turning point for Rajani. When she was able to undo the jams, she began to locate herself within her own body and inhabit her energy more fully. Her stabbing shoulder pain eased, and her heart arrhythmia lessened. Rajani became less afraid to hang out with her emotions and gradually could face issues more directly, which gave her many more options for dealing with them.

There are many varieties of APEP. If yours doesn't seem to fit into Splits or Jamming in, try softening your attention and intending to notice the shape they do take. For example, Lawrence's drooping posture was not only a signal of his anxiety and depression. It was also his Automatic Protective Energy Pattern. His back collapsed, and the energy drained away in the front, forming gaps near his heart where none should have been, as well as a bristle brush of hardness below. His shoulder area looked like an overripe banana—mushy and grey. He needed to become aware of the shape these made together—a bristly pit inside an overtired fruit.

How to undo APEPs

Undoing splitting out: If splitting out seemed to resonate with you as a way that your system protects itself, first breathe, ground, and center. Really focus on being aware of inhabiting your entire energy field. Make sure that you are connected to the earth. Settle into the place where you feel yourself being (although lots of folks who split out have trouble centering).

Your intention needs to be based on a clear message that you want to reconnect with your long-lost aspects. Remind yourself of the benefits of having your energy wisp come back: you'll feel more whole and cohesive, more of your resources will be available, you'll be more present and less caught in the past, you'll learn more effective ways to protect yourself, and to feel freed of that threat. Clearly state to yourself that you want it to return.

Ask your intention to locate a split, like a wispy tissue-paper version of yourself, and then settle into receiving the answer. You know that sense that someone is near you even when you can't see them? Splits feel like that. Take the first indication that you get. Where is it? Is it behind and up from the back of your neck? Is it out in front of your chest? Is it off to one side? If you think about it too much, you will get yourself in a tangle of doubt. If you cannot sense a direction, just try in front of your chest.

Next, you know how you can get a small child (or even a large friend) to come to you by opening your arms? It's as if your intention and your arms opening create a vacuum that draws them to you. Do that to the split. Invite it to come to you, and intend that it will. Be gently clear that this energy of yours will reunite with your body. You can make gathering-in motions with your hands, if you want. Feel it coming toward you.

It may be that, as it comes closer, you have a memory flash of the situation that catapulted it out in the first place. Notice it, but do not get side-tracked. You may sense the event slightly differently. Let that new information wash on by as you keep your attention on re-enveloping the split. (If the memories seem too powerful, it may be helpful to go back to the BWITSY chapter and work it.) Your job now is to give the split-out aspect a chance to discover that it is safer to be home with the rest of you, and that, oh-by-the-way, the precipitator isn't occurring anymore.

Continue to draw it toward you until you sense, or imagine, it merging into your body and settling. Close your eyes and notice how it feels to have it home.

Then see if you can sense another, maybe from another direction. If you can't, play with it. Imagine them and practice pulling them in. People are often a little nervous about pulling splits in. They imagine that they are pulling in an abuser. Remind yourself that you are inviting back your own energy. It is not some stranger's sneaky missile. You are clearly asking your Self to come back into wholeness. Chances are, if you feel nervous, it is the echo of the original event that you are hearing. It is understandable not to want to pull the event back to you. Relax. You can't. It ended. You simply want your scared child-self to come back home and find out that the coast is clear.

Check in. Do you feel calmer, more whole? More awake? The same? Worse? Just notice what you do feel, having gone through this process.

Undoing Jamming in: The first step in releasing a jammed-in area is to check the chakras. When I work with someone, I ask their Higher Self which chakra areas are jammed in. That then tells me what types of energy they have been protecting and which functions are being affected. Practically everyone who jams in has one in the root chakra area. (Each chakra is the locus of a type of human energy. Take a minute to read the extremely minimal explanation of the chakra system at the end of the chapter. If you want more information, there are lots of books written on the subject.) It isn't that the disruption occurs in an organized way, but it does help to make sure that nothing is missed to utilize the chakra system.

If jamming in resonated with you, first breathe, ground, and center. Really focus on being aware of inhabiting all of your body and energy field. Make sure that you are connected to the earth. Settle into your center. Then, be sure to spend a moment musing about the importance and desirability of being whole and cohesive, of having your energy freed, and flowing, and available to you, of being more in present time rather than caught in the past, of learning better ways to protect yourself, as well as really feeling that the threat is over. After all, you can't really protect yourself if energetically you are hiding in the closet.

Let yourself be aware of the value of being more open to your own energy, of inhabiting all of your body, of undoing constrictions so that discomfort doesn't collect there. Okay, now start at the base of your spine, at the first chakra. Intend to become aware of any spot in that area that is so clenched, so closed in on itself, that it is like a small rock or even a tiny black hole. Take the first place that occurs to you. (This is practice anyway.) It usually is a tiny spot that you skip over and do not include when you do a body scan.

Did you ever buy those little, brightly-colored sponge capsules to persuade some small child to take a bath? You plunk them in the tub (the kids and the capsules) and right before their eyes, out blooms a dinosaur, or ship, or flower. Magic! Sponges from nowhere! Urchins transformed into clean cherubs! Your breath is a form of energy. Sense the energy of your breath as light, or warmth, or bath water. Breathe *around* the hiding place. That lets it know that you see it and that your intentions are loving. Gradually have your energy seep in and feel the jammed-in place start to soften and expand like a magic sponge. Gently slide your awareness within it as if you too are sliding into a warm bath (if you like baths. If you do not, try a vat of warm chocolate sauce). Keep moving your energy into it until it is open and relaxed and no longer separated from the area around it.

When you can no longer sense it as a distinct spot and your energy seems fuller and easier in that lowest portion of your torso, move up to the second chakra, below your navel at the level of the top of your pelvic girdle. Ask to become aware of a jam anywhere in this area. In the spirit of investigation, practice clearing jams in the first four or even five chakras. The most common ones to be jammed are from one to five, since five has to do with speaking your truth and bringing your gifts forth.

Repeat the process at each level up, at least the first time. Then sit with your eyes closed and scan your experience of yourself. Do you feel fuller? More present? More alive? The same? Worse? Just notice what you do feel, having gone through this process. Hopefully you feel less tied to the past and more comfortable in the here-and-now.

It's always a leap of faith to tell a client what I see as their APEP. Connie's reaction was heartening and typical of most people. When I suggested that she jammed in, her face lit with recognition, as if she had known it all along but only now was able to recognize it. Even though she doubted her ability to perceive energy, she was able to sense the location of each one before I corroborated. Gradually she washed it with her energy, then settled into it and asked it to ease open. Some were harder than others. The ones in her pelvic and abdominal area took a lot of patience and gentle feeding of energy. There was no rush, though. We took as long as she needed, and gradually the APEPs released their spasmodic hold. As they softened, the energy trapped within swelled and then blended with the energy around it, moving into the natural flow.

After she had them all open, Connie said that she felt reconnected to herself in a way that she hadn't felt in years. She recognized each part as it opened up as a long-lost part of herself, as if finding something she'd lost in childhood. She stood straighter and had more presence. Later, she watched how she felt walking down the street. Surprised, she realized that people noticed her, and she not only was not being knocked into by mistake, she felt more comfortable saying hi or nodding as she passed. This greatly improved her comfort in the world.

Lawrence was a guy who tried to force things when stressed, so he had to learn not to predetermine how the undoing would happen. As he watched with intention rather than willpower, it felt as if energy was being sucked into the bristly area, until it became spongy and started to melt. Then it flowed into his back, up his spine, and out his shoulders to the mushy places, filling them in with warmth. It was a perfect example of the importance of not telling your Higher Self how the release should occur. His energy body knew more than his mind did and followed the path that worked best for his whole being.

Then the underlying collapse in his lower back became apparent. That APEP was the soggy fruit that sagged his lower back into an arch, over the top of his pelvis, then down the front and in, pulling at his sacrum. He moved his attention to this area and watched as his energy filled each part in reverse order, expanding until it detached like a balloon lifting off, releasing his sacrum to move into a more upright position, then on around to connect his gut with the top of his pelvic bone and his navel. For the first time, his front seemed connected to his back, and his lower stomach muscles engaged and provided support for his lower back. His entire pelvic area then acted as a foundation for his chest and shoulder area, giving his torso a chance to act as a unit.

When Lawrence learned to undo his APEPs, he also unpinned the basis of his repetitious, anxious behavior and moved into a more whole, unified sense of his energy. This is what truly enabled him to establish a new sense of empowerment. While he still hadn't dealt with the trauma of ongoing torture by his brother, he felt more capable of addressing his old patterns.

Since self-preservation is innate, APEPs easily recur. With time, though, you'll develop self-protective mechanisms that work better for you and support your feeling unified and competent. As you become clearer how it feels to undo either jams or splits, you may begin to notice when you tend to invoke your APEP. You'll be able to feel when you've done it again. Eventually, you'll sense when you are about to, and you'll then be able to stay present in yourself. When that happens, notice how it changes your experience of a tense moment. Notice what options you have that you would not have seen before, or what it feels like to stay present and supportive of yourself, even if you can't change the situation. Eventually you will find that you do not split out or jam in nearly as often as before, that your sense of self is more whole and capable. Then you'll know from first-hand experience that it is safer to stay open and present than it is to leave your poor body to deal with stuff with less than a full toolkit.

Endnote

1 People with dissociative disorders split out to an extreme, combining it with a jumble of other APEPs in order to disown unacceptable aspects of themselves, solidify the personality positions, and then become seemingly different people when those aspects demand to be heard. There's always a clamping down in order to keep the parts separate. Pulling in splits is one tool that helps tremendously in the outcome of therapy with these souls, although it still takes years of work to help them release the pain and the fear of being present that has been intolerable, and to integrate their identity into a whole.

Appendix
A quick explanation of the chakras

#1 the root chakra, is located at the front of the base of the spine, at the level of the fourth sacral vertebra, so right above the cleft of the buttocks, but in toward the center of that area. The energy it governs has to do with the most basic physical survival, as well as with the most primitive definition of the self and identification with the world—that of the person alone, or by extension their immediate family. Its color, its part of the vibrational spectrum (meaning type of light, as opposed to paint), is red to red-orange.

#2 is in the plane 1½ inches below the navel. It correlates with the *dan tian*, the 'Sea of Qi,' as it is called in Chinese medicine. This chakra has to do with physical energy. For this reason it is sometimes described as sexuality, meaning animal energy and aliveness. It has to do with sex that comes from primitive urges (rather than a desire to connect with a loved one or a sense of oneness). Since it rules physical energy it is about power. Misused, the energy may confuse power with sex or become a desire to want power over others. The color is pink.

#3 is at the level of the solar plexus, the diaphragm, as well as the eighth thoracic vertebra (if you're into counting down your back). It rules the adrenals, spleen, pancreas and liver, as well as the energy of the emotions and also of growth. Having strong emotional reactions, as well as how you relate to your emotions, are rooted here. There is variation on how different practitioners see the color of this one: I see it as golden yellow. One of my teachers, Jack Schwarz, saw it as green.

These first three are considered the base chakras. They have to do with the physical body and basic experience. They are involved in instinctive functioning. With number four, the heart chakra, the scene starts to change.

#4 is at the level of your heart but more in the center of your chest. It is the first chakra of higher energies and acts as a bridge to the upper realms. It governs the heart and also the thymus gland. It demarcates the beginning of empathy and caring, awareness of others and of their having their own points of view. It is involved with integrity, seeing clearly the integrity (or not) of things and people, the beginnings of identifying with a larger entity than oneself and of caring for more than the self. So it is the beginning of identifying with a group and seeing the group's welfare as necessary to one's own wellbeing. I see it as green. Jack saw it as gold.

#5 is located just above the base of your throat, at the level of the fourth cervical vertebra (which puts it in the area below your Adam's apple). Its gland is the thyroid. It governs the energy involved in having your own voice, bringing forth your message, of self-expression and speaking up for yourself. When your throat feels clamped because you're holding back an emotion, you're impacting your fifth-chakra energy. The most common link in all the people with hypo-thyroidism that I have seen is that they stifle their self-expression. Often people who overly express themselves, without discipline or self-regulation, have a disturbance closer to hyper-thyroidism. Its resonating color is lightish blue.

#6 is often called the third eye. It is just below the center of your forehead and governs the pituitary gland. It rules basic psychic energy, synthesizing information from different levels, intuition, and therefore seeing that we are not limited by purely physical constraints. The pituitary gland synthesizes and balances various opposing functions in the body, so the sixth chakra also governs the balancing of energies. Becoming aware of the act of balancing, of weighing differing factors and opposing concerns, leads to insight and enlightenment. Its color is indigo.

#7 the crown chakra, is the door to universal energy. It is located in the center of the top of your head. It governs the pineal gland. The color is violet, a mixing of the indigo and blue of fifth and sixth, with the red of the first. As Jack Schwarz said in his book *Voluntary Controls*, *"When the base chakra is expressed and then purified by the totality of the whole body, the result is all colors, or white. White added to the red and blue makes pale purple, the color of total integration. At the crown chakra, there is no longer a question of synthesizing, metabolizing, preserving, or promoting life. Total enlightenment results in pure white; the first has become light."* (Remember here that he's talking about mixing colors of light, not of paint.) The seventh is where Universal energy enters your body and then is refracted by the chakras to become the different energies of your physical, mental, and emotional systems. The seventh is your connection point with higher energies.

Beyond the seventh are the astral, etheric, and higher levels, the next levels of consciousness including group consciousness, in which the individual is not lost in the mass of others but self-defined while fully identified with and open to ever larger connections.

Some systems go beyond these seven to map the energies of higher orders of awareness and being, including those of the etheric and astral bodies. I work with fifteen chakras, which includes those of your etheric body. In the chapter on decording, you'll use the eighth, which has to do with boundaries and a sense of your electromagnetic field as both as an area that defines you and can also protect you. As well as feeling it around your body, the eighth chakra can be accessed in the physical body in the hollow in front of each shoulder. Sometimes it can be felt to wrap around the back of the shoulders and neck, which is the connecting shape between the two, especially when there are issues in this chakra.

A lot more has been written about them. If you'd like more information about the chakras, look in the bibliography at the end of this book at Jack Schwarz's or Caroline Myss's work.

Never give from the depths of your well, but from your overflow.

—Sufi Saying

Cords and Decording: 13 releasing the burdens and unhealthy connections

JOHN HEADED FOR the water cooler, hoping that Yuri and Maria would be taking a break too. He felt crappy. He'd been up all night replaying the latest fight with his ex-wife. Man, could he use some advice! He really believed in the old saying that a burdened shared is a burden halved. As he neared the cooler, Maria and Yuri looked up, did an exaggerated double-take at the clock, and scurried to their offices. They'd been lending sympathetic ears to John for months, but he never seemed to heed their advice or move on. John felt hurt and took it out on them for the rest of the day, sniping as he passed, and handing off some of his work to Yuri.

Lawrence viewed his empathy as a defining personal characteristic. At work he was known as the one who cared about the lives of others, who was concerned about how people felt in meetings. It actually was something we had to work on, because his effectiveness as a manager of people was compromised. He'd get distracted by his concern over someone and completely forget what he was doing. He didn't maintain the larger picture for his team and didn't provide supervision or leadership. His underlings took advantage of this.

234 From Hurt to Joy

Here was another downside to his warm but unstructured heart: he hid from his own pain by being trying to make nice to his abusive brother, Clyde. "Well, he's another human being," Lawrence would say, at the same time that he'd belittle his own feelings of being trapped and hurt. It's imperative to see the humanity in others. But it is not healthy, nor does it allow for forgiveness, if you don't hold the abuser accountable, which includes facing squarely the fact that they did what they did and seeing the damaging effects.

Also, as long as he made excuses for Clyde, Lawrence was tied to him in a way that sapped his own life and kept him stuck in defeatist patterns. It kept his energy locked in that abusive pattern. Lawrence needed to disentangle from Clyde, view him more accurately, heal, and move on.

Has this ever happened to you? You're at a party. Although no one has mentioned it, you can tell that Bob and Joan have just had a big fight. There Bob is by the fireplace, trying to look nonchalant, while Joan is in the kitchen talking just a tad too brightly. Although they're not aware they're doing it, people are walking carefully around the huge black cord twanging between the two.

Have you ever had a time in your life when you feel you can't get by on your own; are preoccupied with someone who is needy or you're in conflict with; or you are really worried about someone? Then you will relate to the people in the examples above. They are being drained energetically by unhealthy connections with others. This type of pattern is called cording.

Most everyone has corded at some time, because we have all felt overburdened or panicked. What is it, though, that makes us feel bound for so long afterward?

Let's look at how to decord yourself from people who have unconsciously grabbed at your energy. We'll also look at how to undo cords you may have sent to others. We'll then look at how to protect yourself from cords in the future.

What is cording?

Cording is a natural, universal, but unhelpful attempt to resolve situations in which we feel overwhelmed by need, helplessness, despair, shock, violation, or pity. It is an Automatic Protective Energy Pattern in which your energy is diverted from its original purpose to reach out to another. Shamanism and other traditions speak of the same phenomenon. Cording is the energetic result of an overwhelming situation, an effort to resolve something seemingly insurmountable, or to meet a need. There are three major types of situations in which cording occurs:

- You desperately wish you could help someone.

- You are afraid you are inadequate to a task or event.

- Your system is overwhelmed by an assault, so it cannot properly process and resolve it.

We throw cords to others or accept cords from them, try to give or take energy, in order to save ourselves or them. Babies and mamas cord each other often. Babies feel discomfort and don't know what to do, so they reach with all of themselves toward relief. Parents often feel desperate to meet the needs of their screaming, unable-to-communicate-by-talking infants and so may cord them. But it is not just something that babies and "weak" people do. Couples arguing for long periods of time cord. Frustrated bosses and unhappy reports do. Some of the most pervasive corders I have met have been very powerful business men. So obsessed with their work, with so much of their energy tied up in winning power-struggles, they often have no idea at all how to connect with another person when it comes to relationships, so they cord them in an attempt to make contact or get their needs met. Rapists and their victims cord each other, on the rapists' side due to the monstrous extent to which they cut off from their own internal life and relieve themselves by attacking others, and on victims' side by the enormity of the catastrophic disruption of self that occurs when being invaded by so much hostility and sadism.

Although they are thrown during attacks and violence, cording is not inherently a pathological thing to do. Sympathy, as opposed to empathy, causes people to cord quite often, because sympathy involves slipping into feeling the way someone else does. The problem is, then you may feel responsible for their needs, pulled into their concerns, with your energy dropping to match theirs. If you feel guilty or have an unconscious belief that you are to blame if someone else is not happy, it's likely that you will cord. A combination of feeling responsible and helpless is one primary setup.

The predominant emotion that triggers cording is helplessness—feeling unable to get through to someone or to tolerate a seemingly unbearable situation. The helplessness often sits way below the person's level of awareness, completely masked by patterns designed to make them feel strong. It can be a child's feeling unable to gain her mother's approval, or a mother feeling helpless to soothe her child's misery. It can be a powerful politician's buried fear of being out of control, or a wounded woman's hypervigilance. A rapist feels helpless to connect intimately or to face his own deep feelings of hurt. Connie had corded the man who raped her, and he had corded her as well, out of the buried holes in his psyche that led to his being unable to relate to a woman as a person. Helplessness can be overlaid or combined with other feelings.

What is cording not?

Cording is not unusual. Everyone does it at some time. The cord is not the loss or the helplessness that one feels. It is an effort to do something so as not to feel helpless or inadequate. Mary Pat called yesterday. She is always upbeat and level-headed. Yet, yesterday, she said that she felt scattered and upheaved, unable to settle down to anything because she didn't feel like her usual self.

The day before, she and her husband had taken her best friend to the airport after a five-week visit. Rosario spent the time at their house in the country recovering from months of treatment for cancer. Mary Pat had traveled to Louisville to support her each time Rosario had gone through chemo. Yet, having her in their own tiny house for weeks impacted Mary Pat more dramatically. Rosario left feeling much better than when she'd arrived, but Mary Pat felt as if she'd been run over by a cement truck. After leaving her friend at the airport, Mary Pat had gone to work out. But yesterday, she felt scattered, tired, and upset. I explained about cording and guided her through the exercise to release the ones she had thrown to Rosario. She began feeling more like herself right away, but then she said, "At least there was a value to the cording. Rosario so clearly improved during her stay. It was a joy to see her feel better."

I had to explain that it was not the cording that benefited Rosario. Mary Pat, her husband, and their country locale did. It would have been better for all concerned if Mary Pat had been able to deal with her gut reaction to the realities of her dear friend's trouble and had not tied her own energy in knots.

Cords are not the authentic part of a relationship

We grow the most within the context of our relationships, yet even in the closest families, there are times when interactions snag. Ideally, family members do not resort to disconnecting from or grabbing each other metaphorically by the throat in reaction to stress. They stay present in themselves and with each other while dealing with intensity and misunderstanding. In actuality, they often cord each other.

When we hit rough patches, we tend to cord each other. The relationships are then further dragged down by the cording. Yet, when I suggest that they be removed between children and parents, or other family members, people usually fear that they will lose the love bond by doing so. Decording does not remove the true connection. It cleans it up, removing the tangles and obstacles that come from feeling stymied about how to get along.

Often removing the cords saves a fragile relationship. When family members feel released from being drained, stifled, pulled on, or worried out of their skins, they have more room to breathe and to be themselves, and to learn how to relate respectfully and openly.

To untangle such a relational morass, it is important to step back and see what is occurring from a larger perspective. If you feel drained by a person or situation, have you become overly invested? You may have been propping them up so they'll take care of business, or so they'll reciprocate and be supportive of you. But, from their point of view, why should they? It's easier to lean on you and have you do the work. You need to recognize that you are not helping them, nor are you benefiting from it. The other person's cords drain you the same way that someone pulling on you constantly with their hands would drain you.

Clearing cords can free up relationships. You can help all parties move along in their development by releasing the energy stuck in the past, or in helplessness. When you clear cords, love and connectedness have more room to surface, freed from the matted weeds of unresolved situations.

Whether you have corded another or allowed yourself to be corded, your focus needs to shift back to yourself. Here are some questions that will help you discover what led to cording in the first place:

- What in your past has led you to think that you need to rescue people or be rescued?

- What do you get out of being the strong, caring one, or by believing that you can't handle life?

- Do you feel obligated to tend to the emotional needs of others, no matter at what cost to yourself?

- In the past, what did you fear would happen if you didn't?

When you have answered these questions, you'll be more able to see that the present situation is not really resolving the past or the future. It is better to allow the future, even the next hour, to be what it is, than to attempt to stave it off.

If it's natural, what's the problem?

Cording is problematic for several reasons.

- The first relates to the Sufi saying at the beginning of the chapter, "*Never give from the depths of your well, but from your overflow.*" Cording uses your well. It takes energy that is supposed to be for your own maintenance, not the extra which you can give freely. Because cording is a desperate attempt to resolve a seemingly untenable dilemma, it drains you. The cord itself is comprised of energy that is supposed to be in your body being a foundation and taking care of your needs.

- Cording does not actually help others. It is not the same as praying or sending healing thoughts. Those do not rob you of energy. With cording, the other person cannot really be nourished the energy you commit. If you cord because you rather desperately want to help, say, your moaning child or worried father, your target has no conscious idea that you are offering her or him anything. The energy you lose is not deposited into their account. It goes into maintaining, fighting, or grabbing for the cord itself, depending on whose idea it was. The energy is simply tied up.

- It does not help you. Not even babies can actually receive energy by grabbing it from others. If you unconsciously cord someone else, it drains you. It subtracts by tying up some that has already been earmarked for, say, your immune system, or calming yourself, or winning the neighborhood charades championship. If they accept the cord, it drains them.

- Cording binds you to the past. Rather than resolving the stressful situation, saving your child, or making you feel safer, it keeps you trapped in a visceral reliving of some old event. Freud talked about people with unresolved past issues a shaving their energy cathected, or tied up in the painful material and therefore unavailable. Cording, APEPs, and the energetic noose of old beliefs show that he was right.

- Trying to grab energy from others or allowing them to take it from you holds you in a subconscious belief that you cannot make it on your own, and neither can they. You'll be solidifying the notion that you don't know how to relate directly, or that you can't tolerate standing toe-to-toe with your own issues. It keeps you focused away from the responsibility of working to better your own situation and augments any beliefs that it is others' obligation to bail you out.

🐾 Any overwhelming event that triggered cording in the first place is not resolved completely as long as cords still bind you to the event or person. If you still feel strapped to it, you probably are. Cording keeps you tied to the very person or emotion you most want out of your psyche. A sign that you are corded is that thoughts of them keep intruding, hijacking your attention, and draining you of energy, freedom, and hope.[1]

How NOT to decord: cutting cords

Some traditions suggest that you cut the cord. I don't advocate this, because I've seen many people who have been to a practitioner who has done so, and the cord is still there, flapping around. The client doesn't feel any better. They don't feel completely free of the bothersome situation. They have not resolved the urge to throw or accept cords. And their energy is not fully re-integrated.

Cords are made up of real energy. If you simply cut them you have not resolved the energetic issue of having sent your energy outside your sphere in the first place, or of having allowed someone else's energy into your field.

In order to change the energetic event and learn to establish your boundaries in a healthier way, it is necessary to undo the stasis holding them in place, complete the energy's return to its original pattern, allow the pattern that led to their being set up to undo, and then seal any rift in the field.

Before working with me, Mary Pat had experienced several forms of healing and shamanism. She is a therapist who works with clients with personality disorders (serious and difficult patterns such as narcissism and OCD), she could feel their attempts to cord her. She also sensed that the cords locked them in their own painful patterns. "I would start snipping when working with borderlines (a diagnosis for people like the character Glenn Close played in the movie *Fatal Attraction*). But the way you're teaching this is more complete and more connected with what's really going on."

How to decord

With babies and parents, decording is usually quite simple. They often are released when the baby's needs are met, and the parents feel successful in soothing their child. The merged warmth between them works for all concerned, and both parent and child settle into an experience within themselves of happiness and satisfaction.

In other situations, it takes some work. Cords aren't thrown in an organized fashion. They involve various kinds of energies, depending on the events and the unconscious needs or reactions of the person involved. If people have been attacked (or have attacked others), the cords are sticky and locked in. If people are really needy, or the relationship is a long-standing and conflicted one, cords may have been thrown in a tangle or as a jumbled blanket.

To make sure that you release all the types of energy involved, decording is best done systematically through the chakras. (To review the explanation of the chakras, look at the end of chapter twelve.) The first five are most commonly involved because they are the sites of the physical and emotional energies that we usually use with other people: survival, aliveness, sex and power; emotions; integrity, connection, responsibility, and love; and self-expression. Also frequently roped in is the eighth, which has to do with boundaries. (I work with fifteen chakras, all told.) To practice, we will go through each of these. Eventually you will be able to tell where you are corded and where not.

There are four basic kinds of cords:

1) The ones you throw because you are trying to help another person

2) The ones another person grabs at you with to get something from you

3) The ones you throw because you feel overwhelmed and hurt by someone else

4) The ones they throw at you because they have been trying to avoid some of their own baggage by taking it out on you.

Take a moment to clarify which kind you have. To clear the cords, it is important to be able to see the generating situation accurately. (If you have difficulty in getting a sense of the origins of yours, enlist the aid of a therapist or someone highly trained in Energy Medicine. You'll want someone who knows how to work with your particular issue.)

First, it is important to align your intention with the task by stating clearly that you want to decord, that you want your energy back, and that you'll no longer tolerate being drained by others. Become clear about any hidden assumptions that say you're obligated to rescue others at the expense of your own wellbeing. (Once you're completely cleared of cords, you'll experience more directly that it is not helpful or healthy for either of you.) This will establish your intention and your system will begin loosening the locks on the cords and supporting your process.

Suspend any disbelief you might have about cords' existence, much less your being able to perceive them, and use your intention to become aware of the energy that you have invested in your problem person, and/or that they have tied to you. Be playful, exploratory, or anthropological in your experimentation. Give yourself a chance. The biggest inhibitor to your ability to use your energy consciously is your self-doubt.

Settle into yourself by taking three deep breaths into your abdomen. Ground and center. Let go of all outside concerns. Become as aware of your body as possible. Move down into your core, into the back of your legs to your feet, through the fullness of your torso, into your shoulders, arms, and hands, up your back into your neck and head. Moving through the inside of your body, pay special attention to any areas that are tight, that you tend to skip over. Take a moment to stop and be in that area without trying to change it. Just be next to the tightness or blank place, and then ask your energy, light, or warmth, gently to move into that place. Intend that the energy move in enough that you awaken in that part of yourself as well as in the easier places. Become more settled into the inside of your body.

Now, picture a person you feel stuck and conflicted about. In your mind's eye, place them out in front of you. When I teach people to do this, we always clear the cords from the other person before pulling in the ones the client has sent. So look at that person in your mind's eye and sense the stuckness in the form of cords from them to you. Depending on the history you have with them, you may see them looking at you from their usual helpless, hurt, accusing or hostile eyes, or acting as if you owe them, or as if they own you.

Imagine that their hold on you is a cord from their first chakra, at the base of their spine, to you. It usually will land somewhere in your first chakra area, but not always. Just take what you get in terms of sensing where it connects to you.

How it is attached? Is it like a USB plug? A fish hook? A latch? The plug at the end of your headphones? Maybe it's like a suction cup or a claw hook. Whatever it is, imagine yourself unhooking, unplugging, or just gently tugging it out of you. Feel the energy within the cord as palpable and send it back toward the other person. Use shooing motions with your hands, if you want, as if you are brushing crumbs off your lap, and keep that energy moving all the way out of your extended space, your public space. Sense it retracting into the distance. *It* is not your job to force the person to reclaim their energy! You don't have to reengage with them to that extent. In fact, it is better if you don't. It is their responsibility to deal with their own energy and with their own actions. It's only your job to sweep out your own space. Stay grounded as you do this, so you stay in your body and don't get too involved in the energy as it goes back toward them. (You don't want to get too fierce when you're doing this. If it were like a chair you were pushing, you'd have to keep holding onto it in order to do the pushing. You want to let go, dust your hands off, be done with it.) When it's gone from your space, it is out of your realm of responsibility.

Now check their second chakra. Imagine a cord from about one-and one-half inches below their navel to you. Unlatch it from you and send it away. Remember that you're not responsible for getting them to take it back all the way, only for getting it out of your space. So, feel your

244   From Hurt to Joy

aura out to the further edge. Being conscious of occupying your own space helps get it out.

Sense a cord from their third chakra, solar plexus/diaphragm area to you. Unhook it from you and insist on its moving out and away towards them. Intend that it go all the way out of your extended space, so it disappears into the distance toward them. Notice how your energy feels without it, having your energy in your own sphere unimpeded by theirs.

Continue with fourth, at the heart level, removing their cord from you and sending it out.

Then fifth, at the lower part of the throat.

Then try the eighth, at the hollows in front of the shoulders, below the collarbone. Unplug their cords from your field and insist on their energy moving out of your space.

Settle for a moment without those cords draining you. Close your eyes, if you've opened them, and breathe into your stomach and hips. Make sure you're still grounded.

Now, send your awareness down to your first chakra area, at the bottom of your torso, and imagine that your involvement with your problem person, whether from worry or feeling assaulted, as a cord, and your survival energy is affected. Notice how the conflict between you has been siphoning energy to them that you can't afford to waste. When you pull in your own cords and bring your energy back into your own sphere, you will actually be more energized and more fully present within yourself (and with other person, if you choose to be).

Insist that it return. Unhook your cord from them and see yourself reeling it back toward you as if it's a fishing line, or a hose on a reel. As it comes toward you, remind yourself that it is made of your own energy, even if it has spent quite a while away. It is not the other person's energy. It is not something alien or dangerous. People have a tendency to stop when the energy has reached their skin in the front. It belongs melded into the energy system inside, so invite it all the way in. As it comes toward you, take a deep breath into the center of your pelvic bowl. Breathe all the way to the back and exhale down your legs into your feet. After a moment of "Oh yeah, here I am, home at last! Phew!" it will go back to doing what it was doing before it was pushed out of your system in the first place.

Once the first one feels completely re-integrated, imagine that you have a cord to your conflict person from your second chakra, below your navel, to them. Unhook it from them and invite the energy back with some insistence. Allow whatever you become aware of emotionally just to be there as you reel it in. Breathe into the back of your sacrum and let it rejoin your energy system.

Now imagine there's a cord from your solar plexus level to them. Unhook it from them and insist it come home. Feel free to use your hands in gathering gestures. Gently insist that it come in through the space in front of you, and then let it settle inside. Take a deep breath up and down your spine.

Continue on with fourth, at the level of your heart, the **fifth** just above the base of your throat, and then **eighth**, in front of your shoulders and below your collarbone.

Remember that the other person is responsible for his or her own life and sustenance. Let them have the opportunity to learn about their own patterns by not taking over for them. They'll survive having to deal with their own energy. When you feel as if your energy is back where it belongs in your system, let that person fade from your awareness.

It is possible to be corded to others who haven't corded you in return. You may be upset or obsessed about someone who is not at all touched by you. That's okay. Go ahead and pull back your cords from them. You want your energy and focus back.

When you're done, breathe and check in with yourself. Feel how it feels not to be corded to them. Feel the distinct edges of you as a separate person, not as a stuck tangle.

How to keep cords from occurring in the future

With practice, you can keep yourself from being corded in the future and cut down on your tendency to cord. The more you clear cords, the more you'll be able to recognize the feeling of wholeness that occurs when your system is free of such quagmires. You will also find yourself noticing more readily when they've happened again and be able to decord before any lasting problematic patterns are set up or you feel drained and resentful

Sometime when you feel free and clear,

🐾 Ground and Center. Feel your energy as a sphere that includes your physical body as well as the space around it. (This is your aura.) Feel the edge of your field as having a protective coating by investing some energy there.

🐾 State your intention: "This is my space. I am fully present, fully willing to relate. Friendly or loving energy is fine with me. I accept all loving energy coming toward me. I do not allow negative or draining energy, or any energy that is not to my benefit. Neither do I drain myself of the energy that I need to be healthy and whole. This is my energy sphere and I need it and deserve it to be free and clear. I will keep it so."

🐾 Notice the resonance when you clearly put this message out into the world. Feel the statement as a golden shimmer on the surface of your aura, and feel if your system relaxes, spreads out, whether your stance feels firmer and more as if you put your foot down, demarcating your support for yourself. You may feel more awake, more present as you did when you first grounded and centered, because your energy is more thoroughly lodged in your own sphere.

You'll find over time that the sense of your own energy free of any cords is clearer and stronger. You'll feel less vulnerable, more empowered to control your own sphere and walk around unimpeded, more able to protect yourself.

Some further notes about cording and decording

As you decord, you may get a flash of the incident that led to its being formed in the first place. People often have a wave of feeling, a picture, the look on the other's face, a sense of the other's internal strife, or their unconscious reasons for cording. This is a normal function of engaging with the energy of that event. These flashes often lead to greater insight into the reason that cords were thrown in the first place. Marisol commented, "I love grounding and centering, but once we got to cording, I lost my center and felt very uncomfortable at first." As we'd worked on decording, she realized that she'd glimpsed the motives of an abuser. Once the cords were gone, she felt freer than she had in years. If you run into memories or images, don't let them side-track you. Keep going as if moving through a curtain. If you have already been with these emotions, they should be familiar enough and attenuated enough that you can tolerate them, so simply nod and say, "I see you" and keep on going. When you have undone the cords, you'll experience the blessing of life without them. When Kendra decorded from her ex-boyfriend, she said, "I felt a chill, then a softening when his energy went back to him. When I pulled mine in, I felt that I was safe and comfortable again, and then tall!" (She's petite).

As you pull your own energy back in, don't get sidetracked by flashes then either. Let them wash on by. The image or memory is like a stationary veil that you brush through, in front of you and then it's past, if you don't stop to tangle with it.

Lawrence said, "At first, decording felt like a loss. Then I realized what I was losing was a fantasy I'd hidden behind of having a positive relationship with my brother. I started being much more aware of myself—of the inside of my own body. It was as if I'd been out of town all my life and was just getting back. It was clearer what had happened to me. He really had done those things I remembered. I couldn't pretend it hadn't happened." Lawrence looked more present as well as more vibrant. His energy was much more available to him from this point on.

There is often a sense of loss when you decord. Whether of something desired or hated, our systems seem to register any loss as painful. The sudden absence of any connection registers, while the fact that the connection was jerry-rigged out of our essential energy, or that it was damaging, does not make it onto the screen.

A comment on centering and cording

When you practice centering, it becomes clear that one of the benefits is in freeing yourself from being drained. So, it should be clear that when people cord or are corded, they are, by definition, not centered. To throw or grab at essential energy, they must lurch out of themselves and become overly involved with the other person, or lost in their belief about their own inadequacies.

Here is an example: Samir thought he had trouble removing cords. He asked, "What if it feels as if it's everywhere—as if you're on pins and needles, and you want to escape?"

I asked him, "Does your body feel as if your survival is threatened? Emotionally do you want to get away? If you can't get away, what does your body, your primitive emotional triggers (rather than his practical mind), hold as an expectation?"

He answered, "The weight will crush me more and more until I surrender to this person."

When Samir grounded and centered, he was able to explore that sense of being suffocated rather than fighting it. When he stayed with it, he felt as if he were sinking, and then his perspective changed. Rather than being a threat, the weighted feeling became his system's prompt to move more solidly into himself. He suddenly felt as if he grew inside his skin to be bigger and more vibrant. With that, rather than feeling vulnerable to the man by whom he'd felt tormented, he saw unequivocally that the man was self-serving and was not the powerful figure he portrayed himself to be. Samir felt free for the first time to reject this man's pressure and to turn away.

Traumatic events affect you on numerous levels. You may remember them in one way, your adult awareness and the growth work you've done may lead you to think about them in another, and then your body reacts to them in its own way, which is affected by three things at least:

1) the unconscious or energetic intent of the other person, (was their behavior "for your own good?" Did they want to hurt you? Were they just clumsy or ignorant?);

2) how your primitive system read it—your reptilian brain and your limbic system, your-body-as-an-animal-reacting-to-a-threat and its mandate to protect you, and

3) how your system encodes the event based on your history.

So, to counter all these effects, it works best to respond through the body's energy. You'll deepen your connection with your essential self by breathing, grounding, centering, and releasing the trapped, resentful or too-obligated feelings by decording and using other skills. Then you'll be able to stand within your own field and see the other person as separate, outside your personal space. You'll be protected more effectively by having put in place the prohibition against energy thievery, while allowing freely flowing, friendly interactions. When you center, you are much less likely to cord others or allow them to cord you.

When you are able to remain centered, you are better able to tolerate sensations of helplessness, or urges to rescue or be rescued, and simply wait and watch them go by. If events were overwhelming in the past, a centered person is better able to do the work of house-cleaning and plumbing repair that resolves the old event.

A few weeks after Gwyneth learned to decord from her abusive and neglectful parents, her selfish siblings, and her dismissive ex-boyfriend, she came in all in a dither. "After being on my own for seven months, I've become interested in a man, and I want to know how not to do the same old patterns that I've done in other relationships.

"I've always been with somebody. Since breaking up with Max, I've only been interested in working on me. You know how agitated and uncomfortable I was at first being just with myself. But lately, I've been having a great time! I find myself interesting and entertaining. I go on lots of mini-dates with myself. I've tried dragon-boating, and water-skiing, and I'm in a kick-ball league. I don't want to lose that by getting too wrapped up in somebody else. Now that we've decorded, I can see a different way of connecting with and finding myself. I see that I couldn't make a genuine connection until I decorded. It's the first time that I feel genuinely interested in connecting with someone else in a long time. And I can see more clearly. The other people I've been out with I'm not interested in at all. They're just friends.

"And you know what else? When I see Max out somewhere, I can see his attempts to cord me—he seems so much more angry and resentful than I noticed when I was with him. I can feel him pulling on me, even though he doesn't want to talk to me, and I don't approach him. I can feel the stuff he puts on me. And I used to think it was all my problem!

"The decording made all the difference in how I relate to my brother and sister now too. I just don't get sucked in. I find I can just approach them directly, without worrying about their tantrums, and lo-and -behold, they act better around me, because I don't unconsciously ask for that stuff. So, how do I stay out of the old patterns? I'm really interested in this guy." (We'll find out how she did in the next couple of chapters.)

Back to the example (at the beginning of the chapter) of the fighting couple at the party: there's nothing inherently wrong with being angry. Anger is valuable. It gives you important information. It's what you do with your anger that makes it positive or damaging. But this couple, instead of taking responsibility for their conflict, dragged it, in all its toxicity, to infect a group of their friends. They have yet to learn that the main power we have as humans, and also a crucial one as far as becoming free to live as we want, is to change our perceptions and our attitudes.

For those of us who have been traumatized, we want to realize that we are not helpless, that we don't have to remain overwhelmed. Decording shows us that new tools can effectively change our experience by giving us the space to consider what happened and strategize what the optimal outcome would be. It is freeing and empowering suddenly to feel unencumbered by a draining person and able to define situations differently. How cool is that?!?

As for Lawrence, after decording from his brother, his recurring depression disappeared. He felt more together than he ever had, more connected to Spirit, to his body, and to his perceptions. He was more able to stay grounded in himself when someone else experienced an emotion. He started learning to question his assumptions about their feelings and not project his own onto them. He learned to be a better manager by remembering that work is a place to do business, and that the more he provided helpful structure for his people, the less they devolved into personal reactions and focused on doing a good job. His natural joie de vivre stayed with him as he felt a rich satisfaction in being in his own skin.

The more you return to being centered, with your energy wholly within your system, the more you can sense your own energy and clearly define yourself. You'll feel less jumbled with others or, on the other end of the protection spectrum, less needing to be distant and cut off. When you're present, you can be connected to yourself and others, and when you're not present, you can't. It comes down to that.

Endnotes

1 Several therapists and professors of psychology have asked me where cording stands in relation to clinically understood defense mechanisms. The translation may be a little difficult, because psychology looks at how people respond to emotional situations based on their history and their accommodations to that history. (In some theoretical traditions, one's social network and the systems operating around the person are also factored in.) Here, we are looking at emotional and historical material not only as emotional events and mental constructs, but as energetic experiences that impact and grow out of one's physical reality—one's body. With Energy Dynamics, we look at the ways those emotional situations affected one physically, spiritually, kinesthetically.

That said, and to answer the psychologists' questions, cording is a combination of transference and merging. Cording is the mechanism by which the client is still tied to someone, and so disrupts attempts to resolve painful issues, while keeping clients in old patterns of reacting to current interactions as if they are the old one, because they are the old one as far as their system is concerned. Their energy is still cathected to the old events.

We cord when we are not clear about our boundaries as separate and individuated people, so we act on impulses to blend energy with another's. When we do so, it is not clear whose energy is whose. To that extent, cording is (a) form of merging, but not all merging is being corded. Think babies and mommies, or lovers, or cozily cuddling on the couch. These are all healthy examples of merged energy. But, cording occurs when helplessness is overwhelming, when longing becomes obsessive, and when feeling desperately uncertain of your survival, or when you feel run over by another person and you can't put yourself back together. Chances are, you're corded with any of those people about whom you think too much, to whom you feel tied even when you don't want to be, or about whom you can't resolve things. It's as if you can't completely coalesce an integrated sense of yourself, because you have issues with that person and thoughts of them keep intruding and affecting how you feel about yourself.

The value of perceiving the real energetic effects, as well, as the psychological constructs, is that you have more choices for releasing the transference or developing beyond a merged self-definition, as well as working through traumatic memories and events that have been stuck, unmoving, in the brain.

You can't be brave if you've only had wonderful things happen to you.

—Mary Tyler Moore

The best lightning rod for your protection is your own spine.

—Ralph Waldo Emerson

The Physics of Self-Protection: 14
learning to feel safe around
difficult people

NATALIE WAS IN intelligent, successful business woman, in charge of her life, her work, and her home. But not of her mother-in-law. From a traditional culture, Nirgah thought Natalie should stay home with the babies and do everything to make her son's life easy. Natalie's husband, Bayuul, wanted Natalie to work, so that the burden of finances was not solely on his shoulders for their growing family, but he hadn't really looked at what that meant. His assumptions about marriage were based on his mother's traditional model. Anyway, Nirgah would not have been satisfied by Natalie's staying home. Nirgah saw Natalie as a rival for her son's affections, so nothing Natalie did was right. Nirgah accused her of ludicrously bad behavior and made scenes in front of other family members. Natalie felt so cornered and misrepresented that she started shouting back. She then threatened to keep her in-laws from visiting. She accused Nirgah of undermining her marriage, since Natalie's husband sided with his mother. Nirgah of course took all of Natalie's upsets as proof that Natalie was out-of-control and totally unable to be a "good wife." Natalie felt more and more helpless. She took the baby to her parents' for a few months, because she felt so alienated from Bayuul and saw him as under his mother's thumb. She dreaded any family gatherings.

On another note, National Public Radio's humorous show about the week's news, *"Wait, Wait, Don't Tell Me,"* had a quiz question which involved guessing which unlikely corporate training was real. The right answer involved a bank. Tellers were trained to notice signs that the customer in front of them was in fact a robber. This particular bank trained their staff to respond to the would-be robber by going overboard to take care of them. Before the thief took any incriminating step such as pulling out a gun, tellers were instructed to become very sweet and helpful, to smile and lean forward a bit. "Hi! How's your day going? Anything I can do for you? What would make things easier?" Very friendly. The robber in the story ended up simply paying for a roll of quarters. That teller effectively disarmed the criminal by staying present in herself. She took control of the emotional tone of the interaction, redefined the situation, and changed the outcome. Comedian and contestant Paula Poundstone wisecracked, "Whoa, they were that nice? Maybe they could try that with their regular customers???"

Obviously, it is great to feel that we can protect ourselves. Yet, if we have been through shocking events, we do not necessarily feel competent to take care of our safety or assume that everything will be fine. If something were to happen again, we fear that we wouldn't be able to stop it this time either, so we often react fearing the worst.

Even if a we have not been traumatized and have had not had our ability to deal with repercussions blown away, even if situations are simply irritating, it is tremendously helpful to feel that we can take care of ourselves in such a way that we will not be as vulnerable to others' emotions or behavior as we may have been in the past.

Protecting yourself better would be handy when?
There are several types of events in which it is particularly a good idea to know how to protect yourself energetically: when you feel threatened, either by attack, by someone's violating your boundaries (more on that in chapter fifteen); when others want to use you or take advantage of you, or you feel you should let them; and situations in which you feel disempowered and plugged into old patterns.

The second type of situation includes feeling so much sympathy for another person's plight that your energy is drained when around them. This happens a lot to therapists, health-care providers of all sorts, fire-fighters, police, teachers, and school personnel. Listening to horror stories all day, or seeing the effects of unconscionable events, wears down and overwhelms the helper's defenses. It is imperative to know how to maintain and protect your own energy successfully from the emotional tribulations of others without building such an impenetrable wall of hardness that cease to care about others. You cannot help them if you have allowed yourself to be drained.

The third type also includes those times when you're overwhelmed. You may feel vulnerable because your car broke down on the freeway; you're juggling a hard week at work with a child with the flu while your partner is out of town; your son's soccer coach thinks you volunteered to make potato salad for forty; or you can't remember the last time you had a chance to brush your teeth. Any of those times when you are depleted can lead to your suddenly being slammed with some reaction to the straw you didn't see coming.

There is yet another kind of situation in which it is helpful, if not imperative, to know how to protect yourself, which we has to do with decording. This kind deals with energy vampires—the colleague who incessantly talks about her personal problems during work time; the neighbor who leans on others constantly for support; the brother-in-law who can't structure his own life and so brings all his emergencies for your advice but never acts on it; the friend who feels oh-so-much-better-you're-such-a-lifesaver, yet after she leaves you feel depressed and exhausted. These are the ones that draw you into their pain, who pull for sympathy and seem to need to be taken care of, or the ones who put on a valiant front, such as my mother, who projected an image of enthusiasm which veiled a deep well of feeling fury, depression, and demand that others be what she wanted, so she wouldn't have to feel her feelings. I've watched others be drawn to her enthusiasm-masking-valiant-sadness only to find out too late that her plea for care-taking actually masks a deep hostility that lashes out whenever people don't handle all her feelings for her.

To work effectively with others in a helping capacity, it is imperative to be able to differentiate between your feelings and that of others, between your stuff and theirs, your energy and theirs, because you'll feel both sets in your body. If you can't distinguish between theirs and yours, you'll think that it is all your stuff and then take it on, or you'll block it all, project on others, and be clueless about your own feelings. When you can stay present in the moment and in your body, you can remember who you are, what your stuff is, and where your boundaries are. You can use your sensitivity to notice what is happening in another person.

For now, we will talk about the first three types of self-protection situations. If you have an energy vampire in your life, revisit the last chapter on decording.

How to protect yourself with your Energy Dynamics

Think of someone with whom you already have history, around whom, or from whom, you want to protect yourself. It may be because you feel threatened by them, or your sympathy with their situation leads to your energy being drained. It doesn't matter for this practice if it is because you have a strong emotional reaction, the boundaries are not clear, or it is someone who feels invasive, negative, or who makes you feel badly about yourself.

Notice where in your body you feel the impact of this person. Notice what the sensation is. To Katrina, her heart felt tight, while for Bill, his heart felt compressed from the front. John's and Natalie's stomachs felt tight, while Marisol's chest felt constricted. Ming felt a sinking feeling from his chest into his abdomen, with pressure behind his eyes. Notice what it feels like to you. Don't do anything with the sensation.

Ground yourself. Turn your attention away from the sensations and see if you have pulled away from the earth, lost your connection with your feet and legs, stiffened your diaphragm. Make sure that your heels and the back of the legs are connected to the ground. Relax back onto earth and soften your Achilles tendons. Keep your feet in your awareness while I talk for a while, and then we'll get to ways of protecting yourself that do not disconnect you from yourself or limit you, but instead maximize your options and empower you.

The physics of energetic self-protection

Remember our automatic, lizard brain call-to-action. When put on alert, everyone freezes their diaphragm, surges energy upward to rush hormones, to the heart, lungs, and brain, as we discussed in the chapter on breathing. If we don't pay attention to having done so, we get stuck in crisis mode (remember mom here, telling us our face is going to freeze that way), thereby disconnecting from most of our energy, and limiting the amount of space and freedom our energy has. And these days, living in modern, "civilized" societies, fighting or fleeing is not the proper reaction, so our posture remains frozen in a chronic pattern of low-grade crisis. Our energy and chemistry do not have a chance to return to neutral, to rest, to balance. So they are not available for more appropriate or complex responses.

The hard part is that our instinctual protective mechanisms do not protect us very well, I guess because we are not lizards, and we expect to live longer than a season. Going on automatic, cringing, or coming out punching only keep us back in patterns and self-images that keep us down. When we hold ourselves in a chronically low crouch, we feel as if we are beleaguered and alone. In order to protect ourselves effectively, we want to be able to stay in charge of ourselves and define the tone of an interaction, choose our responses, be pro-active, empower ourselves by pausing and strategizing what will work better and what keeps us centered and alters the interaction for the better. Sounds like an awful lot, but think about it: isn't this what happens those times when you are able to affect outcomes positively?

We're back to physics again. Our lizard brain triggers our systems to contract, to tense. When energy contracts, it pulls in (obviously), taking up less space, and incidentally creating a vacuum in the area in which it used to be. Nature truly does abhor a vacuum, as your high school science teacher said. The pulling-in-tightly causes a sucking action (like the one that cleans your rug—not mine very often though. That's a task I have a hard time bringing myself to do), so it pulls other energies, as well as dust bunnies, into it. The flashiest example is a Black Hole, in which a star has imploded, creating a very powerful vacuum which then absorbs all the energy that comes into its field. Flinching, ducking, and tensing actually are counterproductive as protective measures, because you're more likely to draw the bad-guy energy toward you, the very energy that you want to protect yourself from. I'm sure you saw this played out on the playground when you were a kid. There's always one kid who, when loomed over by the bully, winces and cries, "Don't hit me!" and then invariably gets pummeled. With coworkers or friends, if someone reacts by wimping, it is really hard *not* to feel more aggressive, if only because they had the gall to imply that you would ever bash somebody!

Energy waves have two characteristics: frequency, how often they come, meaning how close together they are, and amplitude, how big or small they are. You can have a wave that goes up and down a lot, as well as being very long. This is a high-amplitude, low-frequency wave.

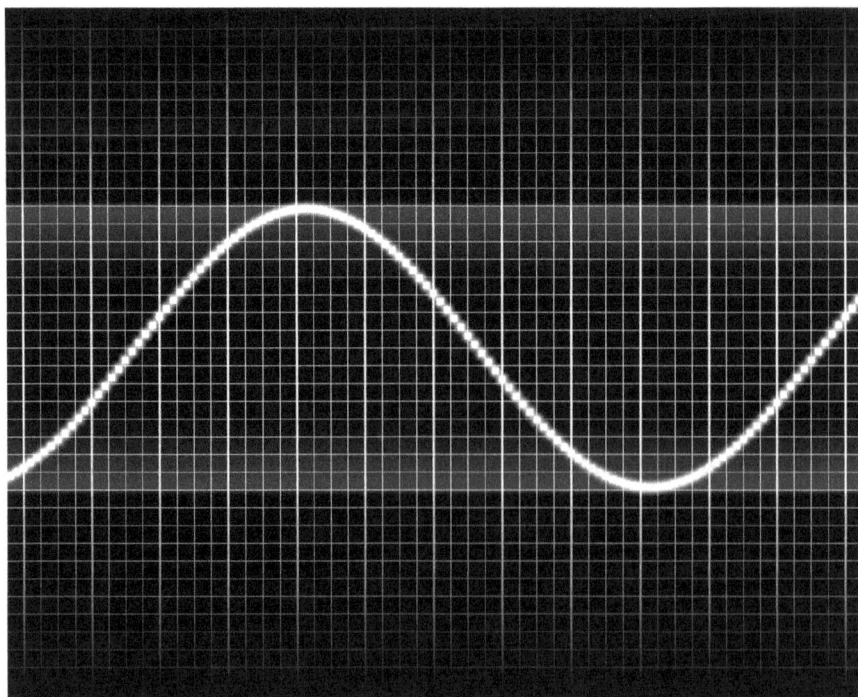

@ 2009 kgtoh bigstockphoto

Having our energy in this wave corresponds with our feeling peaceful, happy, contented, meditative.

The opposite, a tiny, very short wave has low-amplitude and high-frequency. These tend to be the energies of disease germs, fungi, etc.

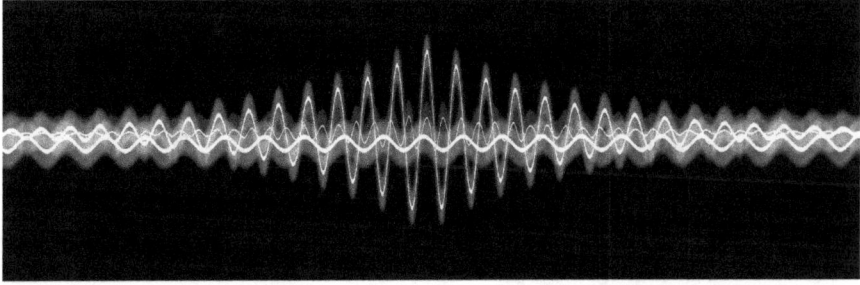

© 2007 Eraxion bigstockphoto

Feeling very agitated or anxious is the outward sign of a low-amplitude, high-frequency wave, while depression and apathy can be low-amplitude, moderate-frequency or low-amplitude, low-frequency.

You know how you get tight when you're angry? Even though anger can help you access your energy, it always is high-frequency, because the energy tightens you up somewhere. Anger can have various amplitudes depending on how worked up you get.

Being ill lowers your amplitude and may either raise your frequency or lower it, depending on the type of illness. Also, if you hurt your foot by dropping a hammer on it, a toe fungus may have set up residence, because you have lowered the amplitude of your toe by injuring it to the level fungi love. Once the fungus moves in, it keeps the amplitude in your toe at the level it needs to thrive, not the level you need for health.

The Aura

When we talk about protecting ourselves by paying attention to the energy patterns in our bodies, we're talking about our electromagnetic field as a whole. The energy in our systems has a measurable (now that sophisticated enough instruments have been developed) charge. The field can even be photographed through a process called Kirlian photography.

All objects and beings have such a field, since all things have some sort of electromagnetic charge, even if at a very low level (called ELFs—extra low frequency fields). Ours is significantly larger or stronger than, say, rocks, although it's less than those of planets. Terra's electromagnetic field has layers that extend from her core beyond the surface, including the layers of the atmosphere from the troposphere, closest to the planet's skin; through the stratosphere and mesosphere, which make up the ozonosphere; to the magnetosphere and then the ionosphere and exosphere, which make up the thermosphere, the exosphere topping out at 10,000 kilometers out. There are other cool names, such as the plasmasphere, the geosphere, on out to the magnetopause, the outer edge of the exosphere at which the earth's magnetic attraction gives up. Don't you love this stuff?

Anyway, our bodies have electromagnetic layers that extend out beyond our skin too. The layers are called by different names, depending on the school of thought. Jack Schwarz, in his book *Human Energy Systems,* calls the layer that permeates the body the physical health layer. Then comes the ovum, like an egg encasing the body, then the emotional, mental, and paraconscious layers, then the causal, and then two layers of cosmic-spiritual, one of which other traditions call the etheric. In these other traditions, these layers are called the aura. (See? Not so airy-fairy now, huh?) It extends beyond your physical body anywhere from a few inches to a few feet, depending on who you are, and what is going on with you. People usually aren't aware of the different layers. They just access them when doing activities that use those energies.

The way people usually sense their energy fields is by being aware of what has also been called their "personal space." You probably know that you stand closer or further away from people depending on how well you know them and what kind of relationship you have with them. The study of proxemics was developed in the late 1950's and early 1960's by Edward Hall, so that now we tend to know that Americans choose to stand roughly four to seven feet apart when conversing, while Europeans feel more comfortable with half that. Hall defined three spheres around people's bodies:

❧ Intimate space: the bubble defining the up-close-and-personal realm. We only accept people this close when they are intimates and very dear friends. Imagine sitting or standing near your lover, partner, beloved spouse or child. Feel when she or he moves from nearby to within your intimate space, as if coming in for a kiss. You can sense where the line is, as your body reacts by softening and receiving. If anyone else moves in, you probably stiffen or try to move them back.

❧ Social and consultative spaces: the circles in which you feel comfortable in day-to-day interactions with acquaintances or strangers. You can notice the outer edge when they come nearer to talk, and then the inner edge if they move into your intimate space to hug you or pat your knee.

❧ Public space: the distance for impersonal or anonymous interactions. I think this distance is also for the acquaintances you don't like very well. You can easily notice outer and inner edges if those to whom you have not given permission to be friends or intimates come too close to you anyway.

Another great way for city dwellers and visitors to become aware of the personal spheres is to notice in subways, lines to get into a night club or sports arena, and other crowds. You will notice how you have to adjust your boundaries to protect yourself in order to stand crammed in with strangers. What you are doing in those lines (besides waiting to spend a lot of money on a night out) is voluntarily adjusting your personal space levels, and often stiffening up your intimate boundary, and maybe shutting down, zoning out, in order to minimize the effects of being crowded, or getting a bit excited if the person next to you is attractive!

Paying attention to these social spheres gives us ways of perceiving our auras, as we note our energetic awareness extending beyond our skin. There is a lot more that has been mapped and explored about auras. It is possible to see or sense an amazing amount of information about what is going on with a person. That would be the topic of another book. For our purposes here, it is valuable to practice sensing the boundaries of the spheres, because successful protection involves these layers.

The secret to protecting yourself

The way to truly keep yourself safe is counter-intuitive in one vital point. The key to energetic self-protection is that a high-amplitude, low-frequency wave pattern repels energies that have higher frequencies and lower amplitudes, while lower-amplitude fields allow in equal- or higher-frequency fields. If someone is aiming at you in anger, hurt, blaming, their energy field is operating at a lower amplitude than yours, *if* you can maintain a calmer, more expanded state-of-being. Lower your amplitude by contracting—getting tense, angry back, or scared—and they've gotten you. Keep yours elevated, and they will have little or no effect on you. *Hah.*

It is not a matter of barricading yourself inside an armor of tension, contracting, or vacating, it depends on your radiating your energy, expanding and feeling calm and empowered. The secret is to inhabit your energy, to expand throughout your entire body and aura. If you pervade your extended space, and you do that by enhancing your energy, by bringing light, warmth, fullness or airiness in, then other peoples' energy doesn't have the same chance to interfere with yours. This is really cool science-fiction force-field stuff. If your energy is vibrating at a high enough amplitude, lower amplitude energy cannot penetrate it. The negative energy of the other person operates, by definition, at a lower amplitude than your expanded, centered, calm energy. It literally bounces off. Remember the playground taunt "any bad words you say bounce off me and stick to you?" Kids would singsong that hoping it'd get the other guy to stop saying mean things, all the while cringing inside and hoping they were as tough as they made their faces look. That saying *is* true, *as long as* you don't tighten defensively, but rather you inhabit your energy field fully, and stay as present as possible.

How to protect yourself energetically

Okay, now let's get back to what actually to do to protect yourself effectively and improve your circumstances at the same time. There are many ways to protect yourself energetically. The ones I include here are simple and highly effective ones. We will talk about some others in the chapter on boundaries (chapter fifteen). (In a future book and CD, I will describe more ways to protect yourself especially in certain types of situations.)

Breathe, ground, and center

You've been keeping your feet on the earth while I've been rattling on about science and stuff. Now, take some deep breaths, let them out with audible sighs, and move your attention into your interior landscape. Check that you have your hips, legs, and connection with the earth. Hopefully as you've been reading the book, you've been practicing, because as you do, you will develop deeper levels of grounding ability. (When I first learned to ground in this specific way, every time our group met we spent at least half an hour checking each other's grounding—where we were missing, obstructed, too impacted, whatever kept us at that moment from being fully in our bodies and fully connected. It not only taught us to read other people. It really helped us be more fully and completely awake and humming along in our own bodies. When I teach a class, either on the phone or in person, I always begin by checking what people are doing specifically, at that moment—where they are, where they aren't, what parts they're leaving out, where old habit patterns are being held and are holding them back from fully being present in that moment.)

As you align your energy more, and your energy works out old patterns, you will want to watch your connection in the moment, rather than assuming that grounding will always land you in the same experience of yourself.

When you feel grounded, ask yourself to center and watch how your energy responds. Try centering softly. Soften behind your jaw. Breathe up and down your throat behind your jaw, so that the energy can flow smoothly between your head, neck and shoulders, and on down your spine. Feel yourself extending through your body and including the whole egg-shaped area of your aura. Make sure you have the back, under your feet, behind your neck and around your head—all the places we don't normally pay attention to. Visualize yourself enlivening your energy within the bubble of your space. It may be as light or sparkles, warmth or tingling when it shows up more.

Golden Bubble

(This is a fuller explanation of the method I described in the decording chapter.) Now that you have your energy fully enlivening all your space, feel the sphere around you all the way to the outer surface of your social space. Make sure you include your back, under your feet, around your head. Continue to feel your energy pervading all of your space within it. Imagine or intend that its surface become golden and shining. Sense it shimmering like a soap bubble or glowing in the sun. Make sure you have shimmers and glows all around.

How does it feel to have this golden egg-shape lightly encapsulating your energy? How does that change your feeling state? Do you relax? Does your breathing become fuller? Do you fill out even further into the area behind you, as if settling into a bean-bag chair? Or include your left side more? Or expand your chest?

When you are ready, bring into your mind the person around whom you'd like to protect yourself. Stay in this great, sparkling bubble while you imagine your difficult person in front of you. Keep your feet. Keep breathing! Notice how it feels to be in front of this person while in the golden bubble. How might outcomes change, because your way of being is different from your usual stance with them? Even a tiny bit of alteration in your stance will make a big shift in future interactions, without their necessarily being aware of anything. They may respond less arbitrarily or more openly. They may simply be puzzled, not able to put their finger on what's different. Is it your hair? Even if they don't, you will not feel as vulnerable to their behavior. You'll see that they are outside the bubble, not invading your private space and affecting your well-being. You will more easily be able to watch them acting out and simply think to yourself, "Wow, what a strange and painful way they've chosen to go through life."

Golden Roses

When feeling on edge around others, people tense the back of their neck and hunch their shoulders. It's an animal thing to want to protect your spine and neck. As well, the way that energy enters the fifth chakra—self-expression—at the base of the neck, and the sixth chakra—psychic energy and intuition—is at the base of the occipital region. So people feel vulnerable to invasion there energetically as well.

This is a very important area to protect by expanding the energy rather than doing the shoulder-hunching thing. Imagine a bouquet of golden roses facing outward behind your neck. The benefit of roses as an image is that it helps you to soften there. See it glow, and know that that sensitive area is being protected.

Imagine talking to your difficult person with this glow going on behind your head (or when you're sitting on a bus or in a theater with wise-acres behind you). See how it changes your perception of the interaction.

Examples: What did you notice? Natalie said of her manipulative and belittling mother-in-law, "It feels good! I'm smiling even when imagining her mannerisms. It's fun to be in this standpoint. I saw the bubble as crystals, and suddenly I felt really protected and was having fun—the opposite of what's usual with her. This doesn't make sense! But you can have all the fun you want when you're freed from the interaction you expect. I'm imagining dancing with these crystals all around me and not being impacted by this very difficult person at all."

Ned said that he felt light and humorous. "There was a blue and light energy coming out from me, then I began bouncing like a ball around this person. Not heavy and dire and as if I can't move."

Kendra had felt undermined by her ex-boyfriend whenever they had contact. "I'd dread talking to him. I'd draw into myself. Now I don't feel dread. Now I feel totally free of the obligation to react. I can choose what *I* want to do in the circumstance."

Jane brought up an interesting type of situation. Challenging types for her are those sugary-sweet people who seem too nice to be true (which is accurate, because these people have major control issues.

Everything has to be the way they want, so that they don't have to face any uncomfortable feelings. If things aren't exactly the way they want, they lash out, sweetly of course, so sometimes it's hard to know you've been sliced.) Many people are taken in by the surface sweetness and can't see the controlling nature beneath the sugar-coating. So, while others are extolling their virtues, Jane feels their falsehood.

Can you use these same protective strategies in situations like these? Yes. You can choose to define the moment and take charge of the interaction by moving your energy to a positive, centered response, by not losing your perspective in reaction to their behavior. Dealing with them by enhancing and enlightening your energy takes care of you, no matter what is going on, and you empower yourself. You don't lose your right to move on your own behalf. You're not making someone else bad or wrong, even if you may need to say no or set a limit in order to take care of yourself and stay inside your energy.

White Lotus

Breathe, ground, center. Fill with your energy. Then, see or feel yourself sitting in the center of a large, white lotus blossom of energy. Feel the petals curling up, the energy of the flower creating a force-field around you. Within the White Lotus, you can spread out. Feel how your energy responds to being in the center of this flower.

If someone aims negative energy at you, don't get sucked into being hypervigilant, focusing too much on the problem person. Know that the flower is there and move your attention back into your center. Simply beam while sitting in your lotus, or use the energy of the lotus to send positive energy toward them, your 'yes' to counter their 'no,' your radiating to counter their constricting. Even if they seem to want to overpower your rights with their agenda, you can say yes toward them and sit within the radiance of the lotus. You can acknowledge their separate existence, and their right to be on this earth. As you expand outward with your 'yes,' your insistence on higher-amplitude energy, an affirming energy pervades the interaction, and their power trip will often dissipate. Most people simply want to be recognized anyway, so you are defusing the situation by giving them what their vulnerable self wants, rather than reacting to their outward tough-guy, defensive act. It does require not going to 'no' in yourself, not contracting. As Bob said, "Where I shut down my energy with my problem person, that's where I've given my energy away." You're not saying yes to their power trip. You're saying yes to the personhood, and if you can, to their soul or being. Most importantly, you are saying 'yes' to yourself, to your right to maintain your equanimity and power and to a connected and whole sense of your own field.

Have the intention that the White Lotus stay even when you're not attending to it. Doing so gels it, makes it set in position to protect you. Feel freer, more empowered in this protected, safe space. Leave others outside the petals where they belong.

Weeks later, the results still held. Bob talked of keeping his intention to expand his energy, rather than contracting when the power-trip person came toward him. Kendra taught the Golden Bubble exercise to her sister, who was dealing with a nasty manager in her corporation. Kendra also taught it to her counseling client who had an abusive ex-husband. Rather than collapsing and being easily swayed by the ex-husband, her client was able to stay more present within herself, to assert herself and protect her kids much better. She felt stronger and more empowered.

Matilda really got how it changed her inside experience. "Every cell tingled and I was happy and excited. I felt intensely energized at the protection and potential it infers. I feel I can be more comfortable with the creativity of uncertainty rather than feeling exposed and vulnerable."

When Natalie decorded and strengthened her aura's protective ability, she felt stronger and more protected. Her toxic mother-in-law seemed much less threatening. Natalie could envisage laughing to herself when Nirgah wigged out. Then she said, "The energy around my pregnancy suddenly seems stronger!" The cathected energy had been rededicated to work that supported her body's important work.

Later, Natalie was surprised when she had a conversation with Nirgah that was genial. When you change your own energy, the energy around you changes. Nirgah didn't know that Natalie had worked on her energy dynamics, and it didn't matter. Natalie said it this way, "My new knowledge of self-protection gave me other ways of looking at what was going on with her, and so I said to myself, 'I'm not going to let you overwhelm me anymore.' It makes such a difference seeing that there are options, looking at it from the viewpoint of energy, and then learning that there are things that I can do, when before I felt helpless and done-to by this hostile woman."

Important Note: You now have a new memory from doing these exercises. Your body will not forget. You can access it, experiment with it, build on it. Remember brain plasticity? You *can* change your reactions. Notice any new reaction in touchy situations. Even if the circumstance seems the same, if you feel differently, the outcome will shift.

If it really protected you to tighten and react defensively, well hey, go for it. But if it only cuts you off from yourself and allows you much less energy and creativity at your disposal, then it doesn't do you any good to constrict. Even if it seems rash, it's worth a try expanding into all of your energy field in the way you want to be—calm, empowered, radiant. Wow. That will attract the kind of energy you really want!

Strong boundaries, no limits!

—Douglas Brooks, yoga teacher and professor of religion,
University of Rochester

The Right to Say No: 15
boundaries are vital

GWYNETH HAD BEEN so eager to be loved that she was easy to take advantage of. Sure, her sister paid plenty of attention to her when she became a teenager—she called on Gwyn to provide free childcare for her nieces and nephews. Gwyn babysat after school and at least an entire day every weekend.

Lawrence had tried to appease his abusive older brother, hoping to avoid being violated. Later in life, that pattern, along with his natural concern about others' feelings, led to his overloading himself with projects and requests. He felt obligated to everyone, so he felt overwhelmed at church, at home, and at work.

What Tani found that she did, instead of investing in her own life, was unconsciously to assume that she had to shoulder all the responsibility in any situation, and that she had to be hypervigilant to help others. Now, it's great to be thoughtful and helpful, but Tani took it too far. This was a sign of having been damaged in her sense of self by having a narcissistic father and a borderline mother. Often she exhausted herself by taking on too much. She didn't ask for help. Sometimes she even got herself into dangerous situations or hurt herself by jumping in to be helpful too fast, without looking. What she did not do was consider herself—her safety, her wellbeing, whether some activity would be good or bad for her. In her intense concern about what others thought, she left herself out of the picture.

The destruction of one's sense of physical integrity and safety is one of the most painful aspects of trauma. It is no coincidence that many folks with unresolved hurt often have boundary issues in many areas of their lives, not knowing what to put up with and when to put their foot down. They find themselves reacting to what comes at them and do not know how to stick up for themselves, define their own space and goals, or set limits with others.

Growing up with a narcissistic or borderline parent will also lead to having a very distorted sense of how much room one has a right to take up, and to believing one doesn't have a right to stick up for oneself or consider one's needs or best interests.

It is vital to our process of uncovering and building the joy in our lives that we recognize our right to have clear boundaries and to maintain them. It is our responsibility to do those things that promote our lives and our well-being. Ultimately, we each must depend upon ourselves to keep us safe and to honor our right to be. Recovering this ability to set limits and boundaries is a crucial step in rebuilding a sense of wholeness and a healthy entitlement to act on our own behalf and to expect positive outcomes. In order to establish our own stance, it is necessary to have a positive sense of ourselves and actively to support it (more about that in the next chapter).

If your boundaries have been violated or compromised, over and over, you may not realize that you have the right to say no. If you were coerced into going against yourself and were required to act as if it was acceptable, or even enjoyable, then as well as living through the abuse itself, you have had a triple whammy to your sense of autonomy. The idea of your right to protect, support, and enhance yourself may seem foreign. This leads to severe existential crises.

Many people come to me because they have an illness, pain, or upsetting thought patterns as a result of absorbing some energy that was not theirs. Other people's issues affect them without their being aware of it. They

THE RIGHT TO SAY NO

often feel woozy or jumbled, because the mechanisms by which they define and locate themselves have been trashed, tossed about by things going on around them, seasick. They have lost their grounding and their center, and their energy has been sapped. Their immune system has taken a hit. (Nothing undermines it more than depleting your life force by going against yourself.)

They often argue against their healthy, self-honoring thoughts, trying to get themselves to go along with someone else's agenda. Next thing they know, they're being taken advantage of, ignoring their needs, sacrificing too much, and feeling disempowered. They reenact old, maladaptive beliefs and react to current events as replications of painful situations in the past.

The importance of saying no

As two-year-olds so ably show us, before we can identify what we want, we must first learn that we can say no. We then learn to identify what we do not want. We must first eliminate the non-contenders to make enough room to perceive the distinctions between possibilities. Only then can we say yes to something.

We enhance our wellbeing, raise our energy levels, and view life positively when we stick up for ourselves. We also trust ourselves more and become our own best friend. More possibilities open up, and obstacles in the way of what we want are lowered. It's easier to get where we want to go when we stop getting side-tracked by what doesn't work for us. Therein lies the skill of prioritizing, which is only possible when we clarify the noes and yesses.

It is also better for others when we say no. They know where we stand, and it feels less burdensome to them if we make it clear that we take care of ourselves. Have you ever been around a person who will not express an opinion? All the work of directing conversation and making decisions falls on you. My mother-in-law was like that. She "didn't want to be a bother," so she in fact took up the lion's share of the emotional energy in any event, as everyone tried to figure out what would be okay with her. Rather than being polite, she was abdicating responsibility for herself and was burdening others.

So often we are worried about hurting others' feelings by having a firm stance, but in the long run, it is much cleaner, and therefore emotionally less taxing, to have things be clear.

Boundaries help you stay centered and not get riled or thrown off so easily, know what your limits are and not let others step on you, or not leap to help others without thinking. Your immune system gets a boost every time you support yourself.

If you learn that you can protect yourself effectively, then you'll feel safer letting more good stuff in. The chapter on beliefs is vital, because it is necessary to develop and strengthen life-affirming core beliefs that support your sovereignty and your optimism. Self-defeating beliefs hold incorrect definitions, and therefore inaccurate ideas of boundaries, in place. Those beliefs are the justification for inadvertently violating your own boundaries. As you get better at valuing yourself, at being present with yourself and your experience, your self-awareness grows, and your sense of the natural boundaries will also. You will find yourself being clear about realistic boundaries— both yours and those of other people. Your interactions may improve, if you have been unclear about other people's boundaries.

Getting better at saying no

More than anything, Connie wanted to feel safe again. She wanted to be able to assume that people would respect her rights. The first struggle for her was simply to move protectively, rather than freezing and sobbing. Racing away from men who looked like the attacker, jumping into the street, rather than staying on the sidewalk—these were growth steps for her in the beginning. Later, she progressed to speaking protectively—saying no—instead of using her entire body to react to fears of danger. Giving herself permission to say no to strangers took some time, but it marked her learning to put herself before what others thought about her.

Giving herself permission to say no then led to Connie's setting appropriate limits. While it became easier over time, with each new step, Connie had to wrestle with the psychological effects of having had her sense of sovereignty ruptured so badly. She had to work to know she had the right to feel autonomous—to feel her psychological boundaries as whole. Each time she worked to return to a sense of healthy entitlement within her own space helped her build an awareness of healthy boundaries and self-care. Asserting herself at work, clarifying what didn't sit right with her in social situations, being more aware when she became tired or when it was time to stop some activity, at what distance to interact with different sorts of people, how she wanted to handle altercations, or when it was time to call it quits—she wrestled with the concept and actuality in all sorts of situations, and this helped her develop a sense of her own autonomy.

Lawrence was able to face the actuality that he had been tortured by his brother and decord from him. When he allowed his shock, hurt, and betrayal to surface, he realized the connection between his past and his lifelong pattern of trying to please people. It took longer for him to become comfortable with the idea that he had the right to limit his obligations and save some energy for himself. As he experimented with saying no (which was scary at first), he found that he did a better job at work and was actually more available emotionally, not less.

While he'd always done enjoyable things, it was only when he focused on setting boundaries and crafting his life that he started enjoying himself and seeing his life as his own creation. "It's amazing, but now I have this feeling that living is fun. Who'd have thought that doing a bit less would lead to enjoying myself more?"

As it is with children, the best way to train yourself to be more self-reliant is to honor yourself as an individual who has the right to be treated respectfully, even though you're a work in progress (welcome to life!) when you make mistakes or even screw up royally.

Feeling you have the right to draw the line comes from having a clear center and from being grounded. It comes when you are firm about supporting yourself and knowing your value.

The skills discussed in this book will help you stick up for yourself. Having more understanding and compassion for what you went through, and learning more what boundaries are about, will certainly go a long way. Releasing pent-up emotions and old beliefs will allow you to set and affirm healthy limits.

Other chapters will be related to the issue of boundaries as well. As you read about perceiving the optimistic interpretations of events; as you turn toward the kindness in people's responses rather than anticipating hostility; as you practice uncovering and building joy; your awareness of healthy boundaries will strengthen.

But first you must know that you not only have the right to say no, you have the obligation. It's your responsibility to take care of yourself.

Using our energy dynamics gives us many more options for improving our experience. For example, I tend to lose some aspect of my boundaries when in doctors' offices. Even if I come across as an adult, I feel like a vulnerable child. I noticed it in a recent eye exam. Maybe because I'd been working on this chapter I realized that I could toughen up my boundary—consciously thicken it—in order to remember to center, so I didn't slide into wanting mothering from my doctor. I did so and found that I immediately felt stronger. I had said no to my habit of becoming a bit needy in healthcare offices. I said yes to my power to change my energetic structure and feel like the adult I was.

How do you learn to support your boundaries?

What's your Bottom Line?
Violating your boundaries makes you give up things that you really shouldn't—that are necessary for your own well-being, whether they are morals or your right not to give your energy away. Below your bottom line are those values and needs that are necessary for your integrity to be maintained, your sense of your own autonomy, your health, and safety. These are not negotiable. They are not ones that on which you can slide with impunity. If you violate one of them, there are repercussions, because you have violated your true self.

It is important to clarify where your bottom line is. Stealing probably is below your line, or allowing your father-in-law to badmouth your children, or being treated with contempt. Above your bottom line are the extra energy you have to devote to others, events or opinions that are not crucial to you, someone's thoughtless comment that you let slide when they are having a bad day.

To identify the location of your bottom line, first (as always) ground and center. Then, answer these questions to help clarify your values, desires, and vision for your life, as well as those items that for you are egregious:

- What is below your bottom line, that if you do it, you feel you've violated or drained yourself? What is not okay with you?
- What do you *not* want to put up with from others?
- In your living situation?
- In your work?
- What drags down your energy?
- What keeps you from your goals?
- What makes you turn against yourself?
- What leads to your getting sick/migraines/too tired/your back going out?
- What leads to your thinking that it's no use, or to that you'll just have to put up with slogging day-to-day?

Who are you? The next step is to find out what defines you:

- What matters to you most?
- How do you want to be treated?
- How do you want to treat others?
- What do you want to exemplify, to bring into the world?
- What do you want your life to be about?
- When you're at your eighty-fifth birthday party, what do you want to be happy that you accomplished?
- What do you want others to say about you at your party?

- How and where do you want to live? Where? With whom? And in what situation?
- What do you really want?
- Emotionally, spiritually, intellectually
- Physically, financially
- What are your dreams?
- If you could do, be, or have anything, what would it be?

What works against you? Then, think about situations in which it's hard to stick up for yourself:

- What happens in your body? What sensations do you have?
- And what thoughts? What do you tell yourself?
- Do you lose sight of yourself, because you're so focused on what else is happening?
- Do you lose a sense of your rights?
- Where does your attention go?

Build your sense of self: Then think about these questions and write at least one answer for each situation that you identified:

- What values are important to you in this type of situation?
- How does the situation step on those values?
- What is okay for you, and what is clearly not okay?
- What do you need to become more clear about?
- What do you want to stand for?
- What limits do you want to place?
- What will you do to put that in place more firmly?
- How will you practice?
- What will you say?
- To whom?
- How will you assess whether it worked?

Rules about boundaries

- One way of hiding our vulnerabilities from ourselves is to violate our own boundaries, acting tough and hyper or a bit too giving, as if we are bigger and more armored than we are. Do not think you must say yes to prove something. The most important thing which you want proved is that you are your own best ally.

- It is your responsibility to take care of yourself by sticking up for yourself and insisting on being treated with respect. For now, err on the side of caution. Do not divulge things that make you feel emotional or shaky about yourself to people you do not know well, or especially to those who have already proved that they do not have your best interests at heart. Keep your inner processes private until you know whether someone is a good recipient and is also in a place to hear something that's sensitive for you.

- Treating yourself badly only attracts abusers. Valuing yourself highly gives others the message that they must treat you well also. It attracts healthy people who want to relate to you. Being picky increases your chance of getting what you want. Have compassion for slip-ups. Be gentle and persevering. Support your own learning by giving yourself a chance to learn over time.

- Grounding and centering are the major tools for helping you have, grow, and maintain healthy boundaries. The more you practice, the more your awareness will develop. The more you practice other skills in the book, the more you will increase your ability to use your awareness to sense where your extended energy is, and then you'll be clear where your boundaries need to be.

Setting limits helped Lawrence's performance at work tremendously, for now he was committed to giving himself time to see where he was and what was important. Before, he rushed, became overwhelmed, and lost his grip on his workload. Now, he accepted that he couldn't do everything and took some tasks off his plate by getting better at delegating. Then he addressed his problems managing others. Before, his team had been in dire straits, because he could not bring himself to criticize anyone or make demands. His team felt undirected and resentful and took to saying no to requests. These were the wrong kinds of "no!" As Lawrence addressed his fears and his need to appease, he saw that he was letting down the team by making excuses for them. The hardest obstacle for him was to risk "hurting" staff by holding them accountable, setting expectations, and giving constructive, pointed feedback. Within six months, his department more than doubled their output and calmly managed the successful completion of vital projects.

One more thought: Boundaries do not keep out loving people. They define where you stand and what you honor.

Part V

Moving On: Creating the Life
You Really Want Requires
Changing Your Outlook

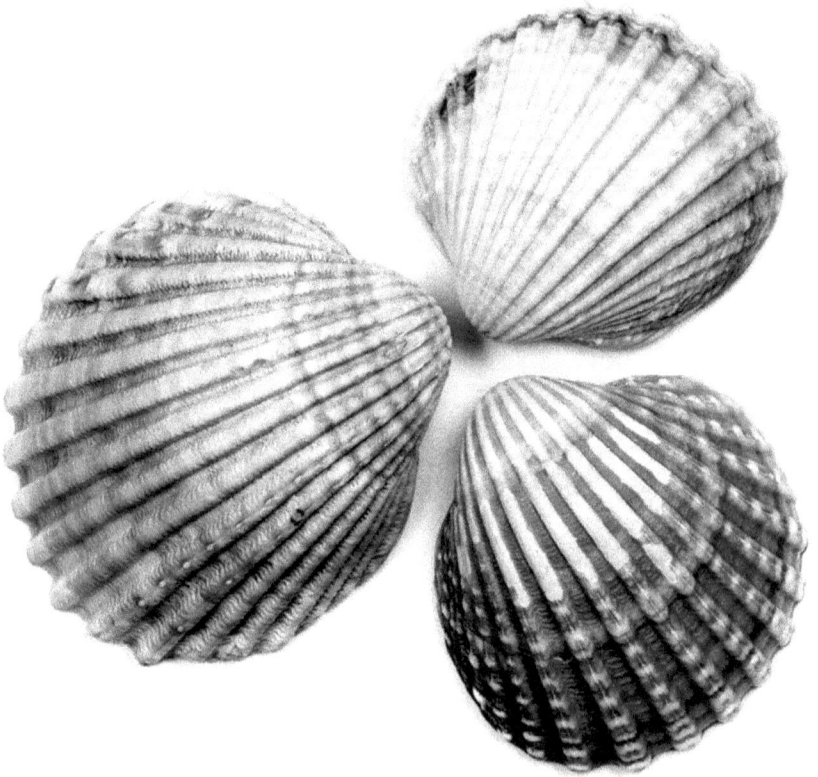

What you do for yourself—any gesture of kindness, any gesture of gentleness, any gesture of honesty and clear seeing toward yourself—will affect how you experience your world. In fact, it will transform how you experience the world. What you do for yourself, you're doing for others, and what you do for others, you're doing for yourself.

—Pema Chodron

Value Your Self Highly 16

DAME JUDY DENCH, arguably one of the best actors in the world, has primarily played sure-footed women. She was being interviewed on National Public Radio to introduce her latest series, "Cranford," as I wrote the first draft of this chapter. One of the things she said of her acting career was, "Those characters are not who I am. Everything I have done has brought up such anxiety, so much anxiety."

No one is free of doubts and critical inner voices! Dame Judy was anxious because she had to wrestle with her worry about failing. Self-doubt is part of the human condition (except in psychopaths and those people who blame others for everything), and it is impossible to eradicate completely. As a great actor, Dame Judy is an example of someone who clearly knows how to deal with her anxiety and move forward.

When I was younger and struggling with my own healing, I could function well at work and with friends. I felt competent when dealing with a project or interaction. I could (nervously) stand up in a courtroom and contest a ticket. I could speak in public, with preparation. But I did not have a sense that it was *my* life. I was caught in old beliefs and injunctions from my upbringing that said that I didn't have the right to live for myself, that I had to focus on what others thought and wanted

281

and make them not be mad. I unconsciously assigned myself the position of person-who-has-to-fix-it-if-anything-goes-wrong. I second-guessed myself constantly. I could find myself sweeping the kitchen floor while thinking that really, it was not the best use of my time, I should be writing an article, or cleaning the bathroom, or researching a concept. I'd utilize my gifts for clients or friends, but not for me.

Why wasn't I able to value my strengths, even while I was helping others heal from pain and embrace bright futures? What does it take to build and maintain a sense of self that supports us through anxiety, opposition, and stressful situations?

As we saw in the BWITSY chapter, releasing hurt makes change much easier, although realistically we cannot erase all pain forever. It never goes away entirely. And really, it needs to be there, at least as a distant whisper, to remind us what we have learned. If it were gone entirely, we might try to be someone we are not, someone who never had to work through the things we have, those things that led to some of our most important qualities, such as compassion, understanding, commitment, caring, dedication. We are no longer the people we were before those traumatic events. True healing is marked by our having accepted and integrated the hurtful memories into the narrative of our lives, and then by our building a freer and fuller sense of ourselves. It is important to see that we are grander, deeper, stronger, softer (i.e. less armored), more compassionate, concerned, and empathic, because of what we have gone through. Accepting the lessons and the strengths that we developed is a clear indication that we have come to terms with the past.

Even when we have done the work of facing painful feelings and restructuring self-defeating beliefs, many of us continue the habit of questioning ourselves unnecessarily or turning against ourselves when something goes wrong. Self-doubt is a habit that no longer serves a protective purpose. It only undermines our efforts to build self-assurance and a new outlook by uncentering us and thus disorganizing our sense of ourselves. We must see that self-criticism and shame are not based on the reality of who we are but rather are attempts to control our pain without dealing with it directly.

If our old sense of self is based on criticism and self-hatred, we must be emphatic in treating ourselves positively in order to build a stance based on a realistic appreciation of our worth. It isn't overcompensation. It simply feels that way if we've had a taboo against being on our own team.

Three things turn the tide

Here's what turns us from a life based on self-criticism, hurt, or disappointment to one of joy and fulfillment:

1) Giving feelings the time they need to be acknowledged and to flow through, and not despairing that they will never end, simply because they are not going fast enough to assuage our impatience. When they have subsided enough (not disappeared for good—that's an unrealistic goal) we will not fear being swept away by them when they are triggered, because they are no longer overpowering and we know how to handle them. They won't run us. We'll be in the driver's seat of our lives, and then we can turn our attention elsewhere freely and grow new habits. (This we talked about in the BWITSY chapter.)

2) Turning our attention *toward* a palpable experience of self, with a rich sense of being firmly in our core and valuing what we find there. (We started building this in the Centering chapter.)

3) Building a new internal structure based on a strong belief, staunchly practiced, in our own value. This is what we are learning in this chapter.

To be life-affirming and experience-altering, centering needs to be based on a belief that we are wonderful!

When they first truly center, people are often amazed to notice that they feel grateful for what they have and who they are. As we continue to practice, this sense of a full self builds into a solid core. We then can experiment with a different response pattern, taking the stance that we are fine, good, and wonderful, and behaving in line with that conviction. This is a crucial step in uncovering joy and really changing how we feel in our lives. Developing the habit of feeling ourselves, at our core, to be valuable and good is the key to building a new personal reality.

Our center continues to strengthen over time as we stop ourselves from going down old, worn paths of self-blame, excessive apology, or excuse-making—whatever our automatic artillery is. Then we must insist on taking the stance that we are fine. We can then see what life is like when standing in our "worthy" position, noticing new options that appear—not just our old usuals.

Trancing out

To be truly centered is to be awake and aware, which brings up the subject of trancing out. Most people take mini-hideaways by staring or blanking out, a bit asleep behind the camouflage of their open eyes. It can be prompted by a dull meeting, dinner at the in-laws, or feeling despair. It happens when we feel trapped. It can seem like a safe little closet to go into when we feel buffeted by events or want to tune out extraneous noise. Teenagers are professionals at it. Anytime you are really pressed to get through to them, watch their eyes glaze over, and they're gone...off in their hiding-from-annoying-adults-place.

Lawrence wasn't even aware that he tranced out. He did it by getting distracted and then dithering while his mind went numb. He fooled himself into thinking he was wrestling with some problem. The trance state was attractive and seductive, because it was quiet. The chaos and demands ceased. "It's like a pseudo-center," he realized. "It seems to be the quietness in the midst of the noise, but it isn't really. It's like putting in earplugs so you can't hear the blaring of the TV, but it's still there yelling at you. You clamp down on your brain, so you just aren't aware of stuff."

After getting better at truly centering while in the midst of situations, he added, "Now I see that trancing out actually kept me stuck in being disorganized. Rather than finding that calm place in which I could really be aware of myself, I zoned out to get away from stress. So I didn't get any better at handling gnarly situations, and I kept feeling crappy about myself."

On top of the usual human tendency to blank out periodically, many people who have been traumatized do it to escape when feeling threatened or overwhelmed. In our bad old days it was pretty smart to protect ourselves when we did not have any other option. In the present, it is liable to get us into trouble. When we zone out, we have dissociated. We are not centered or grounded, by definition., so we can't be clear about what's going on around us and don't necessarily act in our best interest. When we trance out while interacting with certain types of people, we may swallow that other person's interpretation of events and not figure out our own. We may ask the other person to make decisions or go along with things that we haven't thought through. It is no wonder that the next thing we know, we feel disempowered. Trancing out is tantamount to giving up our ability to act on our own behalf and to protect ourselves. To value ourselves highly, we need to stay present.

In her wonderful eponymous book, Tara Brach develops the concept of "radical acceptance." She discusses the internal critic as ubiquitous. Beyond accepting ourselves though, those of us who have had our sense of self disrupted more seriously need to develop staunch and consistent self-championing.

Valuing ourselves is not just a nice idea. It is crucial in order to turn away from those deeply grooved pathways of self-doubt, second-guessing, anticipating disaster, and despair. We cannot wait for circumstances to pop self-confidence over our heads like a new sweater. We must train our minds to see ourselves as valuable and precious.

Joy is not an externally induced event, which actually is a great relief. Our joy is not dependent on events or other people. Even if it feels as though we're breaking taboos, and the wrath of all the gods will pour down on our heads for doing so, we can choose to invest in a true, positive sense of ourselves.

Turning your focus toward your good qualities connects you with your true self. Really. When you do so, you can see that self-negation is not accurate at all. It's been loaded heavily with the weight given to negative thoughts. When you see that those self-doubting voices are merely an attempt to keep you out of trouble by keeping you from taking risks, you can calm them down and begin to let your old self-image slip off your shoulders.

Getting your nervous system to help build a new sense of self

How your neurology can help your efforts is clearer if you understand the physiology of adaptation. For example, the reason that you get out of shape if you lie around on the couch is that human bodies readily adapt to changes in circumstance in order to survive. If you had to wait out the winter in a cave or a yurt, your body would reduce all internal activity to a much slower state, closer to hibernating. It accomplishes this by dismantling or reallocating quite a few synapses from action-oriented to being-on-hold, and transforming your muscles into fat as fuel storage.

This same physiological mechanism can be used to help you build a new self-definition. Your internal structure—either based on self-criticism or on self-support—builds or atrophies based on usage, just as your muscles do.

It's a miracle of being human that the more conscious awareness you bring to any system or function, the more development occurs in that area, because awareness sparks energy, and more energy can build more structure. To help that old-view-of-you atrophy, you need to champion your healthy view of yourself staunchly, even fiercely. Especially when you're in the middle of some stressful event, it takes committed effort to combat old fault-finding thoughts. Insist on seeing yourself as good and valuable by rehearsing affirming messages, even if they seem artificial at first. After a while, your self-perception will start to shift.

Own your own power

To staunchly support ourselves we must own our own power. To do so, we must first identify when and how you have given it away to others. Sometimes we may not even know what power is rightfully ours, thinking that we have to please too many people or be too good.

We may forget that it is our job to stick up for ourselves. When we don't know what power is rightfully ours, we may drain and belittle ourselves by avoiding responsibility and giving the decision-making or action-taking to others, or by trancing out, taking refuge in numbness.

We must activate our energy, come back to the present, insist on seeing ourselves in a positive light, and refuse again and again to go down those old paths that say that we can't do it, or don't deserve to get it, or might as well give up, or can't count on anyone, or (what's yours say?).

When we build a habit of being our own champion (and who better to do it, I ask you?) we can let our gifts blossom. The more we support ourselves, the more they grow. As we remove the constriction of negative thought patterns, more energy is freed up to apply to our talents, and they develop even more. We deserve to treat our gifts as precious and sacred and to do whatever is needed in order to protect and nurture them.

Being centered with a positive self-awareness allows us to relax into ourselves, giving birth to a profound peace, which in turn uncovers the joy waiting for us in our core. Returning to it, or staying with it, demands that we continue to support ourselves insistently and repeatedly. The earlier and more chronically that trauma happened in our lives, the fiercer we have to be in supporting our sense of ourselves as worthy.

As we claim our right to determine our own opinion of ourselves, the past can slip into less importance. Abuse, as well as other people's criticisms, can become more peripheral to our self-concept. Freedom does not, ultimately, have to do with our circumstances. It is in our power to keep from continuing to imbue events with the urgency or horror that have thrown us off in the past. True freedom lies in seeing that we are in charge of how we interpret events, of our attitude, and in how we choose to be within ourselves. Freedom and peace come when we do not let events, either internal or external, knock us off our center for too long. Then joy is uncovered, at first for a minute, then, with practice, for longer stretches of time.

Centering, setting boundaries with others, and taking better care of himself were the keys that led to Lawrence's learning to value himself and put his own needs higher on his priorities list. He no longer allowed his brother's abuse to govern how he perceived himself. He continued to be surprised that his department worked better, and even his home life became smoother. His fear that he'd hurt people's feelings by taking a stand turned out not to be true. It had "hurt" them worse when he wouldn't put his foot down, because he wasn't being responsible communicating, which burdened others. By acting as if they couldn't handle his limits, he also wasn't treating them as functional adults.

The benefits spiraled. As he insisted on valuing his truths, he felt more confident and relaxed, and took up his own space in the world more clearly. He looked clearer! He experienced more peaceful, joyous feelings.

Exercises for valuing yourself highly

A note about the following exercises: While you're building the pattern of viewing yourself as awesome, this is not the time to worry if you might be mistaken, if maybe you aren't perfect when you blurt out what you think, or are too timid, or disagree with someone. You have the right to practice a new skill. The world will not come to an end if, for the purposes of these exercises, you think better of yourself than you imagine you deserve. What Nelson Mandela said about relating to others applies to your relating to you: *"It never hurts to think too highly of a person. Often they behave better because of it."* Try it. It's good practice. See what happens. I'll bet that after a month, you'll relax, handle situations more gracefully because you're not in danger of seeing yourself as a bad person. Maybe you'll thereby find yourself calmer around others as well.

Once you have tried any of these exercises for a day, try it for two. Gradually work up to a week, and then to a month. Don't dwell on any lapses. It is the gentle gathering of your attention and returning to the new focus that retrains the brain.

Noticing that you have gotten off-track and then gently moving yourself back into a centered, self-affirming stance is evidence of tremendous progress! Do not play Russian roulette with your well-being. Do what you need to do to feel happy, calm, grounded, and centered in your own goodness.

Practice: For starters, just today, center and then tell yourself clearly that you are precious and valuable. Here's the mantra:

> *I am wonderful and am supported and valued by the Universe (or deity of your choice) exactly as I am.*

Old, negative thoughts may surface at first, but keep saying this one, until you can hear it and the old ones clear out. If the negative ones really argue, take it gently. You might want to modify the affirmation to:

> *I want to know that I am wonderful and am supported and valued by the Universe, exactly as I am.*

Repeat it as you walk, or bike, or swim, or iron—any repetitive motion during which your mind tends to wander. Try it while out in Nature, if possible. Keep saying it until the phrase it takes on a life of its own and repeats in your mind as your background noise. It doesn't take too long—five or ten minutes maybe. When it does, it takes the place of the automatic and unexamined negative thoughts that your mind may have as muzak—the ones that pull you down without your being aware of them. Watch how your insides respond to your muzak being consciously chosen and helpful. Breathe. Enjoy.

Practice: Maybe you know a very self-confident person (who also is a good person) who seems impervious to guilt or self-doubt. You can learn a lot by watching how they carry themselves, how they interpret events, and how they respond to difficult situations. The point is not to compare yourself with them (which is a road to perdition) whichever way the comparison goes. But, with your new awareness of your energy dynamics, can you imagine your way into their energy dynamics and feel what it feels like to be that confident? Do they feel warm and settled, and therefore not raw in the places you do? Do they slough off unkind words when you might have felt wounded? Do they reply from a sense of being fine and not impacted by others' unkindness or tactlessness? Do they see possibilities where you may only see obstacles?

If you can imagine what it is like to be inside their skin, you play with the visceral experience of confidence. How would it feel to have thicker skin or more certainty about your own value? What in your body would calm down? What would firm up? The goal is not to become that person. After all, they do not have some of the capacities that you do. They may not have your sensitivity, empathy, compassion, or insight. But it might be interesting to play with what it feels like to be more secure and self-satisfied.

Practice: When you find yourself in a difficult situation, insist on treating yourself as a good person, calm, well-functioning, and well-meaning. Insist on being on your own side throughout the altercation. Gather your sense of yourself and don't throw away or scatter your positive feelings. Choose to support yourself emotionally in a circumstance in which you would have turned on yourself. Grit your teeth and insist on being on your own side this time, even if you can't remember why it is a good idea to try it. Don't fall into self-recrimination or taking too much responsibility for the situation. We're not talking here about your turning into a raving narcissist or hothead. I'm betting that you have tilted so far the other way that it'd take a different lifetime to make you callously egotistical or oblivious to others' feelings.

Then see what happens after. Do you make different choices? Does your critical voice keep getting on your case? At first, experiment with just one instance. Then, try it in another situation.

Practice: Support your own decision-making process. Know that your decisions were based on careful thought, that they were the best ones under the circumstances, and *let them be.* Some will work out. Some may not. Difficulties are not a sign that you made a bad decision. They just happen sometimes. You made the best choice you could at the time with the information at hand.

Practice: Support your right to get tired and to make mistakes. After all, you are human. When you feel shaken or find yourself in old patterns of self-criticism, re-center. Refuse to undermine yourself by doubting your goodness. Better yet, take a break, or a nap, or even call it a day.

Practice: Stop putting up with social interactions that feel like body-blows. Just for today, do not invite being re-traumatized by putting yourself in interactions with those that you know trigger you. If that means not speaking to them today, don't. Wait until tomorrow, or until you have had more practice in maintaining a self-supportive stance. If you don't know if you are ready to interact with them, wait. You can manage a few days, and so can they. Eventually, you may choose to remove some of those people from your life. People who make you feel badly about yourself are not worth the effort and may also be abusive.

Practice: Support yourself, even if not everyone likes you. Many will value you. If some people don't like your style, that's great. It means you're not bland, vacuous, or trying to please everyone at the expense of yourself. You don't know what their personal issues are, anyway. The more you build an internal structure based on supporting yourself staunchly, the more you'll be able to stand confidently and let others move away if they need to. It's fine if they do. You then have more room for those who will be more enjoyable and healthier for you to be around.

True compassion arises from a healthy sense of self, from an awareness of who we are that honors our own capacities and fears, our own feelings and integrity, along with those of others.

—Jack Kornfield

Identify and Trust in your Strengths 17

IN HIS RESEARCH, Boris Cyrulnik, a French neuropsychiatrist and ethologist, found that the words used in speaking to oneself or to others affects outcomes of recovery. He has worked with survivors of all sorts of trauma. Women who had been attacked sexually told him that it was being told they were strong that inspired them to recover. Cyrulnik has written that others expressing too much pity or horror can escalate a survivor's pain. From the perspective of Energy Dynamics, the reason for this would be that you'd lose your grounding by being swamped by the speaker's reaction. Your horror would loom large and strengthen the ribbon-on-the-box belief that you cannot handle processing your own feelings. Being told you are strong gives your own horror perspective by having another emotional state act as 'the third point' with which to compare and thereby introduce the possibility of limiting, your pain.

Connie needed people to empathize with her trauma at first, because she did not allow it room or validity herself. But then she needed to know that others saw her as powerful and resilient, the very things she could not access in her own mind until she was reminded of her strength.

There have been plenty of movies of people hurt in accidents who only strive to recover once somebody stops pitying them and expects them to get better.

When I tried to introduce the notion to Katrina, the young woman in chapter eleven who saw herself as broken, that she was valuable and deserving, she kept tripping over her hopelessness and self-loathing. At first, growing her "Katrina-is-wonderful" sense of herself seemed as feasible as walking to Andromeda. We talked about what might be in that new stack for a bit. Then she started to get excited and said, "If I make this pile and I start looking for things I can put in it, then I find myself looking at the stuff in the "Katrina-is-broken" pile and realize that some of that stuff actually belongs in the new pile! It's been mislabeled all this time!" And that was the moment at which she started seeing her "weaknesses" as strengths and positive qualities.

Strengths and Gifts

In order to live life on your own terms, it is necessary to make your view of your inherent worth more robust by identifying and embracing your strengths and gifts. Your gifts are those characteristics that you were born with—musical genius, a photographic memory, brilliance with cake decorating, a knack for drawing horses, the physique to clean-and-jerk 450 pounds, being coordinated, a talent for making furniture out of car parts.

Strengths are more about how you operate as well as what you consider important. Many of them can be seen to have a moral quality. They are innate, in that they are part of who you are, yet they often did develop in response to experience. Chris Peterson, a renowned researcher in Positive Psychology, calls personal strengths "values in action." Examples of these include aesthetic appreciation, fairness, curiosity, spirituality, and leadership.

In his book, *Authentic Happiness*, Martin Seligman describes the difference between strengths and gifts (which he calls talents) this way: "With enough practice, persistence, good teaching, and dedication, (strengths) can take root and flourish. Talents are more innate. For the most part, you either have a talent or you don't; if you are not born with perfect pitch or the lungs of a long-distance runner, there are, sadly, severe limits on how much of them you can acquire...This is not true of love of learning or prudence or humility or optimism."

In Katrina's case, learning about her strengths excited her with possibilities that arose from seeing herself in a different light. She had spent so much time struggling with her pessimism and her self-criticism that it was no surprise that on the VIA Signature Strengths test, her lowest-scoring attribute was optimism.

One of the most powerful findings of Positive Psychology research is the finding that "faults" are reduced more effectively if people build on their strengths than if they obsess about their bad points. Katrina's optimism would improve more quickly if she believed in and built on her strengths of kindness, understanding people, enjoying being part of a group, while her attitude problems would improve, seemingly by themselves. This is because they atrophied from lack of attention or because she was taking care of their real cause, or (my favorite) they could finally be seen in a new light, maybe even as a strength or valuable characteristic. Many "faults" that we struggle against turn out to be our greatest gifts.

It helped Connie to remember that she had gone through hard times before (though not as awful as the attack). She reconnected with her bravery, redefined her scabbing-over tendency as toughness, saw self-compassion as a strength, and used them as teammates in the project of recovery.

When you become clear about your strengths and your gifts, you can fall back on them in times of difficulty. When you are trapped in some thought pattern or are re-traumatized by some present event, it is easier to return to your experience of your being whole, unharmed, and centered when you turn your attention to aspects of your being that enhance the view.

How do you find out what your gifts and strengths are?

Practice: Without editing or judging, make a list of your gifts. Are you a good dancer? Do you have a green thumb? Are you a good listener? Always know which way is north? Good at math? Do you remember phone numbers? Are you athletic? Sensitive with animals? Unafraid of heights? List at least ten positive characteristics.

Now try for twenty. Don't question them. Don't wonder if others would agree with you. Just put them down. No one else is going to see the list unless you show it to them.

List what you see as your strengths, your "values in action." Are you empathic? Curious? Do you love to learn? If you want help with this exercise, go to the website AuthenticHappiness.com. There is a free assessment test you can take called the "VIA Signature Strengths Questionnaire." Once you fill it out, you'll be sent a report listing yours in order from the ones you are strongest in on down. Your top five are called your "signature strengths." You may also take this test by looking in Seligman's book, *Authentic Happiness*. The one on-line is fun, though, because it generates the report for you, free of charge. They do not use your personal identification information at all. They do keep track of results, anonymously, for research purposes to continue to build the field of positive psychology. They want to find out what kinds of trends there are, in different countries, for example.

Muse on your five signature strengths a bit. Do they seem accurate? Do you relish them, or are you arguing with the test results?

Pick one strength which you could use to help to counter negative self-talk. If you have curiosity and love of learning as a strength, how could you use it to help you build a positive sense of yourself and of life? If you have kindness, could you aim it at yourself? If you have justice, could you question the injustice of treating yourself harshly and take a more balanced look at your virtues and abilities?

See how you can use your strengths to support your gifts. When the chips are down, it is the combined list of both strengths and gifts that you want to recite to yourself, over and over if need be. If you find yourself caught in an old, deer-in-the-headlights pattern of self-accusation, breathe, ground, center, and then *gently force yourself* to support yourself by going over the talents and strengths that make you who you are.

Using your strengths can reduce the volume of your critical voices. In one session with my own coach, I found myself in a well-worn groove, off-track from my goal, sliding into a cul-de-sac of second-guessing and over-analyzing. As she turned my focus toward my strengths, the obstructing thought-tangle just disappeared. I then was able to continue toward my goal with enthusiasm (at the same time wondering where all the angst went).

Your strengths are just as valid as your weaknesses. You have a choice as to which to highlight. What you focus on you get more of. The positive psychology research demonstrates that paying attention to your strengths increases your well-being and reduces your perceived weakness more effectively than obsessing about and trying to vanquish your problem areas.

Championing yourself will free you from the quagmire of self-recrimination and lead to your building a sense of joy in settling into your being and allowing yourself to exist as you are. Though, when you think about it, in order to settle and allow yourself to rest in yourself, you have to value yourself enough to find your own insides a worthwhile place to be.

Being inside your valued self will make it easier to reduce the weight to others' opinions, comparing yourself to others, or of being too much on-the-lookout for criticism and danger. You can turn away from that view of life and build another, as we'll see in the next chapter.

Dwell on the beauty of life. Watch the stars, and see yourself running with them.

—Marcus Aurelius

Turn toward Kindness: 18
retrain yourself to see
the good in others

BACK IN THE chapter on self-criticism I discussed how a child treated with chronic ridicule finds it impossible for him *not* to believe deep down that he deserves it. When an adult has been attacked, she tries to gain some sense of control over the fallout by constantly wondering what she did wrong. Victims of violence and abuse react by feeling terrible about themselves and believe that, in some way, they must have deserved it, or it would not have happened.

All this makes perfect sense psychologically and absolutely no sense logically. Instead of realizing that you were in a bad place at the wrong time, human nature has you certain that it was your fault. Meanwhile, the perp gets off scot free! While you hate the thought of him or her, if you are subconsciously saying to yourself, "if only I hadn't done thus and so, they wouldn't have attacked me," then you are not seeing them as responsible for their actions. And, that time working on what is wrong with you and what you need to do next time does nothing to process and release painful incidents which have already occurred.

While we obsess on our behavior in trying to stave off future danger, we are also cementing in ourselves a view of the world as too threatening. Everything seems to have the potential of danger. Besides people who remind us of abusers, we may, especially those of us abused as children, anticipate ridicule or attack from a wide variety of people. We see malicious intent more often that it occurs and interpret incidents as more threatening or critical than they are. It becomes very difficult to see the truth about people or to realize that they have their own preoccupations and motives, or that they may simply be ignorant, having a bad day, or wrapped up in their own worries. The world looks way too dangerous, for we see hostility everywhere. And we miss out on the very things we want—to feel safe and relaxed, accepted and appreciated.

It is useful in crises to be quick to respond to danger. But when we are chronically hypervigilant, we have much less chance of accurately assessing actual crises. Indeed, our adrenal systems get so tired of generating stress hormones, and our hearts and muscles and nervous systems become so overloaded and exhausted, that if a true crisis were to occur, we would respond more slowly and poorly than if our systems had been relaxed when the crisis occurred.

Once when having a session with a healer, my body relived childhood experiences with my hostile and demeaning mother. I felt in my body how my habitual hypervigilance was a fear of missing a possible attack. I felt how she had drawn me to her when she wanted something. Then, if I got close, hoping for some motherly warmth, she'd attack with some vicious word or deed. I felt all the tightness, hurt, and fear that I did as a child.

In this session, I saw that my buried certainty that I was despicable (which I'd spent years trying to improve myself enough to finally vanquish) was itself a cover-up. What became clear that day was that, under the very good distraction of feeling unacceptable was the deeper reality, which was that I had felt hated. Big difference. Feeling hated by my parents, rather than to blame because I was toxic, was a truth which would have been impossible for me to face as a small child. Finally I could see that all my self-doubt had been designed to protect me from feeling despised. It was a huge change to face directly that I had felt hated for all those years.

At that moment in the session, I suddenly felt as if I were a small child being pressed into a huge shoulder covered with fluttering, white garments. I became aware of being held by an angel, seven or eight feet tall. The angel said to me, "*Turn away from the hatred.*" In the moment that I saw the hatred for what it was, I was shown that I had another option. The angel continued speaking quietly to keep my attention until I was succeeded in turning away from being mesmerized by the hatred embodied in my parents, and toward whatever was in her direction.

"*That's right*," she said. "*Turn toward kindness*" as I looked over her shoulder into a view that did not hold recrimination or attack. Pressed into her shoulder, I felt a world that was based on kindness and love, rather on hypervigilance, fear, and attack. She was suggesting that I not wrestle with feeling hated, now that I'd faced what was at the bottom of my self-criticism pattern, because that would just catch me in it again. Rather, I needed to know the truth and right away turn toward the love that was being offered elsewhere in the world.

This is the next task that we need to practice consciously: turning our focus to seeing the kindness in the world and in people. We need gently to insist on seeing them as warm and well-meaning, where before we may have been sure most were critical or rejecting. Rather that assuming that they are selfish or have dangerous opinions, we need to give people the benefit of the doubt. Then it's more possible to see that they are sometimes ignorant or self-absorbed, rather than malicious.

We need to make sure we are not assuming that everyone is like the people who hurt us. If we find ourselves assuming the worst in people, it is a sign that we haven't finished our work with those from our past. We want to make sure that we see people now as they really are, so that we do not miss the beauty, kindness, and caring that are around us. We do not want to hold ourselves in the world-that-was.

Practice: In Eastern traditions, one of the major hooks that keeps us on the wheel of *samsara* (the cycle of birth and death and rebirth, continuing to struggle with worldly pain and pleasure, dominance or helplessness), is that our attention is grabbed by horror, anger, and fear. We release karma and free ourselves once we have worked through old pain and change our experience of the world.

This exercise can revolutionize your perceptions. Use it as an exercise in focusing your attention. Practice noticing and recognizing kindness wherever you see it. Make it up. Ascribe benign motives to people. Choose to their actions from a different perspective. The more you imagine kindness, the more you will see it, and the more you will influence interactions so that they are more positive, through the effect of your attention. Your world will gradually become more pleasant, and your adrenal glands will thank you for it.

Practice: Turning toward kindness also refers to turning to the kindness within ourselves, so that we identify more and more with the positive, the strong, and the valuable within us. It reminds us that our fear, our reactive anger, our tension, are not all of who we are. The more we turn toward kindness in ourselves, the more also we manifest our strengths and respond positively to others. That in turn leads to others being more open and warm towards us. And there we have developed a positive feedback loop!

Practice: Turn toward kindness in your voice. Spend fifteen minutes, then an hour, and two, then a day really watching your tone. Make it softer, calmer, gentler, more even. Or if you tend to hide overly much, make your voice firmer. Drop the note at the end of each sentence, rather than sounding as if you're asking a question. Especially watch when you are riled up by your children, or by some guy at work. Try responding in an even, warm tone and see how it affects the outcome, as well as how you feel afterward.

Caveat: Turning toward kindness clearly does not mean that you should put yourself in harm's way with people who continue to be hostile or belittling. Remember that the angel first said to turn away from hatred. Until you do, you cannot see the kindness. Your eyes will be filled with the old view and with your efforts to combat it. Make sure that turning toward kindness starts with turning away from those who insist on hurting you or defining you negatively. If you have tried to work things out with someone for years, chances are that you have done enough. It ties you into that person's psychological defenses to keep engaging in the same pattern, so stop trying to get through to them, if they do not want to change. Notice that you may be holding your life back by engaging in the old habit of wrestling with them rather than risking a new focus.

We can bring it into being the reality we want to move into by practicing, building it through repetition. Turning away from hatred may lead to feelings of guilt, loss, or danger. You will be breaking some big rules if you do not go along with the old dictates. Release the old situation, and the people, anyway. Let them go and turn to something else. It does not necessarily mean that you will never speak to that person again. But, most likely, your contact will change and become healthier for you.

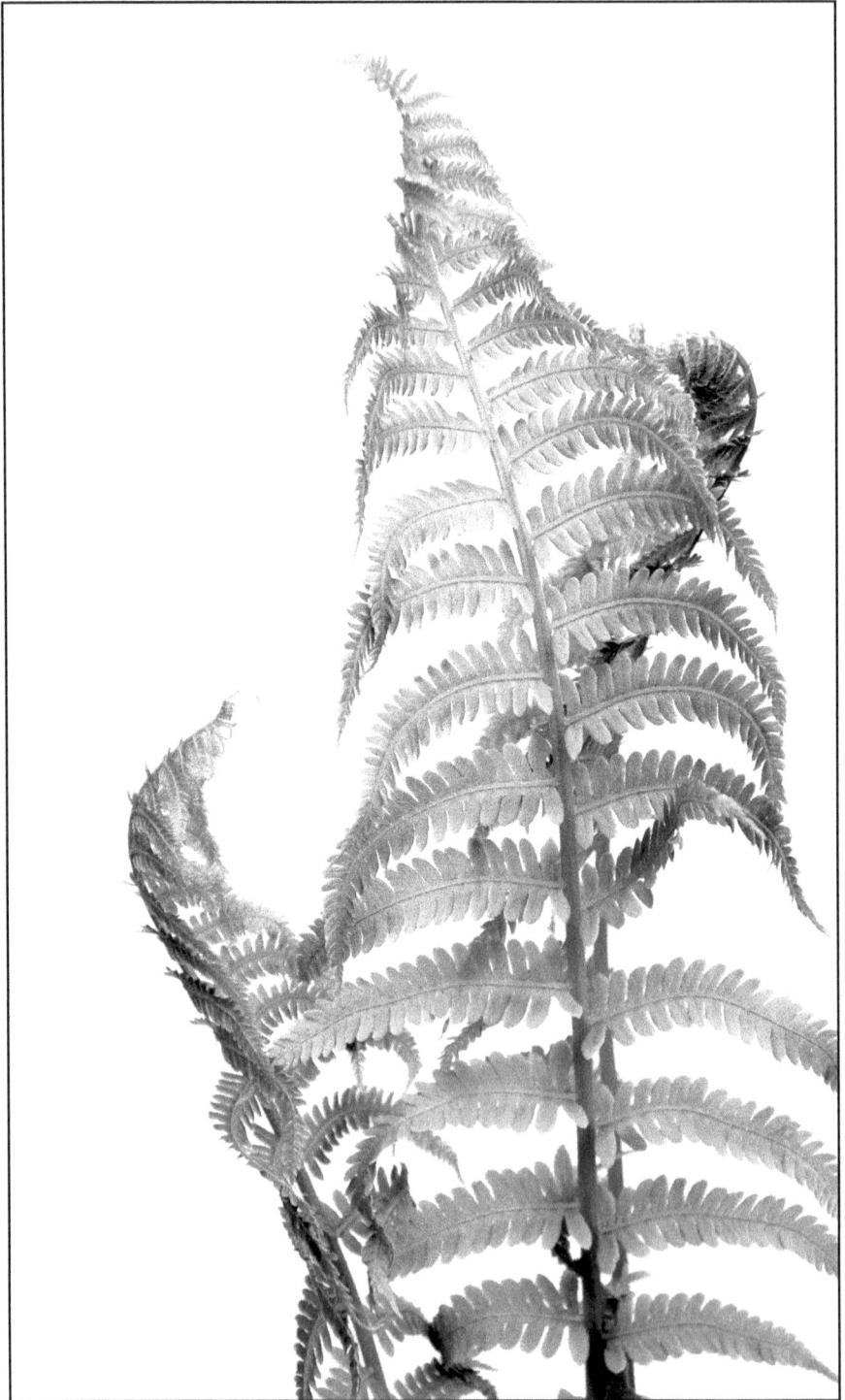

To be hopeful in bad times is not foolishly romantic. It is based on the fact that human history is a history not only of cruelty, but also of compassion, sacrifice, courage, kindness.

What we choose to emphasize in this complex history will determine our lives…To live now as we think human beings should live, in defiance of all that is bad around us, is itself a marvelous victory.

—Howard Zinn

Interpret Events in a Positive Light: 19 how you respond to circumstances changes the way you feel about life

GWYNETH HAD A new boyfriend, Pablo. "I'm trying to do this one differently. I'm trying to take care of myself. This is a much more equal relationship than ones I've had. I speak up; he is concerned about my feelings. But when we spend the weekend together, he goes off by himself at least part of the time. I don't get it. I figure, when we have time to spend together, we should be together. I feel like I'm going out of my way to be with him, but he's not doing the same for me. I can't stop feeling alone and unwanted."

Before we discovered that it is possible to change our approach to life, our unresolved emotions and protective patterns muffled us from an accurate awareness of the present. Our view was occluded by the distorted lens of our old beliefs, which only let us see pain. Only those perceptions which supported our old assumptions were allowed in, so we missed anything that would provide a new perspective. We were steering with the rear-view mirror, so the world kept looking unsafe, we still felt alone, and our protective but maladaptive beliefs seemed depressingly and permanently accurate. If we were hyper-vigilant to boot, we perceived danger more often and in larger amounts than events may actually have warranted.

And then there was that effect on our morale of neural bunching. Once triggered, the litany of similar unhappy memories just seemed to be proof that life sucks. We doomed ourselves to the view that life is as awful as we decided it was *during our weakest, most shattered periods.*

Why continue to give those times so much voting power? In their sway, we inadvertently shut off any possibility of a new life, of change, of release. We missed opportunities, alternate paths, and the chances to relax and enjoy ourselves that appear every day.

Cynics often say that they are more realistic than are perky people, or even those calm and abiding types. Yet, a negative view of reality is not any more realistic than is a positive one. There are many examples of people in similar, difficult circumstances whose experiences and outcomes are radically different depending on their outlook. The reason why the-glass-half-empty metaphor is so prevalent in the media lately is that researchers are finding out that pessimistic people have worse prognoses in health crises, come up with fewer ideas in business, take longer to recover from stresses, and on and on. "Happy people almost always come out on top (of research studies comparing them in varied situations with unhappy people)...They are more successful at school and at work; they have better relationships with other people; and they even live longer....In research...positive psychologists have shown that the experience of positive emotions can actually pay intellectual benefits...happy people are more flexible and creative." (*Peterson, 2006*)

If we build new neural pathways by noticing other aspects of events, we can change our experience of life. Yes, sometimes there is danger. We cannot control everything that happens. We really only have power over our perception of events, our attitude, and how we respond. Yet, that is enough to change our lives for the better. Rather than adding suffering to the inevitable pains that occur in every life, we can focus on meanings that increase our resilience, hope, and faith in life. And changing our attitude and interpretations does open the door for more opportunities.

In the chapter on intention, we looked at the power of focusing our attention in order to manifest what we wanted, whether it was an object or an awareness of some new energy dynamic. In order to uncover and nourish joy, we need to learn to turn our attention away from those old, over-used tapes and focus on perceptions that support the cultivation of a more joyful existence and have the added advantage of being just as true (if not more true) as the negative ones.

Gwyneth's old belief that she had to do everything for others or they would not want her had hidden under it one that said that people never would want her at all—only what she did for them. These beliefs were triggered by Pablo's behavior. But he wasn't being uncaring. He recognized that, even when he loved someone, he sometimes needed a little time alone. It's okay to be tired and rest, even from togetherness.

When Gwyneth learned to look at events positively, she realized that he was simply better at taking care of himself than she was. Seeing it in that light actually helped her take better care of herself. She'd been enjoying time to herself when she was alone. Now she could learn to re-center in herself when with someone else. She started to develop more autonomy in her relationships.

Changing your internal commentary, and thereby your attitude, is the most powerful way to change your experience of life. If you have done the work of resolving hurt and releasing obstructive beliefs and patterns, then you will be able to change the way you perceive what goes on around you. There are several ways to develop this as a skill.

If your habitual viewpoint undercuts your efforts to experience life as you want, make a game of looking for positive aspects of everyday occurrences. It takes practice and rehearsal to perceive things differently. So how can you find and incorporate these positive interpretations?

What follows are the gratitude and three-good-things exercises from positive psychology and then some others that draw from several disciplines. Try them to help develop stronger optimism muscles.

A Positive View of Events

♠ First, catch yourself when you are convinced that the melee in front of you is the same, old, same-old, and *pause.* Notice what you are saying to yourself about the situation. If it is raining, does this "always happen when you need to get something done?" If the kids are crabby, are they "ungrateful" or "too much for you" or "impossible?" If your boss wants it done yesterday, is she an "unreasonable pain in the neck?" or "wrecking your week?" Catch the behind-the-scenes comments that pop into your mind. Notice the flavor they give circumstances. See, also, how they reinstate your old negative beliefs and undermine your establishing new ones.

♠ Then, breathe and ground yourself, turning your attention away from the automatic comments.

♠ Focus on your center. Move to the hub, rather than being flung around in the spokes. Often your notions of your failures, including any failure to be on top of external events, are erroneous anyway. Who labelled you a failure, anyway? They likely had their own troubles or agenda, and were not focusing your best interests.

♠ Imagine yourself in the stance of knowing that you are fine and safe, that there is plenty of time, and that things do not have to happen right away for you to be successful and get things done.

♠ In the situation now, look beyond your first impression. What optimistic or pleasant meanings could there be in what happened? What benign interpretation could you make about others' motives? Chances are, many beneficial factors are present. Use your courage, curiosity, or critical thinking to find a positive interpretation of events. Give

others the benefit of the doubt. See what optimists would see. If your wife was grumpy this morning, rather than seeing her as impossible to get along with, say to yourself that she didn't sleep well, and that everyone has bad days occasionally. If you are fine, then events do not have to be global or signs of character flaws. They can become transitory non-harmful glitches.

🔊 If you can't see any positive way of looking at it, *make it up!* What interpretation would support the view of life that you want to have? What intentions do you wish people had?

🔊 Insist, for your own good, on acting as though that interpretation is true in the situation right now. When you do the tough work of dismantling your old lens, you'll find that people are often kind and well-meaning. They are not the people from your past. You may find, as you practice, that more and more you see likable qualities in the people around you, so the world looks more and more friendly.

🔊 Keep practicing, so that you develop new neural pathways to support this habit. It will become stronger and surer.

As you do, you may well find yourself becoming more optimistic and relaxed. You may also find that you have more power to alter the flow of events toward positive outcomes than you thought. Everyone has stuff going on from their histories and from this morning's push to get to work. Their concern about their fender-bender may have led them not to be careful in conveying what they really meant about your project outline. By acting as if people mean well, very often you encourage them to bring forth the best in themselves. Even if they have been irritated, rude, or selfish, your not reacting to those qualities helps them release them and move to their better side too. At heart, most people are caring, well-meaning folks who want to do their best.

Integrative narrative

One type of psychological work is called narrative therapy. In this approach, the therapist pays close attention to the way that you tell the story of your life and your pain. Together, you investigate the problem spots, what meaning you've given them and how that affects you. The goal is to get to the point of being able to tell the story of your life without feeling that you have to hide some things, to integrate events in such a way that you feel good about yourself, now holding the story of your life as a settled, self-supportive sum of who you are. When you see that there are other ways of viewing events besides the interpretations you made under duress and with only a child's understanding, you have the freedom to integrate your past in a way that builds up who you are rather than breaking you down.

Connie's healing went to a whole other level when she'd worked through the rape experience often enough that it shifted from being the dominant and overwhelming event to having been digested and integrated into the ongoing story of her life. There were important threads that she wove into her narrative of herself: the skills she'd learned and used, how she'd triumphed over the violation and violence by re-establishing her sense of herself as valuable, the deeper and richer sense of who she was, her increased empathy for others, her insistence on her boundaries and safety. All these, and her being able to see her life story as a larger whole than just this one event, enabled her to analyze present events and focus on helpful, happy, optimistic interpretations and gently refute the fear-based ones.

Practice: One way to build the ability to see positive aspects in situations is to go back over your life and tell it or write it as a story in which you draw out different perspectives from your habitual ones. Focus on including the strengths you've gained from going through hard times. Now that you are an empowered adult, you can re-examine circumstances to include such angles as insights into others' psychological problems that led to their bad behavior; or seeing that, as a child, you were not responsible for others' actions; or that of course a child would think that such an event would prove that she was awful, when actually it was not about her.

Keep at it until you can unearth something that you learned, or some skill that you developed, such as empathy, insightfulness, intuition, compassion, or courage. You do not have to be glad that the event occurred. You do want to value your character strengths. Over time, you may want to go over your new narrative until you integrate this view of your history into the way that you think about yourself.

Gwyneth worked with this exercise several times. It was difficult for her. She'd either deny the neglect she'd suffered, or she'd deny her needs. But she kept at it. When she could describe events with an emphasis on what strengths she'd developed, she was more able to focus on her value as a person. It helped her to invest more of her energy in centering in her reality and feeling good about herself, rather than losing herself trying to please others and then feeling bereft. She even started expecting more from her relationships and saying "no" to family members who were used to taking advantage of her.

Gratitude improves your attitude

"Research has been done that categorically shows that the habitually grateful among us are happier than those who are not...Several different research groups have investigated the effects of asking people to stop and reflect on those things for which they are most grateful... The details of this intervention differ across studies, but the results are always the same: Counting your blessings on a regular basis makes you happier and more content with life." (*Peterson, 2006*)

Two exercises in positive psychology were found to have the most universal and long-lasting positive effect on subjects' outlook. They are Gratitude and Three Good Things. They were found to raise levels of happiness and lower amounts of depression for as long as six months, especially for those who continued to do the exercise beyond the (single!) week of the experiment. Participants were benefited so quickly that sixty percent of them continued to count their blessings six months later.

The Gratitude Exercise #1: Write down three to five things each day that you are grateful for. The research done on this exercise shows that better results come from listing only this number, rather than, say, ten. Let yourself really feel grateful as you write them down. Spend a moment savoring the benefit of each thing. Next day, write three to five other ones, if possible. You can keep finding new things to be grateful for. Really focus on a few each day.

The Gratitude Exercise #2: There have been many people in your life who have been kind or helpful to you. Write a letter stating how grateful you are for the way they inspired you, or helped you, or supported you. Describe concretely what they did and how it affected you. If you can, take it to them in person and have them read it in your presence. If this is not possible, then mail or e-mail it and follow up on the phone.

In the studies, this exercise created good feelings in both the letter writer and the recipient with the effect lasting for several weeks. So how about writing another one every week? There is overwhelming evidence from many researchers "that the habitually grateful among us are happier than those who are not." (*Peterson, 2006*)

Three Good Things: For a week, at the end of each day, write down three things that went well. It works best to do it at the end of the day. The items can be as small as "I found the blueberry bushes I wanted to plant in my garden," or as large as, "My work on my resentment paid off. Today I stopped my usual knee-jerk reaction, asked questions of Joe instead, and found that in fact he had a valuable insight into the project we've been stalled on. I'm so proud of myself for not jumping in and blaming him for not getting his part done!" or, of course, "I won the lottery!"

Then, for each one, answer the question, "Why did this good thing happen?" It may be, "I was lucky I stopped at that new greenhouse," or "All my searching and perseverance paid off," or "Good thing my friend told me they were there." If you have an intimate relationship, try sharing your three good things with your partner before going to sleep. You may even make it a ritual that you do together.

Empower yourself by sending positive energy

You can free yourself from feeling impacted or controlled by difficult people by being proactive with your energy dynamics. Sending the other person positive energy, responding calmly and with concern for their wellbeing, can change the dynamic between you.

- Breathe, ground, and center. Invite nourishment from the earth into your energy system. Feel it fill your feet, then your legs, then your whole body.

- When your entire body feels full and fed, while continuing to inhale nourishment in, exhale peace and calm toward the person you're thinking of. Start with someone you care for, so it is easy to send them positive energy even when they are not being particularly positive themselves. Imagine what you'd like to say. (Coming up with possibilities in advance often helps you remember them as options when actually in stressful encounters.) Notice what happens to your interaction.

- When this has become easier to do, you can graduate to someone more problematic, someone you have had difficulties with. If it is too difficult to radiate loving energy, try sending compassion. You can do this alone in your home, and it will still affect the person. When you next have a confrontation with this person, see if you can do it, even if you must be firm or set some limit. Radiate positive energy towards them, while finding a respectful, compassionate way to say whatever else you need to say.

You can also impact larger spheres with this practice. When you want to move to the big leagues, try politicians or other difficult people who show up in the news. Then send it to the world at large. You can have a positive effect on the energy in the world.

A perspective to muse upon

Back in the 1990's, a group of social scientists, educators, and psychologists from several western countries held a conference on health and psychology with the Dalai Lama, the leader of Tibet and of Tibetan Buddhism. Since the Buddha's first noble truth involves the emotional experience of suffering, Buddhism discusses emotions a lot. An American meditation teacher asked him to address the suffering caused by self-hatred. The Dalai Lama looked confused. "What is self-hatred?" he asked.

The therapists in the room tried to explain the concept of self-hatred as it manifests in their clients and students. He became more and more puzzled. "Is this an esoteric mental state that appears in the most emotionally disturbed?" he asked. The teachers and psychologists assured him that self-hatred was not at all unusual in the West, that many people experienced it. He was amazed. "How can they feel that way about themselves, when everybody has Buddha nature?"

A central tenet of Buddhism is the conviction that the core of each person is good, a manifestation of Spirit, and therefore, as expansive, intelligent, and loving as is Spirit itself. People raised in that tradition know without a doubt that, even if they mess up, even if they go against it in their actions, their true nature is goodness and love. So let's adopt that view.

How would it affect how you live your life to know, without a doubt, that your true nature is good, wise, loving, limitless, and bright?

Part VI

Make Joy a Permanent Habit

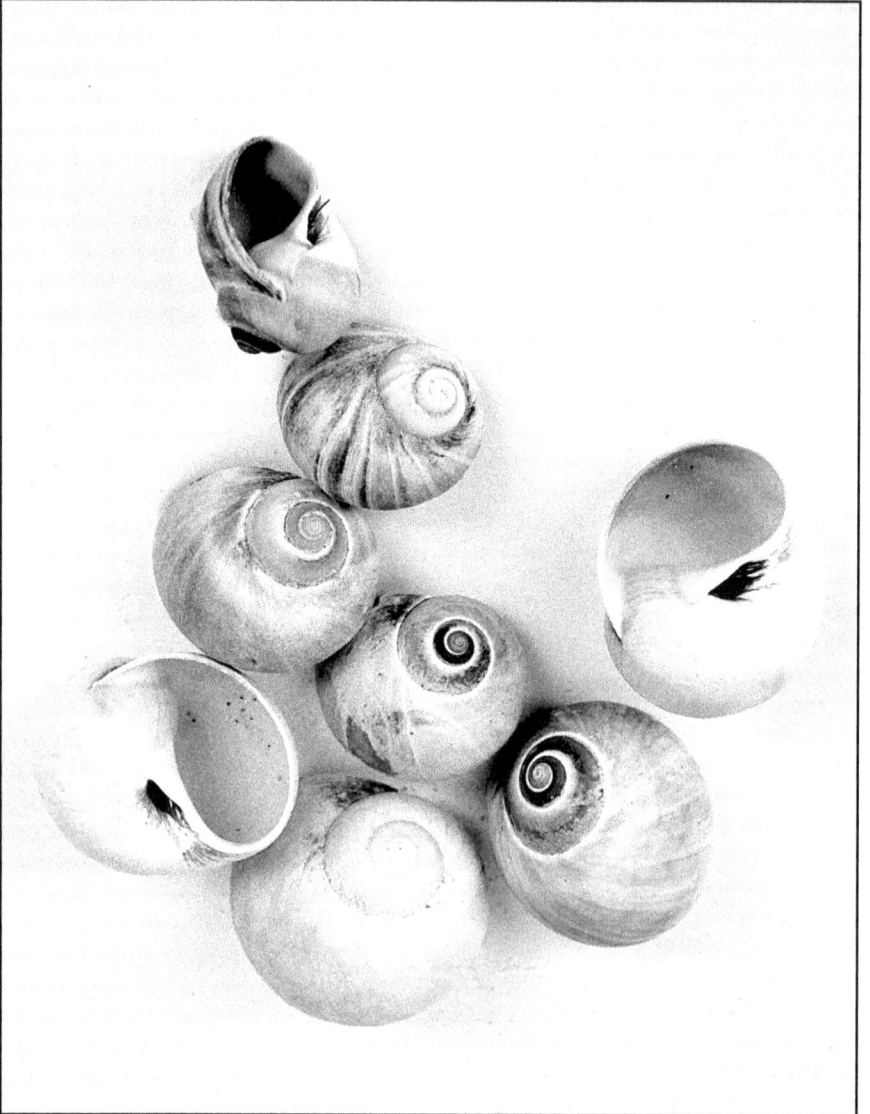

When we let go of our battles and open our heart to things as they are, then we come to rest in the present moment. This is the beginning and the end of spiritual practice.

—Jack Kornfield

How Much Joy Can You Tolerate? 20

TONY, FROM THE chapter on centering, had made great strides. He learned to connect with his body and his emotions. After doing everything for years to please his wife, he eventually decided that the marriage was not healthy for him and filed for divorce. He gained primary custody of his children and then only took consulting jobs that were within driving distance of home. He coached his daughter's chess team, played basketball with some guys in the neighborhood, and found himself more frequently smiling. Then he called again. He was puzzled that whenever he felt truly happy, next thing he knew, he'd be agitated and fearing the worst. "Am I doing something wrong? First I feel guilty, then I get worked up. What's the point of that?" he moaned.

It is disruptive and disorienting to make any changes, even for the better. Tony was breaking some major rules from his past when he focused on what he wanted and then made it happen. He was not committing any crimes. He felt guilty because he was not living in the way that placated his parents or his ex-wife. His nervous system still had the old messages encoded deep-down, and it reacted when he struck out in new directions, trying to herd him back into its safety zone.

After being hurt many times, we may unconsciously turn to our pain as a cocoon that seems safe. Yet that wastes our potential and squanders our energy. When we have outgrown the cocoon, it becomes a straitjacket.

In situations such as this, guilt is not the same moral signal as is remorse. Remorse is the healthy, appropriate feeling you have when you have done something wrong or have hurt someone, and you are sorry and wish you could make up for it. Guilt is a reaction that you were trained to have whenever you weren't toeing someone else's line, meeting someone else's agenda or standards. If you have been developing the skills in this book, and you have been taking the stance that you are a valuable person, and then you find yourself feeling guilty or as if the sky is going to fall, you're on the right track! If you are acting in new ways and then find that others become upset in response, then congratulations! *If you feel guilty when you start, with pure intentions, to act on your behalf in a healthy way, then the guilt is a sign that you are doing the right thing. It is a sign that you are breaking the old patterns and taboos that kept you in line all this time.* Know that you are headed in the right direction. You no longer are succumbing to mandates to erase yourself, to change who you are in order to be acceptable by other people's standards, or so they can be do not have to face their own issues.

Maintaining a calm life requires a different skillset

If you notice that crises keep popping up, take that as a sign to stop and assess. Those of us who are used to upheaval or chronic stress often react to stretches of calm by becoming first bored, then agitated. Our definitions of normalcy, and our self-definition, may have been so wrapped up in reacting to crises that we do not know how to have ongoing calm. We may have become used to life as a raging torrent with unexpected rapids, falls, and obstructing boulders. Or like the Cuyahoga River when I was growing up. It was so polluted with steel mill effluence that fires would flare unexpectedly right on the water. Men working on boats would go barefoot in sub-zero weather, because the river was so hot that the metal boats were like radiant flooring.

Some young people are bored by nice partners and dump them for the bad boys or slutty girls. They confuse the excitement caused by constant upheaval, opportunistic charisma, or danger with emotional substance. A tumultuous relationship provides a distraction from their uninvestigated issues as well as seeming familiar—their sense of life so far is of unresolved crises, so this one feels as if it fits or is meant to be.

Crises demand all our attention and most of our resources. When we handle them, we feel competent and alive. When things are peaceful, we don't know how to feel okay and in charge. Also, when things are okay, stashed-away feelings push up, if only because there is no pressure keeping them down (which is of course why many people stay busy all the time). It's one thing to recognize and work through old feelings when they claim attention, and it's another thing to think we don't have anything to work on because we've kept ourselves distracted by living in crisis mode.

Maintaining a life that flows along quietly takes entirely different skills from fire fighting. If you catch yourself thinking that the other shoe is going to drop, try to identify the old belief that's pushing the worry, such as, "Good times can't last," or "Life isn't supposed to go my way," or "Life will always be hard," or "Chaos is all I know. I'm good at dealing with chaos, so to feel competent, things must be chaotic." That one would be a particularly good one to catch. People have been known to stir things up and create emergencies just to reassure themselves!

Gwyneth thought carefully about the direction she wanted for her career and interviewed with several companies before choosing her new job direction. She took her time, turned down some (although she had to wrestle with her old beliefs to do so, the ones that said "You should fit into whatever anyone else wants or needs," and "Who are you to think you can hold out for something better?"). She then negotiated an opportunity into a position that fit her skills, her vision for her life, and that also excited her. She and Pablo even bought a house together.

After a while in her new job, she found herself working crazy hours, not taking lunch, and taking work home. That all sounded way too familiar a pattern and set off her alarms.

"When I'm not looking, I go back to acting as if something terrible is going to happen if I don't live my life the way I did before. What helps is to talk to someone who knows how far I've come, to reground myself and to remind myself of my worth, so I can feel myself being here in the present, you know, being fine and okay living the way I want to.

"And I have to stop and see that it makes sense that those old fears are churned up again, given all the changes I've made. Then I consciously take time to be aware of the situation, and choose to experience each moment in this way—my way—does that make sense? Oh, and I've been walking in the park on my lunch break, and I got a massage, and I found a yoga studio. "

The important skills Gwyn had developed were to pause and reconnect with herself, see the validity of her feelings, be compassionate rather than judgmental, and simply let them be there for a bit. She had learned to take care of herself—to be with her feelings and then soothe herself, and then to put those feelings into perspective by doing a present-day reality check.

A few months after this conversation, she'd settled in and was blossoming in her new environment. She and Pablo were even talking about marriage. She came to thank me for our work together and said, "You'd think that once I'd been brave enough to make these changes, there'd be no looking back. But I have to remind myself on an ongoing basis that living my own life and feeling good about it takes practice. I have to pay attention. It really is up to me. I find myself being happy for hours or days on end, and then the old feelings will creep in: "are you really okay? You'd better start worrying! You'll starve! There's no one who's really there for you! You're all alone!" It takes paying attention to see when that's happening. I'm much better at re-centering and reminding myself to be in the present.

"For a while, I thought that meant that there was still something wrong with me, that if it wasn't effortless, I was still a basket case. But now I realize that that's our job. We have to consciously build the 'everything's-okay' muscle. The pain was real and will always be part of what made me who I am, but now it's not in charge all the time. Now I can remind myself that the sun is shining, the waves are coming in down by the beach, and life is good!"

Gwyn had realized that we have to not only process and release trauma, we have to counter our old assumption that we're stuck with pain. Instead, we have to build a new tolerance for joy.

It is confusing, when your goal is to have a tranquil life, to feel riled up again. It's a struggle to integrate new habits. It doesn't mean that you're failing or doing it incorrectly. Expending the effort instructs the body to build the neural pathways that will make the new skills easier over time.

How to tolerate joy

If you can't tell whether you are wrestling with a new skill or fighting against yourself and against life, look at what thoughts are sliding by in the back of your mind. Are you reverting to old messages? Or are you practicing supportive thoughts as you build your new way of seeing yourself? It takes time to get there, so give yourself credit and be compassionate!

How much joy can you let yourself have? When we have spent a long time managing the unmanageable, it is quite a shift to relax into the innate joy that is waiting underneath. We have to change our joy set-point. Leading a life in which we allow ourselves to receive goodness and abundance takes confronting our discomfort with change and our old ideas of the way things are. We need to practice long enough to build a new "normal" and gently insist that we relax and soften into the goodness in ourselves and in life.

Practices:

- If, when things are going well, anxiety or agitation bubble up, or you find yourself looking around for what's about to go wrong, stop, and breathe. Go through your body and consciously relax each area. Remind yourself that the agitation is simply because you are moving into new territory and that you want to have a more peaceful life. Say, "I can feel happy. I'm fine." Stay present. Smile. (Helpful chemical reactions occur when you smile. Take advantage of them.) Breathe. Again. If you keep being jittery;

🙠 Focus intently on the experience of being grounded, and then of settling your awareness in your center. Really sense your being in this moment's reality. The more you can be here, right now, the less power your brainstem's automatic fear reactions will have.

🙠 Remind yourself that any agitation is merely a sign that old anxiety needs to be exposed for what it really is—a fear of change, of rocking the old boat, as if the old threats still exist.

🙠 Work through any old beliefs that then emerge.

🙠 Overcome the habit of identifying with your hurt self. Practice identifying with who you are in your best moments. Remind yourself of your strengths and good qualities. Notice how you feel when you step inside your best self. That self is truer than is the version that comes from your weakest moments or from messages from other people. Say to yourself that you will not go into the old shape, the one with the bruised sense-of-self.

🙠 Keep grounding in the present, in the whole of your body and energy, and in your connection with the earth, and thereby, the world, here-and-now.

🙠 Remember that bringing awareness to anything feeds energy to that thing and so enhances it. Your awareness is a manifestation of energy. So continue to focus on your fine self.

🙠 Insist on continuing on your path.

🙠 Be okay with starting again. And again. And again. Perseverance wins the day.

Counter uncertainty and self-criticism with a strong, solid sense of yourself as a person who can tolerate on-going wellbeing. The way to do so is by connecting moment-by-moment with what is primally real and true—the kinesthetic experience of your energy in your body. When you reconnect with your vital energy, you not only strengthen your sense of yourself, you come back into contact with the joy that resides with the still place at your core. So you keep contacting the joy in each present moment.

What if, after all this, you find yourself undermining your progress by whispering in the back of your mind that you will never make it, or that you don't deserve to have what you want? It is not an uncommon problem to have recurring trouble with self-deprecating thoughts. It is helpful to become aware of what triggers it. Work backward to what happened right before you started thinking those thoughts. Can you see a pattern in the things that trigger them? If you bring awareness to the occurrence in that moment, what changes? Then actively counter them by practicing your healthy beliefs. If they keep going, try one of these:

Mantras for getting back on track

- I am safe. I am fine. I relax into the moment.
- That was then. This present moment is not the same.
- I choose to be in my full, free self rather than in my old low crouch.
- I deserve to live my life. I receive support and encouragement to do so.
- I am a valued and valuable person. I am meant to bring my gifts to the world.

For heavy artillery

If your self-criticism artillery is of the really heavy variety, use some gentle force to turn your attention. Recognize that the critical thoughts are not accurate assessments of your worth, but rather are desperate, misguided attempts to keep you safe in what was familiar.

🍂 Say, firmly, "STOP!"

🍂 Breathe. Feel your feet.

🍂 Bring energy into your hands by rubbing them together briskly as you move your awareness into them.

🍂 When the energy is built up and your hands feel hot and tingly, make snatching motions by your head, as if you can pull those thoughts out, and then toss them away. Do this three or four times. Energetically, it does disrupt the waves that the thoughts are made of. (And, if nothing else, it changes your focus from attacking yourself to making some weird motions with your hands!)

🍂 Take a deep breath, and then start at the top of the Practice list and ground, center, and tell yourself that you are fine in the present moment.

Often, we find ourselves fighting off the joy waiting within us. If, as you work with the exercises, resistance takes the form of self-doubt or unworthiness, have compassion for yourself. Come back to a compassionate message over and over. Gradually kindness toward yourself will burn stubborn, residual shame down to a manageable chunk. It will also give your old mechanisms the message that you no longer back down when they flare up, so they might as well back off. If painful thoughts surface, acknowledge them. Be kind to yourself for having them. The more aspects of yourself you can accept with kindness, the more you will accept and support others, and the more fully you will feel joy.

Happiness is not for sissies
Building joy requires that you face down the accretion of tension and reactivity that shouts that you are breaking taboos if you feel calm and happy. Keep practicing, and eventually you will pass through that forest to the clearer place in which you are able to choose your reality.

At that point, you will be able to relax into the present, enjoy what you have, and who you are, and how it feels to be alive, connected, and nourished. You will develop the skills of maintaining a peaceful life, which include acknowledging and being with things as they come up. Your life will be richer and deeper for the lessons that you have learned and the growth that you have committed to. It is okay to have experienced loss. Loss and pain are inevitable parts of life. Don't limit your life in an effort to avoid pain. Be with it, move through it.

The old pathways—your old, knee-jerk interpretations—let them be grown over with weeds. Let the wind of passing days and weeks blow dirt into the ruts, so that your feet do not slip into that worn road. Turn your focus to making your new path the one that your feet find naturally. Smooth the roadbed. Side with your true self. Living well *is*, in fact, the best revenge. Learn to be comfortable with joy. Live the life you were meant to live. Breathe, relax. Intention and practice build the neural pathways that choose joy, calm, and settling into the richness of the present moment. En-joy yourself.

Happiness is the result of inner maturity. It depends on us alone, and requires patient work, carried out from day to day. Happiness must be built, and this requires time and effort. In the long term, happiness and unhappiness are therefore a way of being, or a life skill.

—Matthieu Ricard

Joy Takes Work 21

CONNIE ALSO HAD to learn to tolerate joy. She'd done the work to recover from the attack. With a lot of practice grounding and centering, and time working on her APEPs, she felt much more solidly settled in her own body with a sense of being whole and unified. But she never forgot that it was possible to be attacked—to have her physical integrity shattered by a violent criminal.

At first she looked over her shoulder all the time. Gradually, she got to the point of not dwelling on it every minute, or even every day. Sometimes weeks would go by before something reminded her. She now knew that she could re-knit herself, reestablish her core and her boundaries, and feel encased in her skin. It had taken work, but it was worth it. "I'm not locked in the dungeon of my pain. It's okay to focus and stay centered. I wasn't going to let that scumbag ruin my life. It forced me to really commit to my own life. I had to really concentrate when I was learning to live in my own skin. I had to work really hard to find the still place where I'm fine, even when I still had major freak-out feelings.

"At the time, I doubted whether it was worth it. But it's become a habit. That focus never really leaves me now. I'm really committed to being centered, so I'm really aware when I get off-balance, and I do what it takes to come back as fast as possible. And the more I do, the easier it is. Now it's like a hum that stays in the back of my mind. It's definitely worth it. I feel more alive, more grateful, more careful—more caring of myself."

It's not just luck

Even without catastrophes throwing us for a loop, it seems hard enough to stay happy in an on-going way when everything is copacetic. The little niggling things get people down more than disasters. And if we think that contentment happens randomly—when we throw a really good party, or only when our best qualities and the stars are all properly aligned—then we feel helpless and at the mercy of external forces. We try to woo happiness, grab it, hope it will be bestowed upon us. All this maneuvering takes a lot of effort, expended in the wrong direction.

The fact is that joy—feeling peaceful, happy, and filled with gratitude at the beauty of life—does take work. The rigor of being attentive to our own process in every moment is what uncovers, grows, and sustains it. When we make a commitment to connect with our joy, being sloppy in our mental habits becomes a luxury with too high a price. We no longer can afford to fall unconsciously into old, self-defeating behaviors. We commit to being attentive of our perceptions and attitude, of the world around us, and to working with our assumptions.

Grounding and centering bring you back to your body in the present, making an end run around your frayed, over-worked thoughts. Grounding and centering base your present experience on what is real—not what is seen through the lens of old beliefs, but on your perceptions in the here-and-now. The more you return to your bodily experience, the more you build a truthful definition of reality.

It's your life

People fall short on their New Year's resolutions because either they have not prepared enough to make a successful push; or their busy-ness, combined with old habits, crowd the new goal out of their minds. So often, folks wake up weeks later, smack their foreheads, and wonder how they could have forgotten that they really wanted to lose twenty pounds, or save for retirement, or dig out the mess in the basement, or build a better career.

It takes effort to groove-in new neural pathways. It's okay to fall down along the way. We all do, and it will happen again. In that flattened instant, we have the opportunity to grow our new skills even more strongly. We can use them to stay in the moment, rather than losing our way in self-condemnatory thought-storms. Then we remember our goal of creating the life experience that we really want, start over again, and continue.

Connie was able, after months of hard work, to reconnect with life as a joyous undertaking. She took a lot less for granted and continued to be careful and to keep an eye out for danger, and at the same time, she made sure that she appreciated all the beautiful moments in each day. She had energy to focus on her goals, and faith that she'd achieve them. She started dating again and found a lovely, gentle man. When she caught herself closing down, she put aside time and practiced again being compassionate toward herself and gentle about her reactions. She then checked her assumptions about other people and strove to see them as they really were in this moment. Life, she says, is good.

Practice: Dedicate time to your own enrichment. Build into the ritual of your day time to meditate, journal, spend enjoyable time with yourself, immerse yourself in Nature. Commit to some exercises from this or other books that you find inspirational. Schedule into your datebook, wall calendar, or smartphone time to practice or address your current step. Committing to a specific time to do it, in writing, improves the likelihood of your giving yourself this time by about forty percent, say the time management gurus.

The importance of celebration

So many times we take major steps and then don't give ourselves credit for them. As I was working on rewriting this last section, I found myself resisting getting to work. I pounded the alarm clock into submission, read the newspaper too thoroughly, and discovered lots of errands to do downtown. I realized that I was delaying digging in to finish it because I was daunted by the huge next tasks of finding a publisher and editors, of marketing it and all the rest. My dear friend and first reader, Beth, wisely asked what I had planned as a celebration when I was done. I needed something sizable to wrap up the two years it had taken to put words to paper and rework them into readable form, and also to recharge my batteries before starting the getting-it-re-edited-and-published phase. Even though I was about to rework this very section, I had been neglecting my own need for celebrating.

We tend to focus so diligently on the tasks in front of our noses that we don't come up for air when we have achieved something. Instead of instantly turning our attention to the next task on our never-ending list, we need to take a breather and refill our well. It is important to stop and give ourselves credit and to notice that we do, in fact, succeed. Otherwise life will look like unrelenting struggle. To refine the way we live our lives, we need to raise our heads and notice that effort is not the whole show. There are also benefits that all that work produced, as well as all the beauty and enjoyment available in each moment, and the benefit of relaxing and seeing the larger picture, which puts our efforts into a broader context.

No one schedules recess for us anymore. We have to do it for ourselves. It is important for us to take time to enjoy ourselves, to include fun and relaxation, and to give ourselves credit for perseverance, faith, and skill. Celebrating our successes becomes an important tool that firms up one side of the foundation of our happiness. We deserve to acknowledge ourselves and to feel good about what we have done. Doing so increases our ability to support ourselves when the going gets tough. It builds the habit of seeing ourselves as accomplished and worthy and helps pain from the past slip further away. Cheering for ourselves moves our energy more firmly into our feeling confident and competent.

Practice: Get in the habit of acknowledging and celebrating gains. They can be small—for steps completed, pause to read a chapter of a novel or rock out on the living room rug; or big—when you finish large projects, plan a trip, have a day at a spa, or make a luxury weekend at home. Do not assume that it is enough that you did good work! Find out how it changes your experience if you actually ask a friend to give you a high-five. Notice how it makes you feel about the next tasks you face. Make a ritual of self-acknowledgement something you perform regularly, so that no process is complete without your stopping and giving yourself credit. Spend time in the state of satisfaction, of things going well, of achievement. Let celebration feed you. Let it set your feet more firmly on a nurturing base, raise your energy for the next project, and give you a more balanced, positive, and therefore realistic view of your life.

But is it real if you have to work at it? Shouldn't it just happen by itself?

There's an odd notion about happiness. Many people assume that it isn't real if you have to work at it, that being happy (or loved, for that matter) means getting what you want without having to ask for it. The right partner would know how to make us feel special without being told, we'd get the best job, win the lottery, have the greatest children, and avoid pain. But pain happens in life, in every life, in some way, to some extent. We know, because we have already been through a lot. That does not mean that we are unlucky. It does not annihilate our membership card in the happy-life-club. It means that we are human.

Joy requires that we be responsible for our own lives. We deserve to keep moving forward, no matter what we have encountered. We have the right to activate ourselves—to gather our energy and use it on our own behalf and in service of our talents. We owe it to ourselves and to the world not to let past pain eclipse our gifts. We need to be more committed to our process than to our pain. We need to let our self-doubting voices and old beliefs lose their status as all-powerful "truths" and see them as the clever but futile attempts at protection that they really are. To continue the work that makes joy a habit, we must bring ourselves back into alignment when things happen. As we allow our feelings airtime, we honor our right to have reactions, we learn from our perceptions, and we can resolve situations and integrate them into the grand saga of our history.

"What day is it?"
"It's today," squeaked Piglet.
"My favorite day," said Pooh.

—A.A. Milne

The Life You Really Want 22

THE BASIS OF joy is love. It is a deeply abiding love within us that forms the solid foundation for all the love in our lives. Dismantling our self-hatred and alienation from ourselves is crucial in order to uncover that still place of peace and to live there more of the time. All the work that we have done to heal is what enables us to reconnect with our own spirit. To experience life as we really want it, we need to exert a gentle and firm perseverance in moving forward. We need faith that we can unburden ourselves and partake of the world's goodness, for the world is filled with wonder and love. As Jack Kornfield said in his book, *The Wise Heart,* "The world in which we live is a temple, and the miraculous light of the first stars is shining through it all the time. In place of original sin, we celebrate original goodness.... In every meeting of the eyes and every leafing tree, in every taste of tangerine and avocado, a blessing occurs. This is true mental health."

You are a vital element of all creation, an inextricable factor of all-that-is. And creation is fractal. Every entity within it embodies the whole, within its own size, in the same way that each cell of a feather, seen under a microscope, turns out to be a tiny feather in shape. The Universe is made up of little universes (including you) built into increasingly complex structures. The Universe is made up of itself, an infinite number of times. Your body is made of elements that were created in distant stars

333

eons ago. All the parts add a dimension of richness to the whole, and the whole nourishes and holds each singularity. Each individual part represents the whole. As we are fractals of creation, we have access to all the love, insight, strength and wisdom we need to brave our journeys.

So, in the very act of loving and supporting yourself, truly loving yourself, with kindness and compassion, you radiate love to everything-that-is. The more you value and support yourself, the more your love will radiate into and nourish the world.

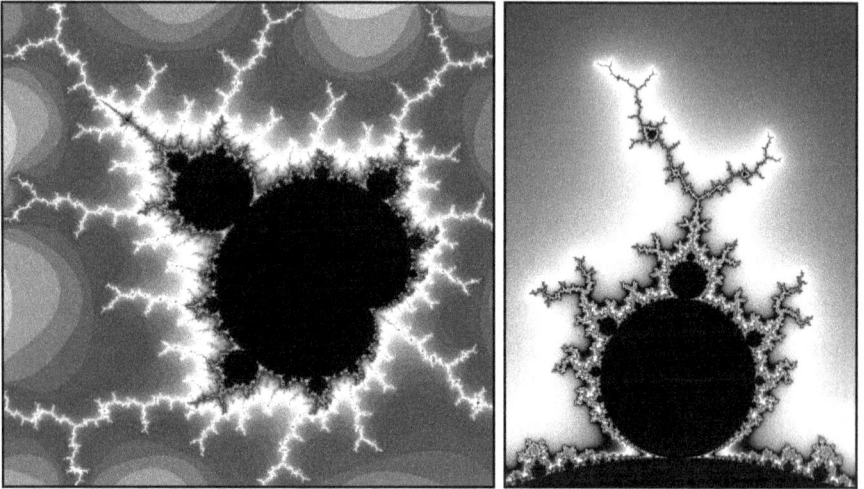

Mandelbrot geode, at X1 and X25 magnification (Note that the black shape in the X25 is the same as the full-sized one. You can see that the smaller round shapes on its surface are the same again.)

Value your heart and your wellbeing. Be more committed to your happiness than to any fear or painful memory. People often ask the Dalai Lama how he can preach loving-kindness and be so happy after being exiled from his homeland and having his people disenfranchised, tortured in the most heinous ways, starved, and murdered. He answers, "After all the invaders have done, should I let them take my happiness as well?" He works every day to stay aligned with his happiness.

Let us not become caught by our pain and mistake it for our real selves and our larger purposes in life. Let us not spend our precious time with our noses plastered against the back corner of a cell made by our past our fears and our un-examined self-protective mechanisms, not noticing that behind us the door is wide open. Let us be brave enough to turn, find the ways to calm our reactions, resolve our emotions, and step through the door into the light of our own nature and of the beautiful world. Even if taking that step breaks rules, or the shining light makes us cry as the crust around our hearts cracks open, with each step we become stronger, freer, more connected and more expansive. There is so much joy in the world and in each moment. And that is the experience of life that we really want.

A meditation to free the heart and nourish joy

Here is a meditation that is a reworking of a loving-kindness meditation from the Insight Meditation and Buddhist traditions. It answers the kinds of issues that we have been working through. Repeat it over and over, for five minutes, an hour, a day, a month, or a year! Find what happens to your experience of life as you do so.

I am safe. I am fine. I am free.
I am well in body, mind, emotions, and spirit.
I open to the oceans of physical, emotional, mental, financial, and spiritual energy available to me.
I receive so much love and kindness that I am filled to overflowing and radiate them to the world.
I am truly happy.

Bibliography and
Suggested Reading

Adams, Jane, *Boundary Issues: Using boundary intelligence to get the intimacy you want and the independence you need in life, love, and work*. John Wiley & Sons, Hoboken, NJ, 2005.

Black, Harvey, "Amygdala's Inner Workings: Researchers gain new insights into this structure's emotional connections." The Scientist 15[19]:20, October. 1, 2001.

Bowen, Murray, *Family Therapy in Clinical Practice*, Jason Aronson Inc., Northvale, NJ, 1978.

Brach, Tara, *Radical Acceptance*. Bantam Dell, New York, NY, 2003.

Bradley, Michael, *Yes, Your Teen is Crazy!* Harbor Press, Gig Harbor, WA, 2003.

Chodron, Pema, *Start Where You Are: a guide to compassionate living*. Shambhala Books, Boston, MA, 2004.

Cohen, Gene D, *The Mature Mind: The positive power of the aging brain*. Basic Books, New York, NY, 2005.

Coleman, James, *Abnormal Psychology and Modern Life*. Scott Foreman & Company, Glen View, IL, 1976.

Cope, Stephen, *Yoga and the Quest for the True Self*. Bantom Books, New York, NY, 1999.

Courtney-Belford, Rosalba, *Buteyko Method*. Copyright 2006 Postural Restoration Institute. Reference: www.Buteyko.com.

Csikszentmihalyi, Mihaly, *Flow: The Psychology of Optimal Experience*. Harper Perennial Modern Classics, New York, NY, 2008.

Cyrulnik, Boris, *The Whispering of Ghosts: Trauma and resilience*. Other Press, New York, NY, 2005.

Davidson, Richard J., and Anne Harrington, *Visions of Compassion: Western Scientists and Tibetan Buddhists Examine Human Nature*. Oxford University Press, Oxford, England, 2002.

Epstein, Mark, MD, *Going to Pieces Without Falling Apart: A Buddhist Perspective on Wholeness*. Broadway Books/Bantam Doubleday Dell, New York, NY, 1998.

Epstein, Mark, MD, *Open to Desire: the truth about what the Buddha taught.* Gotham, New York, NY, 2006.

Follmi, Danielle and Olivier, *Offerings: Buddhist Wisdom for Every Day.* Stewart, Tabori, & Cahng/Harry N. Abrams, Inc, New York, NY, 2003.

Galomb, Elaine, PhD, *Trapped in the Mirror: adult children of narcissists in their struggle for self.* William Morrow & Co, New York, NY, 1992.

Gladwell, Malcolm, *Blink: the power of thinking without thinking.* Little Brown & Company, New York, NY, 2005.

Hall, Calvin S. *A Primer of Freudian Psychology.* Mentor, New York, NY, 1954.

Hall, Calvin, Linsdzey Gardner, & John B. Cambell, *Theories of Personality.* John Wiley & Sons, New York, 1998.

Hall, Edward T, *The Hidden Dimension.* Doubleday, Garden City, N.Y. 1966.

Note: (Hall introduced the field of proxemics—cultural and relational accepted distances between people.)

Hamilton, N. Gregory, *Self and Others: Object relations theory in practice.* Jason Aronson Inc, Northvale, NJ, 1990.

Healy, Jane M, *Your Child's Growing Mind: Brain Development and Learning From Birth to Adolescence.* Broadway Books, New York, NY, 1987.

Henson, R.N.A, Shallice, T., & Dolan, R.J., "Right prefrontal cortex and episodic memory retrieval: a functional MRI test of the monitoring hypothesis." *Brain, a journal of neurology,* Oxford Journals, Volume **122**, Issue7, pp 1367-1381.

Holt, Doug, "The Role of the Amygdala in Fear and Panic." Submitted to *SerendipUpdate* on Tue, 2008-01-08.

Horner, Althea, *Object Relations and the Developing Ego in Therapy.* Jason Aronson, Inc., Northvale, NJ, 1984.

http://biology.about.com/library/organs/brain/bltemporallobe.htm (about the amygdalae)

Hughes, Daniel, *Building the Bonds of Attachment: Awakening Love in Deeply Troubled Children.* Jason Aronson, Inc., Northvale, NJ, 1998.

Hughes, Daniel, *Facilitating Developmental Attachment: The Road to Emotional Recovery and Behavioral Change in Foster and Adopted Children.* Jason Aronson, Inc., Northvale, NJ, 1997.

Jerome, John, *Staying With It: On becoming an athlete.* Penguin Books, New York, NY, 1984.

Kornfield, Jack, *A Path with Heart: a guide through the perils and promises of spiritual life.* Bantam Books, New York, NY, 1993.

Kornfield, Jack, *The Wise Heart: a guide to the universal teachings of Buddhist psychology.* Bantam Books, New York, NY, 2008.

Korzybski, Alfred, *Science and Sanity: an introduction to non-Aristotelian systems and general semantics.* International Non-Aristotelian Library Publishing, Laxeville, CT, 1949.

Maguire, EA, Gadian DG, Johnsrude IS, Good CD, Ashburner J, Frackowiak RS *et al* (2000), "Navigation-related structural change in the hippocampi of taxi drivers." *National Academy of Sciences, PNAS* April 11, 2000 vol. 97 no. 8 4398-4403.

Mandelbrot, Benoit B, *The Fractal Geometry of Nature*. W.H. Freeman & Co, New York, NY, 1983.

Myss, Caroline, *Anatomy of the Spirit: The Seven Stages of Power and Healing*. Three Rivers Press, New York, NY, 1996.

Northrup, Christiane, M.D., *Women's Bodies, Women's Wisdom*. Bantam Books, New York, NY, 2010.

Peterson, Christopher, *A Primer in Positive Psychology*. Oxford University Press, New York, 2006.

Raphus, Spencer, *PSYCH*. Wadsworth Publishing Co, Belmont, CA, 2008. (about axons)

Rapoport, Judith L., and Nitin Gogtay, "Brain Neuroplasticity in Healthy, Hyperactive and Psychotic Children: Insights from Neuroimaging." *Neuropsychopharmacology* (2008) 33, 181-197; doi:10.1038/sj.npp.1301553; published online 12 September 2007

Remen, Rachel Naomi, *Kitchen Table Wisdom*. The Berkeley Publishing Group/ Penguin Books, Ltd, New York, NY, 2006.

Schwarz, Jack, *Human Energy Systems*. Schwarz Publishing, Mendocino, CA, 1980.

Seligman, Martin, Authentic Happiness. The Free Press, New York, NY, 2002.

Time Magazine, online article, Jan 19, 2007 on "Plasticity of the Brain."

Ungerleider LG, Doyon J, Karni A (2002). "Imaging brain plasticity during motor skill learning." Neurobiology of Learning and Memory, 2002 Nov;78(3):553-64.

van der Graaf, Kent M., *Human Anatomy*. William C. Brown, Dubuque, IA, 1992.

van der Kolk, Bessel. In a study published in the *Annals of the New York Academy of Science* entitled *Yoga and Post-traumatic Stress Disorder*, Bessel van der Kolk discussed his findings that hatha yoga helped female trauma patients to reduce the frequency of intrusive thoughts and the severity of anxiety.

van der Kolk, Bessel A, Onno van der Hart, Jennifer Burbridge, *Approaches to the Treatment of PTSD*. http://www.trauma-pages.com/a/vanderk.php.

van der Kolk, Bessel A, *Clinical implications of neuroscience research in PTSD*. http://www.traumacenter.org/products/pdf_files/NYASF.pdf.

van der Kolk, B.A. & van der Hart, O. (1989). Piere Janet and the breakdown of adaption in psychological trauma. *American Journal of Psychiatry*, 146, 1530-1540.

van der kolk, B.A. & Saporta Jose. *The biological response to psychic trauma: mechanisms and treatment of intrusion and numbing*. Anxiety Research (U.K.), Volume 4: Pages 199-212.

Young, Sinzen, *Break Through Pain*. Sounds True, Inc. Boulder, CO, 2004.

Zukav, Gary, *The Dancing Wu Li Masters: An Overview of the New Physics*. William Morrow & Co., New York, NY, 1979.

Index

341

About the Author

Sarah Gillen, MA, LMFT, PCC, holds an advanced degree in psychology, is a licensed Marriage & Family Therapist, and is trained in Asian Medicine and Energy Medicine. Sarah is also a medical intuitive, and a Professional Credentialed Coach with the International Coach Federation.

Sarah developed a protocol for releasing the effects of painful and disruptive physical and emotional events through the energy systems of the body. This method is a synergy of Energy Medicine, Asian Medicines, and several forms of psychology.

For over 30 years, she has helped thousands of people, from babies to adults. Her work has two phases: 1) the Energy Work she does in person or at-a-distance to release stubborn pain and induce healing, and 2) Energy Dynamics—the skills she teaches people so they can help themselves.

These are the same techniques Sarah makes available to you within these pages.